Alexander Crummell

The Future of Africa

Being addresses, sermons, etc., delivered in the Republic of Liberia

Alexander Crummell

The Future of Africa
Being addresses, sermons, etc., delivered in the Republic of Liberia

ISBN/EAN: 9783337308704

Printed in Europe, USA, Canada, Australia, Japan

Cover: Foto ©ninafisch / pixelio.de

More available books at **www.hansebooks.com**

THE

FUTURE OF AFRICA:

BEING

ADDRESSES, SERMONS,

ETC., ETC.,

DELIVERED IN THE REPUBLIC OF LIBERIA.

BY

REV. ALEX. CRUMMELL, B. A.,
QUEEN'S COLLEGE, CAMBRIDGE.

NEW YORK:
CHARLES SCRIBNER, 124 GRAND STREET.
1862.

> "Joy to thy savage realms, O Africa!
>   A sign is on thee that the great I AM
>   Shall work new wonders in the land of Ham;
> And while he tarries for the glorious day
>   To bring again his people, there shall be
>   A remnant left from Cushan to the sea.
> And though the Ethiop cannot change his skin,
>   Or bleach the outward stain, he yet shall roll
>   The darkness off that overshades the soul,
> And wash away the deeper dyes of sin.
>   Princes, submissive to the Gospel sway,
> Shall come from Egypt; and the Morian's land
> In holy transport stretch to God its hand:
> Joy to thy savage realms, O Africa!"
>   —Rev. WILLIAM CROSWELL, D. D.

JOHN F. TROW,
PRINTER, STEREOTYPER, AND ELECTROTYPER,
48 & 50 Greene Street,
New York.

Entered, according to Act of Congress, in the year 1862, by
CHARLES SCRIBNER,
In the Clerk's Office of the District Court of the United States for the Southern District of New York.

PREFACE.

Most of the papers contained in this volume were addressed to public assemblies in the Republic of Liberia, and, at their request, a few of them have already appeared in print. The remaining articles, now for the first time published, relate, in an equal degree, to the interests of Africa and the negro race. They were prepared, on their several occasions, under a keen sense of responsibility, in the new field of duty on the coast of Africa, whither God has called several thousands of the sons of Africa from their former American homes. They are now published with the humble but sober conviction, that the trains of thought they present *are* worthy the attention and consideration of the people to whom they were addressed; if, perchance, they should prove undeserving the notice of others.

The Author, however, feels that they are somewhat fitted to two important ends; namely, *first*, to show that the children of Africa have been called, in the Divine providence, to meet the demands of civilization, of commerce, and of nationality; and, *second*, that they are beginning, at last, to grapple with the problems which pertain to responsible manhood, to the great work of civilization, to the duties and requirements of national life, and to the solemn responsibility of establishing the Christian faith amid the rude forms of paganism.

The Author cannot let this volume go forth to the public without tendering his best thanks to very many friends, both clerical and lay, who, during his sojourn in this country, have either aided him in his collections for the "Liberia College," or have interested themselves in the publication of this volume, or have bestowed upon him personal attention and kindness.

He trusts he may be excused for mentioning, in this public manner, his deep acknowledgments to the Rt. Rev. Bishops Eastburn, and Potter, of Pennsylvania; to John P. Crozer, Esq., of Philadelphia; to Wm. B. Dodge, Esq., of New York; and to Wm. Coppinger, Esq., of Philadelphia; and especially to those two gentlemen who have favored him with great kindness, through many years, in Africa as well as America—Benjamin Coates, Esq., of Philadelphia, and the Rev. S. H. Tyng, D.D., of New York.

CONTENTS.

		PAGE
I.	THE ENGLISH LANGUAGE IN LIBERIA,	9
II.	THE DUTY OF A RISING CHRISTIAN STATE TO CONTRIBUTE TO THE WORLD'S WELL-BEING AND CIVILIZATION,	57
III.	THE PROGRESS OF CIVILIZATION ALONG THE WEST COAST OF AFRICA,	105
IV.	THE PROGRESS AND PROSPECTS OF THE REPUBLIC OF LIBERIA,	133
V.	GOD AND THE NATION,	151
VI.	THE FITNESS OF THE GOSPEL FOR ITS OWN WORK,	175
VII.	ADDRESS ON LAYING THE CORNER-STONE OF ST. MARK'S HOSPITAL, CAPE PALMAS,	195
VIII.	THE RELATIONS AND DUTY OF FREE COLORED MEN IN AMERICA TO AFRICA,	215
IX.	HOPE FOR AFRICA,	285
X.	THE NEGRO RACE NOT UNDER A CURSE,	327

THE
ENGLISH LANGUAGE IN LIBERIA.

Delivered before the citizens of Maryland County, Cape Palmas, Liberia, July 26, 1860, being the day of National Independence. Also in the Hall of Representatives, Monrovia, February, 1861.

"Language, in connection with reason, to which it gives its proper activity, use, and ornament, raises man above the lower orders of animals, and in proportion as it is polished and refined, contributes greatly, with other causes, to exalt one, nation above another, in the scale of civilization and intellectual dignity."—ANON.

"Our language is a part, and a most important part, of our country. * * * * Nobody who is aware how a nation's feelings and opinions, and whatever characterizes it, are interwoven with its language by myriads of imperceptible fibres, will run the risk of severing them. Nobody who has a due reverence for * * * * his own spiritual being, which has been mainly trained and fashioned by his native language—nobody who rightly appreciates what a momentous thing it is to keep the unity of a people entire and unbroken, to preserve and foster all its national recollections, what a glorious and inestimable blessing it is to 'speak the tongue that Shakspeare spake,' will ever wish to trim that tongue according to any arbitrary theory."—REV. J. C. HARE.

"So may we hope to be ourselves guardians of its purity, and not corrupters of it; to introduce, it may be, others into an intelligent knowledge of that with which we shall have ourselves more than a merely superficial acquaintance—to bequeath it to those who come after us not worse than we received it ourselves."—DEAN TRENCH.

ADDRESS.

Two years ago to-day, when we were assembled together here, as now, to celebrate our National Anniversary, I was called up, after the orator of the day, to make a few remarks. And perhaps some, who are here, may remember that, in setting forth a few of the advantages we pilgrims to these shores possess, for a noble national growth and for future superiority; I pointed out among other providential events the fact, that the exile of our fathers from their African homes to America, had given us, their children, at least this one item of compensation, namely, the possession of the Anglo-Saxon tongue; that this language put us in a position which none other on the globe could give us; and that it was impossible to estimate too highly, the prerogatives and the elevation the Almighty has bestowed upon us, in our having as our own, the speech of Chaucer and Shakspeare, of Milton and Wordsworth, of Bacon and Burke, of Franklin and Webster. My remarks were unpremeditated, and they passed from my thoughts as the meeting was dismissed, and we went forth to the festivities of the day. But it happened that, shortly afterwards, I had occasion to seek health by a journey up the Cavalla. There, on the banks of that noble river, fully 80 miles from the ocean, I met with hospitality from a native trader, a man who presented all the signs of civilization, and who spoke with remarkable clearness and precision, the English language. The incident struck me with surprise, and started a crowd of thoughts and suggestions concerning the future; among these came back the lost and forgotten words of our Anniversary of 1858. More than once since, in conversations, speeches, and sermons, have I expressed the ripened convictions which that occurrence created in my mind; and the other day, after I received the invitation to speak before you on this occasion, I concluded to take this for the subject of remark: "THE ENGLISH LANGUAGE IN LIBERIA."

I shall have to ask your patience this day; for, owing to that fatality of tardiness which seems to govern some of our public movements, I have had but a fortnight to prepare for this duty, and hence I cannot be as brief as is desirable. I shall have to ask your attention also, for I can promise you nothing more than a dry detail of facts.

I trust, however, that I may be able to suggest a few thoughts which may be fitted to illustrate the responsibilities of our lot in this land, and to show forth the nature and the seriousness of the duties which arise out of it.

1. Now, in considering this subject, what first

arrests attention, is the bare simple fact that here, on this coast, that is, between Gallinas and Cape Pedro, is an organized negro community, republican in form and name; a people possessed of Christian institutions and civilized habits, with this one marked peculiarity, that is, that in color, race, and origin, they are identical with the masses of rude natives around them; and yet speak the refined and cultivated English language—a language alien alike from the speech of their sires and the soil from whence they sprung, and knowing no other. It is hardly possible for *us* fully to realize these facts. Familiarity with scenes, events, and even truths, tends to lessen the vividness of their impression. But without doubt no thoughtful traveller could contemplate the sight, humble as at present it really is, without marvel and surprise. If a stranger who had never heard of this Republic, but who had sailed forth from his country to visit the homes of West African Pagans, should arrive on our coast; he could not but be struck with the Anglican aspect of our habits and manners, and the distinctness, with indeed undoubted mistakes and blunders, of our English names and utterance. There could be no mistaking the history of this people. The earliest contact with them vouches English antecedents and associations. The harbor master who comes on board is perhaps a Watts or a Lynch; names which have neither a French, a Spanish, nor a German origin. He steps up into the town, asks the names of storekeepers, learns who are the merchants and officials, calls on the President, or Superintendent, or Judge; and although sable are all the faces he meets with, the *names* are the old familiar ones which he has been accustomed to in the social circles of his home, or on the signs along the streets of New York or London, viz. : the *Smiths*, (a large family in Liberia as everywhere else in Anglo-Saxondom,) and their broods of cousins, the Johnsons, Thompsons, Robinsons, and Jacksons; then the Browns, the Greens, the [paradoxical] Whites, and the [real] Blacks ; the Williamses, Jameses, Paynes, Draytons, Gibsons, Roberts, Yates, Warners, Wilsons, Moores, and that of his Excellency, President BENTON.

Not only names, but titles also are equally significant, and show a like origin. The streets are Broad, and Ashmun, and as here, Griswold. The public buildings are a Church, a Seminary, a Senate, and a Court House.

If our visitor enters the residence of a thriving, thoughtful citizen, the same peculiarity strikes him. Every thing, however humble, is of the same Anglo-Saxon type and stamp. On the book-shelves or tables, are Bibles, Prayer or Hymn Books, Hervey's Meditations or Bunyan's Pilgrim's Progress, Young's Night Thoughts or Cowper's Poems, Walter Scott's Tales, or Uncle Tom's Cabin. In many places he will find well-used copies of Shakspeare and Milton. Not a few have enriched themselves with the works of Spenser and Wordsworth, Coleridge and Campbell, Longfellow and Bryant, Whittier and Willis, and of that loftiest of all the bards of the day, ALFRED TENNYSON. Should it happen to be a mail-day, or the " Stevens " has just glided into our waters, he would find at the Post Office, papers from America and England: "The Times," "Illustrated London News," "Daily Advertiser," "The Star," "The Guardian," "The New York Tribune," and "Commercial Advertiser," the "Protestant Churchman," and the "Church Journal." In one heap, "Littell's Living Age;" in another, "Chambers' Journal." Here, "Harper's Monthly;" there, "The Eclectic." Amid the mass of printed matter he would see, ever and anon, more ambitious works: Medical and Scientific Journals, Quarterly Reviews, the "Bibliothœca Sacra," "Blackwood" and other magazines.

Such facts as these, however, do not fully represent the power of the English tongue in our territory. For, while we repress all tendencies to childish vanity and idle exaggeration, we are to consider other telling facts which spring from our character and influence, and which are necessary to a just estimate of the peculiar agency we are now contemplating. And here a number of facts present themselves to our notice. Within a period of thirty years, thousands of heathen children have been placed under the guardianship of our settlers. Many of these have forgotten their native tongue, and know now the English language as *their* language. As a consequence, there has sprung up, in one generation, within our borders, a mighty army of English-speaking natives, who, as manhood approached, have settled around us in their homes from one end of the land to the other. Many of these take up the dialects of the other tribes in whose neighborhood their masters lived, but even then English is their speech. Thus it is that everywhere in the Republic, from Gallinas to Cape Palmas, one meets with a multitude of natives who have been servants in our Liberian families, and are daily in the utterance of English. A considerable number of these have enjoyed the opportunity of school instruction, and have carried back to the country the ability to read and to write English. In many cases, it is, in truth impossible to say whether their attainments should be suggestive of sorrow or of joy. I have had naked boys working for me on the St. Paul, who, when they wanted any thing, would write a note with as much exactness as I could. We all here know *one* native man, over the river, who is a leader in Devil-dances, and yet can read and write like a scholar. A friend of mine, travelling in the bush, nigh 200 miles from Monrovia, stopped one night, exhausted, at the hut of a native man, who brought him his own Bible to read, but alas! it was accompanied by a decanter of rum! The moral of such facts I shall not enter upon; but here is the simple fact, that by our presence, though in small numbers, we have already spread abroad, for scores of miles, the English language, written as well as spoken, among this large population of heathen.

The trading schemes of merchants and settlers, is another powerful auxiliary, in disseminating this language.

At every important point on the coast, Liberian, English, and American merchants have, for years, established their factories. Between Cape Palmas and Monrovia, there cannot be less than 30 factories. In each of these depots, some three or four English-speaking persons—Liberians—are living; in a few cases families have made them their permanent abodes; and thus, what with their native servants, the natives in neighboring towns, the more remote natives who flock hitherward for trade, and the few happy cases where pious young men devote a portion of their time to teaching; there is, and has been, a powerful, a wide-spread system in operation for the teaching and extension of English.

Another process has been for some time at work to spread our language. The interior natives have found out that a home in our vicinity is equivalent to an act of emancipation; and, as a consequence, remnants of tribes who for centuries have been the prey of their stronger neighbors, for the slave trade; and boys and men, upwards of 100 miles inland, who have been held in slavery; crowd in upon our neighborhood for freedom. Behind our settlements, on the St. Paul, there is the most heterogeneous mixture conceivable, of divers tribes and families, who have thus sought the protection of our commonwealth. Numbers of the Bassas, Veys, Deys, Golahs and especially the PESSAS, the hereditary slaves of the interior, have thus come to our immediate neighborhoods. Although I am doubtful of the *moral* effect of this movement upon *ourselves*, yet I feel no little pride in the fact that this young nation should become, so early, a land of refuge, an asylum for the oppressed! And I regard it as a singular providence, that at the very time our government was trumpeted abroad as implicated in the slave trade, our magistrates, in the upper counties, were adjudicating cases of runaway slaves, and declaring to interior slaveholders that, *on our soil*, they could not reclaim their fugitives!

Just here another important item claims attention, that is the *Missionary* agency in propagating this language. The reference here will be, chiefly, to the two uppermost counties of Liberia. Their younger sister, Sinou, I am sorry to say, has not, as yet, made any marked impression upon her surrounding heathen; more we believe through youth, and weakness, and suffering, than through indifference or neglect. Missionary operations, though participated in by others, have been chiefly carried on, in Bassa, by the Baptists. The means which have been employed have been preaching and schools. On the St. John's they have had for years a Manual Labor School, instructed by white Missionaries. This school has passed into the hands of a *native* Teacher, educated at Sierra Leone—a man who is the son of a prominent chieftain, and who possesses unbounded influence, as far as the Bassa tongue reaches. He has, moreover, these three prominent qualities; that is, he is a well-trained English scholar, a thoroughly civilized man, and a decided and well-tried disciple of the Lord Jesus Christ. His earnestness is evidenced in the fact that his work is unaided and self-supporting, and numbers of his tribe are glad to send him their children. Besides this means of influence, ministers have been accustomed to visit numerous towns and villages, preaching the Gospel. And thus, by preaching and schools a multitude of the Bassas have gained the English tongue, with many of its ideas and teachings.

The same Anglicizing influence has been carried on, but on a larger scale, in Montserrada County, but mainly through the Methodists; and they have spread our language widely abroad through that county, by the means of native schools, native children in their American schools, and missionaries residing in country towns, teaching and preaching as far back as the Golah tribe, and now among the Veys: native preachers, too, men converted to the faith, and moved by the Spirit to proclaim the glad tidings to their needy parents, brothers, and kin. I must not fail to mention the fact, that, during the last two years, one of their ministers has carried the English tongue some 200 miles in the interior,* and has spread it abroad amid the homes of the mild Pessas; thus preparing the way for legitimate trade, for civilization, for the Gospel of Jesus Christ, by the means of the spoken Word and the English Bible.

Thus, fellow-citizens, by these varied means the English language has been pushing its way among the numerous tribes of our territory. And thus, in a region of not less than 50,000 square miles, there are few places but where an English-speaking traveller can find some person who can talk with him in his own language.

And now I beg you to notice one point: this English, which we are speaking, and teaching the heathen to speak, is not our native tongue. This Anglo-Saxon language, which is the only language ninety-nine hundredths of us emigrants have ever

---

* The lamented Rev. George L. Seymour, Missionary and Traveller.

known, is not the speech of our ancestors. We are here a motley group, composed, without doubt, of persons of almost every tribe in West Africa, from Goree to the Congo. Here are descendants of Jalofs, Fulahs, Mandingoes, Sussus, Timmanees, Veys, Congos; with a large intermixture, everywhere, of Anglo-Saxon, Dutch, Irish, French, and Spanish blood—a slight mingling of the Malayan, and a dash, every now and then, of American Indian. And, perhaps, I would not exaggerate much, if I ended the enumeration of our heterogeneous elements in the words of St. Luke—" Jews and Proselytes, Cretes and Arabians."

And yet they all speak in a foreign tongue, in accents alien from the utterance of their fathers. Our very speech is indicative of sorrowful history; the language we use tells of subjection and of conquest. No people lose entirely their native tongue without the bitter trial of hopeless struggles, bloody strife, heart-breaking despair, agony, and death! Even so we. But this, be it remembered, is a common incident in history, pertaining to almost every nation on earth. Examine all the old histories of men—the histories of Egypt, China, Greece, Rome, and England; and in every case, as in ours, their language reveals the fact of conquest and subjection. But this fact of humiliation seems to have been one of those ordinances of Providence, designed as a means for the introduction of new ideas into the language of a people; or to serve, as the transitional step from low degradation to a higher and nobler civilization.

2. And this remark suggests, in the *second* place,

the query :—"What is the nature, and if any, the advantage of the exchange, we have thus, in God's providence, been led to make?"

The only way in which, in a fit manner, I can answer this question is, by inquiring into the respective values of our native and our acquired tongue. Such a contrast will set before us the problem of "Loss and Gain" which is involved therein. The worth of our fathers' language will, in this way, stand out in distinct comparison with the Anglo-Saxon, our acquired speech. And *first*, let us speak of the African dialects. I refer now to that particular group of aborigines who dwell in West Africa, from the Senegal to the Niger, and who have received the distinctive title of "Negro."

Within this wide extent of territory are grouped a multitude of tribes and natives with various tongues and dialects, which, doubtless, had a common origin, but whose point of affiliation it would be difficult now to discover. But how great soever may be their differences, there are, nevertheless, definite marks of inferiority connected with them all, which place them at the widest distance from civilized languages. Of this whole class of languages, it may be said, in the aggregate that (a) "They are," to use the words of Dr. Leighton Wilson, "harsh, abrupt, energetic, indistinct in enunciation, meagre in point of words, abound with inarticulate nasal and guttural sounds, possess but few inflections and grammatical forms, and are withal exceedingly difficult of acquisition."* This is

---

* "Western Africa," &c. 456, by Rev. J. L. Wilson, D.D.

his description of the Grebo; but it may be taken, I think, as, on the whole, a correct description of the whole class of dialects which are entitled "Negro." (b) These languages, moreover, are characterized by lowness of ideas. As the speech of rude barbarians, they are marked by brutal and vindictive sentiments, and those principles which show a predominance of the animal propensities. (c) Again, they lack those ideas of virtue, of moral truth, and those distinctions of right and wrong with which we, all our life long, have been familiar. (d) Another marked feature of these languages is the absence of clear ideas of Justice, Law, Human Rights, and Governmental Order, which are so prominent and manifest in civilized countries. And (e) lastly—Those supernal truths of a personal, present Deity, of the moral Government of God, of man's Immortality, of the Judgment, and of Everlasting Blessedness, which regulate the lives of Christians, are either entirely absent, or else exist, and are expressed in an obscure and distorted manner.

Now, instead of a language characterized by such rude and inferior features as these, *we* have been brought to the heritage of the English language. Negro as we are by blood and constitution, we have been, as a people, for generations in the habitual utterance of Anglo-Saxon speech. This fact is now historical. The space of time it covers runs over 200 years. There are emigrants in this country from the Carolinas and Georgia, who, in some cases, come closer to the Fatherland; but more than a moiety of the people of this country have come from Maryland and Virginia, and I have no doubt that there are scores, not to say hundreds of them, who are unable to trace back their sires to Africa. I know that in my own case, my *maternal* ancestors have trod American soil, and therefore have used the English language wellnigh as long as any descendants of the early settlers of the Empire State.* And, doubtless, this is true of multitudes of the sons of Africa, who are settled abroad in the divers homes of the white man, on the American continent.

At the present day, be it remembered, there are 10,000,000 of the sons of Africa alien from this continent. They live on the main land, and on the islands of North and South America. Most of them are subjects of European and American Governments. One growing prominent section of them is an independent Republic.† They speak Danish, Portuguese, Spanish, French, and English; the English-speaking portion of them, however, is about equal to all the rest together. The sons of Africa under the Americans, added to those protected by the British flag, number 5,000,000.‡

Now what is the peculiar advantage which Anglo-Africans have gained by the loss of their mother tongue? In order to answer this query, we must present those direct and collateral lingual elements in

---

* New York. † Hayti.

‡ In the N. Y. Tribune of the 10th January I find the following estimate:—NEGROES ON THIS CONTINENT.—It is estimated that there are some 14,000,000 persons of African descent on this continent. In the United States, they number 4,500,000; Brazil, 4,150,000; Cuba, 1,500,000; South and Central American Republics, 1,200,000; Hayti, 2,000,000; British Possessions, 800,000; French, 250,000; Dutch, Danish, and Mexican, 200,000.

which reside the worth and value of the English language, especially in contrast with the defective elements of the African dialects.

I shall not of course venture, to any extent, upon the etymological peculiarities of the English language; for even if I had time, I lack the learning and ability for such disquisition. Moreover the thoughts presented on such a day as this, should have a force and significance pertaining to national growth and a people's improvement. I shall therefore point out some of those peculiarities of the English language which seem to me specially deserving notice, in this country, and which call for the peculiar attention of thoughtful patriotic minds among us.

The English language then, I apprehend, is marked by these prominent peculiarities:—(a) *It is a language of unusual force and power.* This, I know, is an elemental excellence which does not pertain, immediately, to this day's discussion; but I venture to present it, inasmuch as you will see presently, it has much to do with the genius and spirit of a language. The English is composed chiefly of simple, terse, and forcible, one and two-syllabled words; which make it incomparable for simplicity and intelligibleness. The bulk of these words are the rich remains of the old Saxon tongue, which is the main stream, whence has flowed over to us the affluence of the English language. It is this element which gives it force, precision, directness, and boldness; making it a fit channel for the decided thoughts of men of common sense, of honest minds, and downright character. Let any one take up the Bible, the Prayer-Book, a volume of

Hymns of any class of Christians, the common proverbs, the popular sayings,—which strike deep into the hearts of men and flow over in their common spontaneous utterances; and he will see everywhere these features of force, perspicuity, and directness. Nor is it wanting in beauty, elegance, and majesty; for, to a considerable extent, this same Saxon element furnishes these qualities; but the English, being a composite language, these attractive and commanding elements are bestowed upon it, in fulness, by those other affluent streams which contribute to its wealth, and which go to make up its "well of English undefiled." (b) Again, the *English language is characteristically the language of freedom.* I know that there is a sense in which this love of liberty is inwrought in the very fibre and substance of the body and blood of all people; but the flame burns dimly in some races; it is a fitful fire in some others; and in many inferior people it is the flickering light of a dying candle. But in the English races it is an ardent, healthy, vital, irrepressible flame; and withal normal and orderly in its development. Go back to the early periods of this people's history, to the times when the whole of Europe seemed lost in the night of ignorance, and dead to the faintest pulses of liberty;—trace the stream of their descent from the days of Alfred to the present time, and mark how they have ever, in law, legislation and religion, in poetry and oratory, in philosophy and literature, assumed that oppression was an abnormal and a monstrous thing! How, when borne down by tyrannous restraint, or lawless, arbitrary rule, discontent and resistance have—

"Moved in the chambers of their soul."

How, when misrule became organic, and seated tyranny unreasoning and obstinate, they have demonstrated to all the world, how trifling a thing is the tenure of tyrants, how resistless and invincible is the free spirit of a nation!

And now look at this people—scattered, in our own day, all over the globe, in the Great Republic, in numerous settlements, and great colonies, themselves the germs of mighty empires; see how they have carried with them everywhere, on earth, the same high, masterful, majestic spirit of freedom, which gave their ancestors, for long generations, in their island home—

—"the thews of Anakim,
The pulses of a Titan's heart;"

and which makes *them* giants among whatever people they settle, whether in America, India, or Africa, distancing all other rivalries and competitors.

And notice here how this spirit, like the freshets of some mighty Oregon, rises above and flows over their own crude and distorted obliquities. Some of these obliquities are prominent. Of all races of men, none, I ween, are so domineering, none have a stronger, more exclusive spirit of caste, none have a more contemptuous dislike of inferiority; and yet in this race the ancient spirit of freedom rises higher than their repugnances. It impels them to conquer even their prejudices: and hence, when chastened and subdued by Christianity, it makes them philanthropic and brotherly. Thus it is that in England this national sentiment would not tolerate the existence of slavery, although it was Negro slavery. Thus in New Zealand and at the Cape of Good Hope, Statesmen, Prelates, Scholars, demand that a low and miserable aboriginal population shall be raised to their own level; and accept, without agonies and convulsions, the providence and destiny, which point plainly to amalgamation.* Thus in Canada it bursts forth with zeal and energy for the preservation and enlightenment of the decaying Indian. And thus in the United States, rising above the mastery of a cherished and deep-rooted spirit of caste; outrunning the calculations of cold prudence and prospective result; repressing the inwrought personal feeling of prejudice, it starts into being a mighty religious feeling which demands the destruction of slavery and the emancipation of the Negro! (c) *Once more I remark, that the English language is the enshrinement of those great charters of liberty which are essential elements of free governments, and the main guarantees of personal liberty.* I refer now to the right of Trial by Jury, the people's right to a participation in Government, Freedom of Speech, and of the Press, the Right of Petition, Freedom of Religion. And these are special characteristics of the English language. They are rights, which in their full form and rigid features, do not exist among any other people. It is true that they have had historical development: but their seminal principles seem inherent in the constitution of this race. We see in this people, even in their rude con-

---

* "See Church in the Colonies, No. xxii. A Journal of the visitation of the Bishop of Capetown. Also, letters of the Bishop of New Zealand, etc., etc."

dition, the roots from which have sprung so fair and so beautiful a tree. And these conserving elements, carefully guarded, deepened and strengthened in their foundations from age to age, as wisdom and sagacity seemed to dictate; illustrated and eulogized by the highest genius, and the most consummate legal ability; have carried these states, the old country, the Republic of America, and the constitutional colonies of Britain, through many a convulsive political crisis; the ship of state, rocked and tossed by the wild waves of passion, and the agitations of faction; but in the end leaving her to return again to the repose of calm and quiet waters!

In states thus constituted, no matter how deep may be the grievance, how severe the suffering, the obstructive element has to disappear; the disturbing force, whether man or system, must be annihilated!— for freedom is terrible as well as majestic; and the state emerges from the conflict with a fresh acquisition of strength, and with an augmented capacity for a nobler career and loftier attainments. This fact explains the progressive features of all Anglican political society. Revolution seems exoteric to it; but the tide of reform in legal, constitutional, channels, sweeping away obstructive hindrances, goes onward and upward in its course.

I quote here a remark of a distinguished writer, a lady :—" The original propensities of race are never eradicated, and they are nowhere more prominent than in the progress of the social state in France and England. The vivacity and speculative disposition of the Celt, appear in the rapid and violent changes of government, and in the succession of theoretical experiments in France; while in Britain, the deliberate slowness, prudence, and accurate perceptions of the Teuton, are manifest in the gradual improvement and steadiness of their political arrangements." (Here she quotes a passage from Johnson's Physical Atlas.) "The prevalent political sentiment of Great Britain is undoubtedly *conservative*, in the best sense of the word, with a powerful undercurrent of democratic tendencies which give great power and strength to the political and social body of this country, and make revolutions by physical force almost impossible.* * * * Great Britain is the only country in Europe which has had the good fortune to have all her institutions worked out and framed by her in a strictly *organic* manner; that is, in accordance with *organic wants* which require different *conditions* at different and successive stages of national development—and not by theoretical experiments, as in many other countries, which are still in a state of excitement consequent upon these experiments. The social character of the people of this country, besides the features which they have in common with other nations of Teutonic origin, is, on the whole, domestic, reserved, aristocratic, exclusive." *

The spirit of the above contrast is truly and accurately reproduced in the lines of a great poet:—

> "A love of freedom rarely felt,
>   Of freedom in her regal seat
>   Of England; not the school-boy heat,
>   The blind hysterics of the Celt."

* "[Mrs.] Somerville's Physical Geography," ch. 33.

And another of England's great poets, the calmest, quietest, the least impassioned of all her bards; moved by this theme, bursts forth in the burning words :—

> —— " We must
> Be free or die! who speak the language
> Shakspeare spake ; the faith and morals hold
> Which Milton held!"

(d) Lastly, in pointing out the main features of the English language, I must not fail to state *its peculiar identity with religion*. For centuries this language has been baptized in the spirit of the Christian faith. To this faith it owes most of its growth, from a state of rudeness and crudity, to its present vigor, fulness, and expressiveness. It is this moreover which has preserved its integrity, and kept it from degenerating into barren poverty on the one hand, or luxuriant weakness on the other. The *English Bible*, more than any other single cause, has been the prime means of sustaining that purity of diction, that simplicity of expression, that clearness of thought, that earnestness of spirit, and that loftiness of morals, which seem to be distinctive peculiarities of this language. Its earliest ventures for a true life, were wrestlings with the spirit of the Word. Previous to the invention of printing, pious Kings and holy Priests made their first attempts in English, in their rude essays to write, " in their own language," the words and precepts of the Gospels. Its first lispings were in Scriptural translations, its earliest stammerings in fervent prayers, holy Primers, and sacred minstrelsy. Then when the Press unfolded its leaves, its first pages were vernacular readings of the Word of God. From thence, ever since, as from a fountain-head, has flowed a mixed stream of thought and genius and talent, in all the departments of science, of law, and of learning; but the whole has been colored and leavened, and formed by, and under, the plastic influence of Christianity. The Bible and its precepts, has been the prompting spirit of its legal statutes, its constitutional compacts, its scientific ventures, its poetic flights, its moral edicts. But above and beyond all these, this language has delighted to expand and express itself in Tracts, and Tales, and Allegories; in Catechisms, and Homilies, and Sermons; in heavenly Songs, sacred Lyrics, and divine Epics; in Liturgies and Treatises, and glowing Apologies for the Faith; sweeping along in a pure and gracious flood, which in the end shall empty itself into a blessed eternity!

These then are the main peculiarities of this language, and these some of the rich gifts it bestows upon us. But while, indeed, dwelling as I do, with delight, upon the massy treasures of this English tongue, I would not have you to suppose that I forget the *loss* which has accompanied all this *gain*. Do not think, I pray you, that I am less a man, that I have less the feelings of a man; because I would fain illustrate a favoring providence,—

"And justify the ways of God to man."

No! I do not forget that to give our small fraction of the race the advantages I have alluded to, a whole continent has been brought to ruin; the ocean has been peopled with millions of victims; whole tribes of men have been destroyed; nations on the threshold of civilization reduced to barbarism; and generation upon generation of our sires brutalized! No, my remarks, at best, are discordant; and I avoid collateral themes in order to preserve as much unity as possible, while endeavoring to set forth the worth and value of the English language.

And this is our language. But notice here the marks of distinctive providence. Our sad and cruel servitude has been passed among men who speak this tongue; and so we have been permitted, as the Israelites of old, to borrow " every man of his neighbor, and every woman of her neighbor, jewels of silver and jewels of gold." * But now, on the other hand, as to that portion of our race whose lot has been cast among *other* sections of the European family; what advantages, what compensation have *they* reaped which can compare with *our* riches and our gain? Where do we find among them a Bill of Rights, the right of trial by Jury, or, an act of Habeas Corpus? Where do they know clearly and distinctly the theory of Free Speech, of a Free Press, of Constitutional Government?—where are they blessed with such a noble heritage as the English Bible, and all the vast wealth, both religious and political, of the literature of England and America? It is not in Cuba, nor in Porto Rico. Not in Guadaloupe, not in Martinique. Even in Brazil these ideas are but struggling for life; and their continued existence is doubtful. Time is yet to show whether either the white or black race

---

* Exodus, ch. xi. 2.

there, will ever rise to their full height and grandeur. With all our hopes of, and pride in Hayti, her history shows how sad a schooling she has had! In truth, how could France or Spain train the Negro race to high ideas of liberty and of government, when all their modern history has been an almost hopeless effort, to learn the alphabet of freedom,—to tread the first steps of legal self-restraint? I grant that not unfrequently they present the *individual* black man, refined, elegant, accomplished, and learned, far beyond any that spring up on American or English soil. But in capacity for free government, and civil order, the British West India Isles, Sierra Leone, the free colored men of America, and our own Republic are, without doubt, far in advance of all the rest of the children of Africa under the sun. * Indeed it is only under the influence of Anglo-Saxon principles that the children of Africa, despite their wrongs and injuries, have been able to open their eyes to the full, clear, quiet, heavens, of freedom, far distant, though at times they were!

3. I venture now to call your attention to a few remarks upon the probable destiny of this English language, in this country, and throughout this continent.

And here, as everywhere else on the globe, one cannot but see the most magnificent prospects for this noble language.* Its thought, its wisdom, its prac-

---

* I quote the following from a learned English journal:—" And as of all the works of man language is the most enduring, and partakes the most of eternity, as our own language, so far as thought can project itself in the future, seems *likely to be coeval with the world, and to spread*

ticality, its enterprising spirit, its transforming power, its harmonizing influence, and its Christian leavening, have gone out everywhere in our territory, and are changing and fashioning, not only our small civilized communities, but also gradually lifting up and enlightening our heathen neighbors. By a singular power it is multiplying its own means and agencies for a reproduction of influence, and a further extension of power in wider circles. As an illustration of this, we have here present to-day, by a remarkable providence, as guests—and we are glad to see them in our midst—the Captain and this large company of officers, of the little Steamer "Sunbeam," bound for the upper waters of the Niger; there to introduce trade and civilization, to pioneer letters and culture, and to prepare the way for the ENGLISH LANGUAGE and RELIGION.*

One cannot but mark the finger of marvellous providence, in the divers ways, in which this language is getting mastery over and securing hold upon the masses of natives through all Liberia. Look for instance at the fact that the *only* people these Krumen trust and rely upon, and with whom alone they

---

vastly beyond even its present immeasurable limits, there cannot easily be a nobler object of ambition than to purify and better it."—*Rev. J. C. Hare, Philological Museum*, vol. i., 665.

* The Steamer "Sunbeam" came into the Roads of Harper, Wednesday, 25th of July, and the captain, and his officers and company, joined in the procession on the 26th, having fired a salute in the morning. They all participated in the festivities at a public party in the evening, and went off to their steamer at eleven o'clock at night, amid the loud cheers of the citizens, who accompanied them to the water's side.

are willing to ship for sea, are men who speak the English language. And consider here the bearing of this fact upon the increase of this speech throughout the country. They come from all that section of the coast which lies between Bassa and Beribi, and inland upwards of 60 miles, and offer themselves as seamen. Indeed, the desire for this service is almost a passion among them; boys in scores, run away from their parents for sea-service; I have seen here, in Harper, fully that number together, on a Steamer day; and notwithstanding the hindrances and the monopoly of the coastwise natives, the interior people run all risks to reach the coast to go to sea. The vessels in which they ship as sailors are English-speaking vessels. And in this way a multitude of them are acquiring the habitual use of English. On the coast, between Bassa and this point, there are many large towns where, among adults, it is almost as constantly employed as in our civilized communities.*

Notice here another fact: among all the industrial pursuits of our citizens, trading absorbs as much attention as any other pursuit. Scores of our youth, soon after leaving school, start with their cloth, guns, powder, and tobacco, for the factory, whether on the coast or in the country. Added to this is the other fact, that from Sierra Leone to the Equator, the master commercial influence is English. Liverpool and Bristol, Boston, Salem, and Baltimore rule this coast. The numerous factories which now

---

* "Three-fourths of the population of the Kru country speak imperfect, but intelligible English."—Western Africa, &c., p. 103. By Rev. J. L. Wilson, D.D.

2*

exist, and those which are starting up everywhere along the coast and up our rivers, are English-speaking. So almost universally is this the case, that Dutch, French, and Sardinian vessels find an acquaintance with English an absolute necessity, and are lost without it.

Thus, by these varied means, the English language is gradually extending itself throughout this country, and rivalling the rude native tongues of our aboriginal population. Now all these divers streams of influence, operating daily and hourly all through the country, upon thousands of our native population, disclose to us a transforming agency, which is gradually subverting the native languages of our tribes. The influence is here; it is in operation; it is powerful. Every day by trading, by adventure, by the curiosity of the natives, by war at times, by the migration of tribes, by the hasty footsteps of fugitives— this English language is moving further and further interiorwards its centre, and sweeping abroad with a wider and wider circumference. Nor can it be resisted. It carries with it two mighty elements of conquest: it is attractive, and it is commanding: 1. It is *attractive*, in that it brings cloth, iron, salt, tobacco, fish, and brass rods, and all the other divers articles which are wealth to the native, and excite his desires. Poor, simple, childish, greedy creature! he cannot rest satisfied with the rudeness of nature, nor with the simplicity of his sires; and therefore he will part, at any moment, with the crude uncouth utterances of his native tongue, for that other higher language, which brings with its utterance, wealth and gratification.

2. It is *commanding*, too, as well as attractive. When used merely as the language of trade, it brings to these people the authority of skill, ingenuity, and art, in tasteful fabrics, in finely-wrought domestic articles, in effective instruments of warfare. The acquisition of it is elevation. It places the native man above his ignorant fellow, and gives him some of the dignity of civilization. New ideas are caught up, new habits formed, and superior and elevating wants are daily increased. Then the instruction in schools, and service in our own families for a few years, put the native boy so far in advance of his tribe that he must either become head-man or revolutionist; and if the latter, dividing the nation and carrying his party to a higher mode of living, and to a closer connection with Liberians or foreign traders.

As to the future results of this rivalry there can be no doubt; for, first of all, it is a superior tongue; and in all the ideas it expresses, it comes to the native man with command and authority; next, it appeals to him in the point of his cupidity; and his selfish nature yields to an influence which gratifies his desires and his needs. And it is thus, by the means of commerce, and missions, and government, that this language is destined to override all difficulties, and to penetrate to the most distant tribes, until it meets those other streams of English influence which flow from Sierra Leone on the north and from Abbeokuta on the east; and so, at the last, the English language and the English religion shall rule for

Christ, from the Atlantic to Timbuctoo, and all along both the banks of the Niger.*

Powerful as are these divers agencies in working out the end suggested, they are far inferior to one other, which I must hold up to distinctive notice. CHRISTIANITY is using the English language on our coast as a main and mighty lever for Anglicizing our native population, as well as for their evangelization.

I have already referred, in part, to the work of Missions: but there are some peculiarities in this work which clearly show that Christ is going to put all this part of the coast in possession of the English language, English law, and the English religion, for his own glory. Hundreds of native youth have acquired a knowledge of English in Mission Schools, and then in their manhood have carried this acquisition forth, with its wealth and elevation, to numerous heathen homes. Throughout the counties, Bassa and Montserrada, the Methodists have raised up numbers, in the wilderness, whose daily utterance is English; and they are doing this more at the present time than ever before. We, who are living in this county, know well what a disturbing element, Missions, here, have been, both to Heathenism and to the Grebo tongue. But how great has been this Missionary transformation of the Grebo to English, very few, I

---

* There seems every probability that the whole of that part of Africa, called Nigritia, which includes what is termed the Negro race proper, is to be brought under the influence of the English language, by the agency of black men, trained under Anglo-Saxon influences, at the Pongas Mission, Sierra Leone, Mendi Mission, Liberia, English Accra, Lagos, and Abbeokuta.

judge, have stopped to calculate. For instance, the Episcopal Mission, in this neighborhood, comprises at least 12 stations; and this has been its status for, at least, 12 years. At these stations, what with day-schools and night-schools, for a dozen scholars each; and remembering that, at Cavalla, 100 children, at least, are always under training, in reading, writing, and arithmetic; you can see that several thousands of our aboriginal population have received a common school education in the English language. And numbers of these persons show their appreciation of their advantages, by securing the same for their children, and coveting them for their kindred.

And thus, every year, wave after wave dashes upon the weak intrenchments of heathenism, and is wearing them away; and thus, also, to change a figure, we have illustrated the noble truth, that a great language, like the fruitful tree, yields fruit after its kind; "*and has its seed in itself;*" * by which it is not only reproduced in its own native soil, but also takes possession of distant fields, and springs up with all its native vigor and beauty, in far off lands, in remote and foreign regions!

And now, lest this subject should seem to have but slight connection with the rejoicings of the day, let me point out a few practical teachings which flow from it, and which clearly pertain to our nation's advancement, political and moral, and to its future usefulness and power.

1st. Then I would say, that inasmuch as the Eng-

* Gen. i. 11.

lish language is the great lingual inheritance God has given us for the future; let us take heed to use all proper endeavors *to preserve it here in purity, simplicity, and correctness.* We have peculiar need to make this effort, both on account of our circumstances and our deficiencies: for the integrity of any and all languages is assailed by the newness of scenes in which an emigrant population is thrown; by the crudity of the native tongue, with which it is placed in juxtaposition; and by the absence of that corrective which is afforded, in all old countries, by the literary classes and the schools. Here, in our position, besides the above, we have the added dangers to the purity of our English, in the great defect of our own education; in a most trying isolation from the world's civilization; in the constant influx of a new population of illiterate colonists;* and in the natural oscillation from extremely depressed circumstances to a state of political democracy, on the one hand, and an exaggeration of the "ologies," and "osophies" of school training, at the expense of plain and simple education, on the other. The correctives to these dangers are manifest. (a) *In our schools we must aim to give our children a thorough and sound training in the simple elements of common school education.* Instead of the too common effort to make philosophers out of babes, and savans out of sucklings; let us be content to give our children correctness, accuracy, and thoroughness, in spelling, reading,

---

* Since the delivery of this address a new element has been added to our population. The American Government is now sending recaptured Africans to Liberia.

writing, arithmetic, and geography. I cannot but regard it as a serious defect in the schools in Liberia, that so many teachers undertake to instruct their pupils in Chemistry, Botany, and Natural Philosophy, before they can write and spell with accuracy. It seems to me the wiser course is to ground our youth well in the *elements* of the simple branches, before any thing higher is undertaken. Where it is convenient and desirable, teachers may aim at something more. We are, most certainly, in need of learned men and accomplished women. The State moreover is not too young, nor our circumstances too humble for us, even now, to gather around us the fruits of the highest culture and of the profoundest attainments. But *all* learning in our schools should be built upon the most rigid and thorough training in those elements which enable people to spell and read correctly, and to understand and explain, such simple reading as comes before them in the Bible, the Prayer-Book, devotional books, and common newspapers. (b) But besides this, COMMON SCHOOL *education must needs be made more general, superior masters secured, and the necessities of the case be put more directly within the control of the citizens, than it is at present.* Perhaps there is no defect in our political system so manifest and so hurtful, as that its arrangements allow no *local* interests, whether it be in the election of a Constable, or the appointment of a Schoolmaster. As a consequence, all our growth seems to be the result of national, in the place of local enterprise; a feeling of dependence upon the Capital is exhibited everywhere; and there exists, universally, a lack of municipal pride and energy. It would be quite beyond the limits I have set before me, to enter upon this subject, else, I should venture to point out great and growing evils which are the result of this state of things; in the points, that is, of political ambition, local improvements, roads, and civil order. I confine myself, however to the subject of education; and I would fain call the attention of public men to the necessity of putting the power of common school education *in the hands of the people*, in townships,* with whatever measure of government aid can be afforded; if, indeed, they wish to see inaugurated a common school system in our country, and desire the continuance in the land, of sound English speech, thought, manners, and morals. (c) In addition to the above, let every responsible man in the country, and by responsible men, I mean Government Officers, Ministers, Teachers, and Parents, strive *to introduce among our youthful citizens a sound and elevating* ENGLISH LITERATURE. In this respect we are greatly endangered. There is going on, continually, a vast importation among our young men, of the vilest trash conceivable, in the form of books. They are, moreover, as poisonous as they are trashy. As trade and commerce increase, this evil will increase, and magnify itself; and it is a manifest duty to ward off and forestall this danger, as soon and as effectually as possible. Happily the antidote to this evil is simple,

---

* The wide diffusion of education which has distinguished New England from her earliest times, is owing to this arrangement. Its great and divers advantages are pointed out by De Tocqueville. See "Democracy in America," ch. V.

and easily available. There are a few standard English books which, some for generations, some in recent times, have served the noble purpose of introducing the youthful mind to early essays to thought and reflection; to the exercise of judgment and reason; and to the use of a chaste and wholesome imagination. It is the nature and office of books, to produce these grand results. "For books," to use the lofty periods of Milton, "are not absolutely dead things, but do contain a potency of life in them, to be as active as that soul whose progeny they are—nay, they do preserve, as in a vial, the purest efficacy and extraction of that living intellect that bred them! I know they are as lively, and as vigorously productive, as those fabulous dragons' teeth, and being sown up and down, may chance to spring up armed men." *

The particular works to which I refer, are so masterly, and have become so much the staple of the Anglo-Saxon mind, that in England, America, and the British colonies, numerous editions of them have been stereotyped, and may be had almost as cheap as palm leaves. I do not speak of the brilliant Essayists, of the profound Historians, of the sagacious Moralists. I am referring to another class of books, not less distinguished indeed, but more level to the common taste: works which have been scattered broadcast through the whole of Anglo-Saxondom, and the possession of which is attainable by the humblest persons, by the simplest investment. Any one of these books, which I shall mention, can be bought by any one, if he will practice daily a simple act of self-

---

* John Milton. Oration for "Unlicensed Printing."

denial, for a few hours, or put by, occasinally, a single twelve and a half cents. My catalogue would include the following works:

Locke on the Mind.	Life of Benjamin Franklin.
Bacon's Essays.	Life of James Watt.
Butler's Analogy.	Life of Mungo Park.
Paley's Natural Theology.	History of Rome.
Wayland's Moral Philosophy.	History of Greece.
Bunyan's Pilgrim's Progress.	History of England.
Robinson Crusoe.	Milton's Poems.
Alison on Taste.	Cowper's Poems.
Watts on the Mind.	Burder's Self-Discipline.
Channing's Self-Culture.	Todd's Student's Manual.

The entire list, as several of them are abridged, may be purchased for less than three dollars. But the value of such a Library to a youth, just starting into life, would be incalculable. And no better service could be done the cause of pure speech, correct diction, and earnest thought, than a general effort to put a Library of this kind within the reach of every intelligent boy in the country, of 15 years of age.*

(d) But besides the correct training of the *young*, I beg to insist upon *the great necessity of special care being bestowed upon the culture of the female mind in Liberia*. I feel that I cannot exaggerate the importance of this duty. The mothers, sisters, and daugh-

---

* Just here, while speaking of books, it is no more than duty to acknowledge the vast debt of obligation Liberian citizens owe Benjamin Coates, Esq., of Philadelphia, U. S. A. Scores of persons in Liberia will join in this expression of gratitude. The families are not a few, who, as in my own case, beside other books, have likewise their valuable Coates' Library.

ters of the land, are to train the whole of the rising generation, now growing up around us, down, forever through all the deep dim vistas of coming ages. The influence of woman in this great work is deeper and more powerful than that of man; and especially in those years of our life when we are most susceptible. But no one who looks carefully at the state of things in this country, can suppose, for a moment, that either justice is done to the intellect of this sex, or, that women, in this land, feel the burden of obligation which rests so heavily upon them. The latter fact, however, peculiarly affects me. I must confess myself amazed at the general frivolousness of the female mind in this country. It is one of the most astonishing problems that my mind has ever been called upon to solve, how women can live such trifling, unthinking lives, as they do in this land. When I look at the severe and rugged aspects of actual existence in this young country, I find it difficult to understand how it is that Parisian millinery can maintain such a tyrannous control, as it does, over the sex, from Cape Mount to Palmas.

I do not blame women so much for this state of things; nor do I forget the somewhat pardonable fact that dress is the *only* Fine Art we have in Liberia. The world has been six thousand years in existence, and it has hardly yet begun to do justice to the intellect of woman.* Here, on this soil, this injustice

---

* "It seems needful that something should be said specially about the education of women. As regards their interests they have been unkindly treated—too much flattered, too little respected. They are shut up in a world of conventionabilities, and naturally believe that to be the

cannot be perpetuated with safety. What with the present state of the census,—more than half of the population being females; and the colonization ships, from the necessities of the case, sending us every six months two women to one man; we shall, by and by, reach a state of moral shipwreck; and the sad examples of the heathen, will, ere long, begin to act injuriously upon our social and domestic state, if we are not careful and foresighted. This will surely be the case, especially in the humblest walks of life, if we do not strive to raise our daughters and our sisters to become the true and equal companions of men, and not their victims. He who keeps wide open the eyes God has given him, cannot be blind to some sad tendencies which already show themselves in our social state. And reform, in this particular, cannot commence too soon. Two or three things can be done immediately. (1) Let every respectable householder make the effort to put in his wife's hand some thoughtful Literary Journal, such as "Littell's Living Age," or "Chambers' Journal;" by which both taste and thought may be cultivated, and the mind be started on the track of reflection. (2) Let some influential persons attempt to gather, in clubs or a society, the aspiring matrons and young women, in our communities, for reading, composition and conversation upon improving topics. Let the scheme projected be humble and simple; let it be elementary, even in its nature; and by gradual steps, rise to something more

only world. The theory of their education seems to be, that they should not be made companions to men, and some would say they certainly are not."—*Friends in Council*, B. 1, ch. viii.

ambitious; why, indeed, may not ministers of the Gospel lead classes of their congregations in this intellectual effort? There is certainly nothing unholy in it; there is surely *much* that may lead to and foster piety in it; much that would have the sanction of Scripture. Indeed, is not the religion of Christ to be the great regenerating agent in all *mental*, as well as all spiritual things? Is not the CHURCH to take the lead in all things that are to elevate and dignify man? In any event, and by all means, do not let us go on in the dull, unthinking way we are now treading; and leave the minds of children and youth, in our families, unblessed by that pure speech and strong Anglo-Saxon thought, which come with the most impressive force, from the graceful mind, and the tender voice of cultivated womanhood.* (3) But the master need in Liberia is that of a FEMALE SEMINARY, *of a high order, for the education of Girls.* Already our wives and daughters are in the rear of ourselves and sons, in training and culture; humble as we all are, in this country, in acquirements, yet there is a *class* of men in Liberia who are fully fifty years in advance

---

* I cannot resist the temptation to add here another fine extract from the learned English journal before quoted. "It is a most happy and beautiful provision that children should imbibe their native language primarily and mainly from their mothers, should suck it in, as it were, along with their milk; this it is that makes it their mother tongue. For women are much more duteous recipients of the laws of nature and society; they are much less liable to be deluded by fantastical theories; and it is an old and very true remark, that in order to feel all the beauty and purity of any language, we must hear it from the lips * * * * * of a sensible, well-educated woman."—[*Rev.*] *J. C. Hare, Philological Museum,* vol. i., 644.

of our women, that is, intellectually. The operations of High Schools, now in existence, the High Schools for boys projected, the other educational preparations going on, for Colleges and Seminaries, the return, ever and anon, of professional young men, Lawyers, Doctors, Ministers, who are sent to America to be educated, with the mental training afforded men in mercantile pursuits, political contests, legal affairs and Legislative duty; will place men, before long, a century ahead of our women. Such mental inequality will be a dangerous state for the interests of education and for social well-being. The mental inferiority of women will retard the progress of our children and youth. The intellectual force of the country will more and more decline; Learning and Letters will be without influence; material interests will everywhere predominate; we shall lose the freshness and the force of all our Anglo-Saxon antecedents; and at length, men everywhere, will rise up and weigh their paltry purses in the scale, over against the strongest brains; and all manhood shall cease in the land! No better corrective to this sad tendency can be found than a good, sound, moral, English Education for those, especially, who will be entrusted with the rearing and training of our unborn children. I beg therefore to urge upon public attention, the immediate need of raising the standard of female education in this country. I beg to insist upon the deep necessity of elevating the mind of woman in the republic, and directing it to noble and commanding themes. I beg to enforce the duty of making woman in this land as superior, intellectual, and dignified, as we all would have her beautiful, and attractive, and moral. And to this end all heads of families should strive, at the earliest day, to fall upon some plan, to found a FEMALE SEMINARY, with an able staff of officers and teachers.*

2. The subject we have been considering, teaches the duty of *National* care and effort, that *our heathen neighbors be trained to the spirit, moral sentiments, and practical genius* of the language we are giving them.

I have already affirmed that more natives speak English in Liberia than Anglo-Africans. I wish to add to this, the almost certain fact, that by the arrival of Immigrants, by the opening of interior Stations by Missionary Societies in America, the number of native men and women who will read and write will, ere long, overwhelmingly predominate over us; so that for one civilized Liberian, there will be ten native men who will then speak English. Already our fellow-citizens have, at times, to make strange comparisons. It was only yesterday a respectable citizen told me that his hired woman expressed unwillingness, on

---

* I feel sure that, for the accomplishment of this end, we can, if necessary, look to that anxious and painstaking benevolence in America, which so very generally anticipates the intellectual needs of Liberia. But there are men of means enough in Liberia to start such an undertaking; and there are scores who are able to pay a good sum annually, to give their daughters a substantial, and at the same time, a refined education.

Since the delivery of this address, Rev. Mr. Blyden has been acting in accordance with the above suggestion in England; and has succeeded, I learn, in raising a considerable amount of funds for a female High School in Liberia.

a recent occasion, to attend prayers in his family, because his native boys could read and she could not. Her ignorance of letters shamed her, "and made her feel," to use her own wise expression, "more than ever before the importance of education." These comparisons are becoming too frequent; and by and by they will extend to communities as well as to individuals, unless we provide more fully for the improvement of our own colonists. But I only mention the above facts in order to show how rapid is the advance of the heathen in our own knowledge and acquaintance. And now the question arises, are these people to be quickened by letters to become only *intelligent* heathen? Are we, by contact with them, to give them only an intellectual paganism? Is our influence upon them to touch only the brain, and not life, manners, the family, society? or rather should we not as a Nation, take upon us the duty of so training these people, that as they receive the language, so they may likewise receive the civilization, the order, the industry, and the mild, but transforming influences of a regulated Christian state? The Mission of Liberia, in its civil aspects, is clear to my mind. This nation is to restore society all along our coast; and by restoring society to regulate social life, to quicken in its growth the "tender plant of confidence," in both a direct and indirect manner to elevate the domestic state, to give rise to industrial activity, and to establish good neighborhood. However humble the effort may be, still it seems to me that we ought to have, in each county, an industrial School for *native* boys who are fugitives, or wanderers, or who have been convicted of crime; where they could be trained to the use of the plough and hoe, and receive a good, but simple English education. Our neighbors too, that is, those who live near our settlements, should be bound, by law, to make broad and substantial roads for travel, to keep the Sabbath, and to conform more to our habits of dress than they now do. Moreover we cannot be too early in giving them the benefit of the great Saxon institutions of Trial by Jury, and personal protection. Life should be made sacred among them in the neighborhoods of our larger towns. The Sassy-wood Ordeal should be put an end to, and a due process of law guaranteed to all criminals and suspected parties among them. This I know could not be done in remote places; but in the vicinity of our towns and settlements, sanguinary retaliation, envy, and revenge should not be allowed to show themselves as they now do; nor the awful scenes which take place, almost under our eyes, be suffered to barbarize our children. Indeed, both for their benefit and our own, law and authority cannot be too soon established among them on a firm basis, and *with full legal forms*. It is a matter alike of policy and of duty for us to attempt, though at a humble distance, the same legal reformation among this people that the English have, with great success effected in India. There is no greater disparity *here* in our relative numbers, than *there*, between the Christian power and the heathen masses; while here we have a population at once simple and unenlightened to deal with, and the presence and protection of the three chief naval powers of the world. Moreover we have this encouragement in any such undertaking, namely, that our heathen neighbors are ambitious of improvement, and always welcome the changes and the regulations, which tend to make them "Americans."

3. Finally let us aim, by every possible means, *to make indigenous, in this infant country, the spirit and genius of the English language,* in immediate connection with its idiom.

You all doubtless remember the solemn utterance of St. James that "the body without the spirit is dead."* So likewise a language without its characteristic features, stamp, and spirit, is a lifeless and unmeaning thing, and must, ere long, degenerate into a crude, mongrel, discordant jargon. If the English had educated their West India blacks they would never have committed so great a blunder, as they did before emancipation, as the publication of the Bible for them, in broken English:—a miserable caricature of their noble tongue. All low, inferior, and barbarous tongues are, doubtless, but the lees and dregs of noble languages, which have gradually, as the soul of a nation has died out, sunk down to degradation and ruin. We must not suffer this decay on these shores, in this nation. We have been made, providentially, the deposit of a noble trust; and we should be proud to show our appreciation of it. Having come to the heritage of this language we must cherish its spirit, as well as retain its letter. We must cultivate it among ourselves; we must strive to infuse its spirit among our reclaimed and aspiring natives. And

* St. James, ii. 26.

what that spirit is we have witnessed in the character of the people among whom we have lived, across the waters; in their strong institutions; in the history of their ancestors; in the distinctive features of their governmental antecedents; in their colonies; their religion, letters, and commerce. The spirit of the English language is the spirit of Independence, both personal and national; the spirit of free speech and a free press, and personal liberty; the spirit of reform and development; the spirit of enterprise; the spirit of law, of moral character, and spiritual beneficence.

With these ideas we have been familiar from our youth. Wherever the English language is spoken these sentiments are the daily utterances of men. Even in those cases where there is the widest separation between theory and practice, even there the *idea* of freedom exists and secures expression. The American black man, even in the States of slavery, has been in a school of freedom, from which even the Italian, the German, the Frenchman, the Russian, and the Sardinian, have been separate and alien. He has had unfolded to him, in harangues, in public speeches, in grand orations, in the social talk of the table and the fireside, in the august decisions of Courts and Legislatures, and in the solemn utterances of State papers, all the sublime abstractions of human rights and civil freedom.

You and I have been accustomed to the utterance of the noblest theories of liberty, the grandest ideas of humanity, all our lifetime; and so were our fathers. And although we have been shorn of our manhood, and have, as yet, attained only a shrivelled humanity; still there is some satisfaction in the remembrance, that ideas conserve men, and keep alive the vitality of nations. These ideas, alas! for the consistency of men! though often but abstractions *there*, have been made realities *here*. We have brought them with us to this continent; and in this young nation are striving to give them form, shape, and constant expression. With the noble tongue which Providence has given us, it will be difficult for us to be divorced from the spirit, which for centuries has been speaking through it. For a language acts in divers ways, upon the spirit of a people; even as the spirit of a people acts with a creative and spiritualizing force upon a language. But difficult though it be, such a separation is a possibility. And hence arises the duty of doing all we can to keep alive these grand ideas and noble principles. May we be equal to this duty—may we strive to answer this responsibility! Let us endeavor to live up to the sentiments breathed forth in all the legal charters, the noble literature, the religious learning of this tongue. Let us guard, even here, the right of FREE SPEECH. Let us esteem it one of the proudest boasts of this land, and, to appropriate the happy language of a heathen—esteem it "the rare felicity of our times that, in this country, one can think what he pleases, and speak what he thinks."* Let us prize the principle of PERSONAL LIBERTY, as one of the richest jewels of our constitutional diadem. Let us not shrink from the severest test to which a heathen

---

* "Rara temporum felicitate, ubi sentire quæ velis, et quæ sentias dicere licet."—*Tacitus*, *Hist.*, lib. 1, cap. 2.

and degraded population around us, may at times strain it. Let us, amid all the extravagances of their crude state, guarantee, even them, the full advantage of it. Conscious of the nobleness of this great constitutional principle, may we allow it full force and unrestricted expression. Let us rejoice that our Republic, diminutive as it is in the group of nations, is already a refuge for the fugitive; and congratulate one another upon the fact that we can already apply to our state and position, the proud lines of Whittier:—

> "No slave-hunt in our borders, no pirate on the strand,
> No fetters in Liberia! no slave upon our land."

Let us endeavor, by the reading of their Journals; by close observation of that venturesome enterprise of theirs, which carries them from " beneath the Arctic circle, to the opposite region of Polar cold;"— by a careful inspection of their representatives, who visit these shores; and by a judicious imitation of their daring and activity; let us strive to catch and gain to ourselves somewhat the SPIRIT OF ENTERPRISE AND PROGRESS which characterizes them, in all their world-wide homes. Moreover, let us cultivate the principle of INDEPENDENCE, both as a nation and as individuals, and in our children; as, in itself a needed element of character, as the great antidote to the deep slavishness of a three centuries' servitude, and as a corrective to the inactivity, the slothfulness, and the helplessness, which are gendered by a tropical clime. I am well aware of the exaggeration to which all men are liable to carry this sentiment; but this, indeed, is the case with all the other noble principles which I have alluded to. This possibility of excess is one of the conditions of freedom. You cannot hem it in, nor any of its accessories, within the line of strict propriety, to the rigid margin of cold exactitude. And the spirit of independence, the disposition to modest self-reliance, the feeling of one's being sufficient for one's own needs, and temporal requirements; is just one of those golden elements of character, which needs to be cultivated everywhere among our population. It is conservative, too, as well as democratic; and if it does overflow at times its banks, it will not be long ere it will delight to come back to, and run, in its proper channel. An antidote to its extravagances, will, moreover, be found in the cultivation of another prime characteristic of the English language, that is, ITS HIGH MORAL AND SPIRITUAL CHARACTER. Remembering that "righteousness exalteth a nation, but that sin is a reproach to any people;" let us aim at the cultivation among us, of all that sensitive honor, those habits of honesty, that purity of manners and morals, those domestic virtues, and that evangelical piety, which are peculiarly the attributes of Anglo-Saxon society, States, and homes.

So, by God's blessing, shall we prove ourselves not undeserving of the peculiar providence God has bestowed upon us; and somewhat worthy the inheritance of the great and ennobling ENGLISH LANGUAGE.

THE

DUTY OF A RISING CHRISTIAN STATE

TO CONTRIBUTE TO THE WORLD'S WELL-BEING AND CIVILIZA-
TION, AND THE MEANS BY WHICH IT MAY PERFORM
THE SAME.

*Delivered before the Common Council and the Citizens of Monrovia,
Liberia, July 26, 1855, being the day of National Independence.*

"Even so doth God protect us, if we be
Virtuous and wise. Winds blow, and waters roll,
Strength to the brave, and Power and Deity;
Yet in themselves are nothing! One decree
Spake laws to *them*, and said that by the soul
Only, the Nations shall be great and free."

WORDSWORTH.

"As men in proportion to their moral advancement learn to enlarge the circle of their regards; as an exclusive affection for our relations, our clan, or our country, is a sure mark of an unimproved mind, so is that narrow and unchristian feeling to be condemned * * * * which cares for no portion of the human race, but that to which itself belongs."—DR. ARNOLD.

"No man can, by care-taking, as the Scripture saith, add a cubit to his stature in this little model of a man's body; but in the great frame of kingdoms and commonwealths, it is in the power of princes or estates to add amplitude and greatness to their kingdoms. For by introducing such ordinances, constitutions, and customs as are wise, they may sow greatness to their posterity and successors."

—LORD BACON.

ORATION.

This day is the festival of our national independence; the day of all the year dedicated to joy, thanksgiving, the sober thought of national responsibility, and the earnest pondering upon future destinies. Let us accept the delights and privileges it proffers us; tempering the elastic joy of youth with the calmer reflection of maturer years, and the sage wisdom of age.

I occupy the position to which you have appointed me with reluctance, and stand here to fulfil its duties with painful diffidence; for the brief period given me by the Committee, has not afforded me time to prepare for the duty of the day, in a manner adapted to the occasion, nor with justice to myself: and, therefore, I am sure there will be no expectation of pleasing oratory here, nor of the high gratification which it affords. Perhaps, however, the simple words and the plain thoughts I may present to you may find rather a more attentive ear, especially from more sober years and minds.

For you will remember that the first anniversaries of this Republic have passed away: and the warm exuberance of new-born nationality has given place to care, to thought, to the consciousness of burdened duty, the weight of national responsibility, and the heavy cares of citizenship and government. And, therefore, we may more properly, at this time, think about our duties and our obligations, as a Christian State, and ponder the responsible future now coming quickly upon us.

Moreover, this, I should judge, would be the thoughtful tendency of all thinking men among us. The burdens of State are increasing every day. Deep and weighty questions are constantly arising. More and more are we brought into relation with foreign lands. And young as we are, the future begins to loom upon us with import and solemnity.

Such questions have much filled my own mind since my residence in this country. And during the few days which I have spent in preparing this address, no subject has seemed more deserving of notice than this:—"THE DUTY OF A RISING CHRISTIAN STATE TO CONTRIBUTE TO THE WORLD'S WELL-BEING AND CIVILIZATION; AND THE MEANS BY WHICH IT MAY PERFORM THE SAME." And this is my subject for the day.

With respect to this point of obligation, fortunately for the speaker, as well as for the apprehension of his audience, the idea of duty and obligation is one so common and so manifest that it needs but be mentioned to be felt. The truth comes in upon us from different sources, and in divers streams. The simple details of common culture, the inobtrusive elements of schooling, the plainest fabrics of constant wear, the enjoyment of the staples of daily life, the facts of commerce, and the observations of travel, however limited by individual observation; all, with clearest tone and manifest significance, bespeak the mutual dependence of the different families of men, as also the obligation of all states and commonwealths and empires to contribute to human well-being and the progress of nations.

Among the diverse evidences and suggestions of this principle, there are some few most prominent. Let me endeavor to prove and illustrate the truth, the fixedness, and the universality of this obligation; for the sake of the benefit and the strength of its repetition, and of the internal refreshing which comes from the "line upon line," "the precept upon precept," and which ever proceeds from the iteration of all prime truths, all great and fundamental ideas, all large and noble principles.

I commence this argument, for which I feel and know myself unfitted, with the remark that, *The relations which nations bear to the whole family of man in the aggregate, attest this obligation, and press this duty.*

For there *is* a relation between individual, distinctive, nationalities, and the entire race. There is a significant meaning in that new word just introduced into our language, that is, the "*solidarity* of nations:" for a nation is a collection of men; not of angels, not of demi-gods, not of indescribable celestials; but of MEN—men of flesh, and blood, and bone, and muscle; men "of the earth, earthy;" men of the same make, and nature, and appetencies, and destiny, as ourselves, and the men of all other nations; and, therefore, a nation is but a section of the great commonwealth of humanity, a phase of the common type of being, and no more.

The endless migrations, the strange wanderings, the multitudinous progenitures, and the colonial formations which have originated the nations of earth, eschew the idea of isolation, and show that all are but fragments, separate, broken, detached, from some large parent form, itself of like origin, which has spread itself out, on every side, the common mother of nations and races.

For such is the light which shines even from the gloom of history: from one single pair and parentage —a race; from the dawn of time to the days of Noah. From the deluge, three distinct forms of race and family, which have again budded into life and energy divers nationalities, of immortal renown, of boundless influence, and commanding name, through all the tracks of time. And then, again, since the days of our Lord Christ, and especially since the Reformation, how the Scandinavian and the Norman races have streamed out from their crowded homes or hives in the far north and formed those great and mighty nations; which, notwithstanding the semi-barbarism of ages, and their brutal love of fight, have mastered the world by law, and genius, and learning, and science, and the genial outgrowings of art; and have blessed mankind by the religion which has ever tempered their rudeness! Nor yet is it Europe only that feels the tread of their feet and the might of their presence and their influence. They have gone out in commerce, in trades, in corporations, and in missions; —streaming along the banks of both sides of the North American continent, and leaving, as their footprints, on those mighty shores, cities, and states, and commonwealths, and empires; filling the archipelagoes of both the eastern and western hemispheres with their offspring, their laws, their letters, and religion; dipping down into the far south seas, and sowing the seeds of European civilization among the scattered remnants of the Malayan race, far off in the wide, wide ocean; reproducing their restless energy, their creative intellect, and their vital faith, on the shores of Africa and India; aiming thence to bear them across the steppes of the Altai and to the central regions of this vast continent.

But view this mutual interdependence of nations in other aspects. Look out upon the broad and chequered field of universal history, and mark some few of its more prominent events which illustrate the truth we are now considering. We go back some 4,000 years in time. We tread the sedgy banks of the Nile; and a princely maiden, while taking her morning bath, discovers among the bulrushes an ark of flags, bearing as its precious burden a tender Jewish babe. The infant boy is carried to the Royal Palace of the Pharaohs; and from that palace comes forth, in time, that superior man, the leader of that immortal race so distinguished in the destinies of man, and in the economy of God,—the man Moses; in whose one single name is gathered and included, statesman, lawgiver, general, and prophet. And here we see the rise of that wondrous code of laws, that system of equity, order, and justice, that prolific, as well as mysterious, ecclesiastical polity, which makes the Jewish race the most singular and prominent; but which has ever since influenced the destinies of man in every way, more than any other cause in human history. We pass on to a later stage: and from the eastern side of the Ægean we see the movement of small communities across its beautiful waters, to seat themselves on the fair shores of Greece; whither flowed the streams, now deep, now shallow, of all the world's high thought, its culture and refinement: and Greece stands forth in all history the central point of intellectual greatness, taste, and wisdom. But these existed not for Greece alone: all civilized Europe through the ages, civilizing and expanding Americans, Hindoos, Indians, and regenerated Africans; all men of thought throughout the earth, seize upon, and ponder, and strive to master these fine creations of the Grecian mind, as the great teachers of thought and genius.

The strong, active, energetic Roman rises before us with a fabulous origin, strangely contrasting with the real, actual life and bearing, which mark his strong hand and his iron sway for centuries. But though Roman history is the story of the mastery of might over right, of the abeyance of individual freedom, of the crushing out of national life, of splendid, but barbaric brute force; yet Rome has transmitted the legacy of two valuable principles to man—INVINCIBLE ENERGY, AND THAT OF LAW AND GOVERNMENT.

The Jew, the Greek, the Roman—types of religion, of intellect, and power; they have vanished and departed. But still their spirit remains; for that spirit forms the elements of our faith, of our culture, and of our national rule and State polity. The religion which we profess, the modes of reasoning we adopt, the intellectual methods we employ, the elements of our youthful instruction, our modes of government, the authority and the forms of law, the simplest types of architecture, and some of the commonest modes of manners and refinement, all link the present with the past, and clearly show the unity of the race.

The race, in the aggregate, is to go forward and upward. This is the destiny which God has incorporated in the very elements of our moral being. The failure of *this* type, or the destruction of *that* form, is no prevention of nature's upward reaching. They are as the falling of the leaves in a foreign autumn, in consequence of which, in spring-time, the forest appears, apparelled in beauty, and gorgeously laden with masses of foliage. And to this advancement all the sections of the race are to add their contributions, and to send in their quota of gift and influence. And thus we see that all the preceding generations of mankind, and all the various nations, have lived for every successive generation, and *all* have been the workers for, and the benefactors of, *this* age in which we live, and of this land which we call our country and our home. And so there is no isolation; no absolute disseverance of individual nations; for blood and lineage, and ancient manners, and religion, and letters, all tend to combine nationalities and link them in indissoluble bonds, despite all the lapses of time. In this manner, therefore, we are taught that the Hebrew polity, so wise, so just, and so sacred, was not local in its bearings and intents; but that, in its ultimate ends and aims, it was *our* polity, and the polity of all Christendom, ay, and of all the world. For us, moreover, Greece was raised up with her unrivalled eloquence, matchless wisdom, and fine ideas and forms of beauty. And Rome—imperial Rome—stands before us, immortal! in practical wisdom, in stirring energy, and in her matchless capability of rule!

Indeed it is no exaggeration to say that our life, our culture, and our civilization are but the result of the ceaseless energy of mind and body of all past nations. And of all these nations, if we are grateful men, we are bound to turn to Palestine, Greece, and Italy, with beaming eyes; and, to use the words of Arnold, "draw near with reverence" to them, "as those higher causes which, proceeding directly from the inscrutable will of our Maker, seemed designed to humble the presumption of fancying ourselves the arbiters of our own destiny;"* and, if I may add my own words to *his* profundity and insight,—seemed designed also to teach us, as a nation, that we are not to live merely for ourselves, but to bless the present generation of nations, and to send down the beneficence of our regards, of our activities, and our virtues to other peoples, and to future times!

I go on to show the obligation of nations to contribute to the well-being and civilization of man,

---

* Dr. Arnold. See Miscellanies.

from a consideration of the moral ends and duties of nations.

The primary ends of civil government are the conservation of men's lives, bodies, and goods. But there are also remote and ultimate ends, which pertain to Morals, Duty, Obligations, and Justice.

For moral character is an idea—as true, exact, and absolute, applied to a nation as to a man. A moral system which claims authority only in its private, personal, application to men, but withdraws from them so soon as the individual is merged in the association or the body politic, is nothing but vagueness, darkness, and confusion. "Nations and individuals," says Channing, "are subjected to one law. The moral principle is the life of communities." Under no moral code can the individual eschew truth and justice. Neither can the nation throw them aside, and perform its functions, treating right, and truth, and principle as matters of indifference: for the magistrate and the lawgiver meet the august presence of Truth alike in all the details of administrative law, and in the commonest minutiæ of civil regulation.

We cannot, indeed, speak of the *conscience* of a nation; for conscience is so personal a quality, that it is only by a strong figure of speech that we can apply it to nations. But all those moral qualities which are subsidiary to conscience are so manifestly brought out and recognized in all, even the minutest, acts and offices of government, that it is but a bare, distinct verity, and no metaphor, to speak of the moral duties and obligations of nations.

The internal moral obligations of nations are plain and evident: cultivation of religion, the maintenance of justice, the progress of education, the upholding of law and order, and national growth. All these arise from the *paternal* relation of government: a doctrine as old as it is true, and recognized by heathen nations, as well as by the Hebrew writers.

But now we are led to ask, "Are there not *external* moral duties resting upon nations?" Moral law applies to them in relation to their citizens and subjects; but does it not also apply to them with respect to bodies outside of their own rule and power? Do not nations owe duty and obligation to other nations? Such, we cannot doubt, is the common consent of mankind and the teaching of all national history; though dimmed and obscured in olden times by cruel barbarism and savage wars. We catch a glimpse of this in the leagues, compacts, and alliances of Pagan nations. The treaties they formed for the promotion of commerce, the mutual obligation for aid and succor in times of danger, bespeak a sense of national obligation to benefit and bless. They showed the presence of these principles, in the very article of war, by beautiful displays of equity, of honor, and of clemency. When the thirty tyrants at Athens drove out the very flower of that city, and forbade the other cities of Greece to show them hospitality or to give them succor; the people of Thebes humanely received them, and, by law, threatened those of their own citizens who might refuse to assist these unprotected refugees. "War has its rights as well as peace," said Camillus,* the Roman Dictator, struck with horror and disgust at the treachery of one of the Falisci, against whom he was warring. Indeed, warlike and domineering as the Romans were, they frequently exhibited honor, magnanimity, and justice. Their common practice of siding with the oppressed and of defending the weak may have been policy, but it was also the teaching and the instinct of generosity and high-mindedness. And the equity and the faithfulness with which they generally carried out their promises to the vanquished, show the presence, even in their darkened state, of those large and noble principles of humanity which now are part of the law of nations; and they also teach that which I am endeavoring to elucidate—that is, that it is the moral duty of nations to advance human well-being and the civilization of the race.

Under the influence of Christianity, the idea of brotherhood has been gaining influence and authority; so, likewise, the principle of national good-will has kept pace with the moral progress of the age. Ruthless brute force, unreasoning domination, no longer decide the fate of inferior nations. Moral considerations have now a decided influence in regulating national intercourse. So strong is this influence, that "international law" has become a distinctive branch, commanding the life-long attention of distinguished minds. So pure, humane, and genial is its spirit, that one great authority declares its purpose to be, " to insure the observance of justice and good faith in that intercourse which must frequently occur between

* Livy, b. 5.

two or more nations."* A great moralist of our own day declares that "'international law' is capable of progressive standards; that it must acknowledge the authority of morality, and must, in order to conform to the moral nature of man, become constantly more and more moral."† One remarkable evidence of this genial progress of moral law among nations is the fact that the chief states of Christendom have concertedly, and without the desire of advantage, but from principles of humanity, discouraged and condemned the slave trade. So, likewise, the cause of peace, which once was the scoff of wits, and which elicited the sneer of the great, has now lost all its supposed littleness. For, at this day, gray-haired veterans in states-craft recognize with clearness the binding tie of humanity, and esteem it the highest statesmanlike wisdom, and the noblest achievement of diplomacy, to stay the effusion of blood, and to bind in concord the families of nations. I verily believe that RUSSELL the statesman, would rather have won a peace at Vienna, than have been the hero of Alma, of Balaklava, or of Inkermann; and to gain power, as a Minister of England, that thereby he may stanch the wounds of bleeding nations, is, I feel, a higher object of ambition to the mercurial DISRAELI than all the boast of military renown; and this not merely from considerations of policy or from motives of gain, but because the civilization of England is interpenetrated by the FAITH of England, and her large-minded statesmen recognize the obligation of morality in all the machi-

---

* Blackstone.
† Dr. Whewell, "Elements of Morality," b. vi., chap. 1.

nery of statesmanship. And thus the Christian sentiment of the world forces itself upon states, and diplomacies, and policies, and FIXES the noble sentiment that a nation, even as the personal being, cannot hold itself back from the law of moral responsibility. For, as no individual man can draw himself off from his fellow-man, and proclaim,' '*I am distinct from the mass of humanity*,'' so no nation can set itself off, unconcerned, from the rest of the race. "No man liveth to himself," is a truth as positive in its application to a nation as to a man; a truth recognized everywhere, and in all history; anticipated, long centuries before its sacred utterance, as truly veritable as on the day when the inspired penman wrote it. For the words of the heathen Terence—

"Homo sum; humani nihil a me alienum puto"—

contain just the same spirit as the sentiment of Shakspeare—

"One touch of nature makes the whole world kin."

Once more, I would further add that, if related humanity and moral law teach beneficence as the duty of nations, so, likewise, *the commerce of nations.* For this seems the clear mandate of Heaven: "The nations that will not hold intercourse with other peoples, in trade and barterings, and thus bless the world, they shall suffer and shall die!"

A non-commercial spirit and practice has always stifled the life of nations, or laid them low in ruins. In the history of the "Decline and Fall" of nations, this will yet be shown to have been one of the most potent agencies of national decay; for among the elements of the life of nations some of the chiefest are the commodities of foreign lands, the infused blood of foreign people, the freshening influence of foreign thought and sentiment, and the quickening power of foreign enterprise and activity. We see, in different quarters of the globe, the scattered, broken relics of divers nations. Some, like the inhabitants of the isles of the sea, remained, untold centuries, apart from the world's civilization, until some venturesome navigation brought them into contact with cultivated man; and then they went down at once to speedy decay and swift destruction, the very atmosphere of cultivated life proving too strong for their emasculated natures. It is said that no enlightenment, no cultivation, not even Christianity, can save the Sandwich Islanders; the degeneracy of heathenism, their long isolation from the human family for so many centuries, have so lessened their vitality and vitiated their blood, that there is no hope for them, and they must die out! With their partial civilization, the Chinese stood still for centuries, refusing commercial intercourse with the nations; and God's providence brought forth the penal fruits of their national pride and misanthropy; for, *first*, they were made to experience that saddest of all national ills save death, a wrested, stunted growth, the reversion of that great law of being, the law of progress and expansion—and *next*, turning fierce upon humanity, and refusing that interchange of thought, and sentiment, and trade, which aids the life of both men and nations, humanity rose up in the person of Britain, and inflicted upon her sore and humbling chastisement.

How strongly contrasted is the beneficial influence of commerce! How prolific the favors and the fruits it everywhere begets! How numerous the blessings it scatters abroad on every side! It is a remark of Dr. Arnold, " Well, indeed, might the policy of the old priest-nobles of Egypt and India endeavor to divert their people from becoming familiar with the sea, and represent the occupation of a seaman as incompatible with the purity of the highest castes. The sea deserved to be hated by the old aristocracies, inasmuch as it had been the mightiest instrument in the civilization of mankind."* The page of history proves this. There are few secular agencies so life-giving, so humane, and so civilizing, as is commerce. Let a nation sleep the sleep of a century's dulness, and then some propitious providence draw towards it the needs and desires of the nations; and up it starts to life and vigor. Long, long eras had passed away, vast generations of men had gone down to the slumbers of the sod; and all the while, from the world's infant days, the wild waters of the Pacific had laved the banks of California, undisturbed by the fluttering sails and the flying wheels of commerce. But the report of its gold encircled the globe, and all the world, civilized and heathen, sends its representatives to her shores; civilization crowns and adorns her valleys and her hills; and religion and enlightenment set up their standard along the Pacific shores of America for all future times.

Equally apparent is the elevating and civilizing influence of commerce. Contact and acquaintance

* Dr. Arnold. See Miscellanies.

of nation with nation soften asperities and angularities of character, introduce the better and superior manners of each into the other, and cause the mutual communication and introduction of new, original, and noble ideas.

Its bearing upon system, order, morals, is manifest. The Carthaginian and the Roman merchants were noted for their sterling honesty and their love of justice. People who are uncommercial are given to dissimulation, fraud, and trickery. No class of men who have the true commercial spirit are so; for the more commercial they become, the more honest are they in their dealings, and the more exact and trustworthy.

And thus, from these few hints, we can easily see what a civilizer is commerce; how it binds men and nations to each other; how it promotes good-will, and builds up sterling character. And the consideration of the whole of this particular topic serves to show how, by the order of nature and the will of God, nations are bound to contribute to the well-being and civilization of the great family of man.

II. I pass, now, to the second topic into which my remarks are distributed, and shall attempt to answer the question,—" How, AND BY WHAT MEANS AND AGENCIES, SHALL WE, AS A RISING CHRISTIAN STATE, MEET THE OBLIGATION TO CONTRIBUTE TO HUMAN WELL-BEING AND THE WORLD'S CIVILIZATION ? "

I could not stand here, and, with self-respect, tell this audience that the great powers of the earth wait, with deep concern and breathless expectation, our offerings and our gifts. Bombast such as this tends to the mortification of great minds at home, to our disadvantage abroad, and to that inertness and lack of enterprise which all false ideas are prone to create. We are but a small nation, as yet hardly productive, certainly not self-supporting; but we have nationality, and also the duties and responsibilities which are of twin birth with it. Our nationality is to be carefully guarded and cherished as a most precious jewel; but the obligations which are connected with it are of equal worth, and demand equal interest, and earnest zeal, for their preservation. I have already shown the obligation of nations to contribute to the world's well-being. As an humble member of the great sisterhood of nations, this obligation rests upon us. How shall we meet this obligation and answer the call of this duty?

Now, I have no doubt that while speaking of blessing and benefiting mankind nationally, some here have thought of the material agencies, of trade and commerce, as *the* means to be pointed out, inasmuch as they seem the chief instrumentalities by which one nation comes in contact with and influences others; and I shall not fail to notice these means of good to man. But in exhibiting the main modes and measures whereby we may fulfil our national obligation to the human race, I would urge and insist, primarily, and as of the vastest importance, that *we must cultivate to the highest bent, to the nicest coloring of honor,—we must cultivate* MEN!* This

---

* "Our land is rough and poor," said a New Englander, "we can raise but little produce, and so we build school-houses and churches, and RAISE MEN."

mode of expression may, perchance, appear singular; but there is, in reality, nothing extravagant in it. "Cultivate men!" It is a correct expression, and a *real* thing. Men cultivate fields; they cultivate cattle, and trees, and birds, and fish; so, too, they can cultivate men.

The old Romans understood something about this; with an iron hand the Spartans tried their skill at it; so, too, still more and more wisely, the English in modern times; and some few other nationalities. But, as for the world's history in general, alas! how few know any thing about training and fashioning men! Among the vast millions of human beings on earth, and of all its divers nations, what a minimum of men! Vast hordes of male inhabitants there are, in this country and in that; but that largeness of soul —that quick, glad recognition of noble principles— that love of and reverence for fixed and eternal truth —that eager desire for the work of life, which mark and characterize men—TRUE MEN,—in how many of the human frame and form, in any land, can you discover them?

And yet you can easily see the radical necessity, in this respect, in two ways. For, FIRST *it is only* MEN *who can make a country.* You may have rich, productive fields, vast mines of silver, of gold, and of diamonds; a genial clime; noble rivers, capacious harbors, nay, even large masses of inhabitants; and yet you may fail as a nation. *That* requires citizens with large, expanded minds, a fine culture, with natural or acquired manners, and a constant delicate honor; giving strength and solidity at home, and fair fame, respect, and character abroad. And, NEXT, with regard to ourselves, how this need is pressed upon our heart of hearts! For the truth must needs be confessed by us all, that our natures have been dwarfed and our souls shrivelled by the dread ordeal of caste and oppression through which our fathers, and some of ourselves, have passed. Why, do not *you*, and *you*, and *you*, fellow-citizens, feel the want, the lack, the incompleteness of being?—the idea that something is gone?—that you need something that has been taken away, and you cannot seize upon it? —so that, at times, the heart swells, and the tears come unbidden, and the mind itself becomes bewildered? It is the fruit of that old system, which tracks even freemen to freedom's own domain. It is the remembrance of that old death, which retains vitality and generates agony even in the region of life and blessedness.

Men talk of our having been in training for freedom! that slavery has schooled us for free government! We submit to the severe providences of God, and recognize his wisdom therein; but *they* are nought but vain babblers, who speak as though this were natural sequence, or legitimate result, or effect, which should follow its parent cause—that *death* should be the prime and proper originator of *life*—that *filth* and *pollution* should generate *purity*—that *sin* should be the direct author and agent of *salvation*—that Satan should be the sure guide to godliness and heaven! We reject and scorn all such empty verbosity as this —so disgraceful to the cause of freedom, and so dishonoring to the name of liberty; for I doubt whether there can be found an eminent man in this country who is not haunted by the gloomy spectre of past thraldom, and who would not give thousands of pounds if the whole matter could be blotted out forever, as history and as a remembrance, and become a blank!

We must get rid of all this—get rid of it for the generations to come; and the great means thereto is cultivation. And what a word of depth, of power, of vast import, of broad significance, of profoundest meaning, and of far-touching influence, is this!—a word which enters into the training of little children, the formation of men's characters, the development of women's virtue and moral beauty, the determining the power of laws, and the founding of states and empires!

And if the *word* has such deep and mighty import, so, likewise, the *work* which it implies and places before us; a work which requires all sorts of instruments and all kinds of agencies. For to cultivate men and manhood is no easy task, and can be done by no simple, trivial means, nor yet by any special order or peculiar class in the state. Men look here to the preacher, the missionary, the school teacher, to cultivate and train up the future manhood of the country; and great, I know, is the responsibility which rests upon them. But the cultivation of the manhood of a nation comes from all sources in the commonwealth, and flows in upon the souls of its citizens from all its streams of influence:—from the EXECUTIVE, the prime representative of authority, repressing passion, giving its wonted authority to cool, calm reason, illustrating in his life the quietness, the order, the patriotism, and the character, which it is his duty to promote; from the JUDGES on the bench, forgetful of persons, and passing transitory circumstance, remembering the awful idea of justice above, preserving their ermine unspotted from the stains of spite and prejudice, of personality and partisanship; from the MERCHANT, who, by strict integrity, high honor, business capacity, courtesy, and promptness, incarnates the character of his country in the eyes of the foreigner, and gives pride and hope to his fellow-citizens; from the plodding, enterprising FARMER, married to the soil, and, like a faithful spouse, rejoicing in its fruitfulness; from the MECHANIC and the ARTISAN—types of honest, patient industry, exhibiting daily thrift, skill, and ingenuity, the honest pride of manly energy, and the dignity of healthful toil; from the SAILOR and the TRADER—the latter penetrating the wilderness, and the former ploughing the main, yet both exhibiting that boldness, endurance, daring, and courage, which serve to fill up the hardy element of a people's character and to prompt its youth to ambition and adventure; from the TEACHER and the CLERGYMAN, the representatives of manners and refinement, of culture and enlightenment, of high morals and pure speech; holding the tender hearts of little children in their hands, and training the young, the mature, and the aged in those lofty truths and those divine principles which sanctify *life* in all its phases, and which tell upon *eternity.*

These are some of the sources whence proceeds the cultivation of the men and manhood of a nation. I give but an epitome, for the full detail would be tiresome.

But besides these agencies, we must also consider the cultivation ITSELF : what it is in quality, nature, character, and purpose. This is too large a theme for one day's discussion, but some few simple things I may say. In this cultivation of manhood in a nation, boys and girls are to be our main material to act upon. And I would say that they should have every item of culture, every element of instruction, all the treasures of science and learning which we can possibly command. I hope there is no man here to-day who fears that learning will spoil our youth!—who, poor father!—

("The booby father claims a booby son"—)

trembles lest his child, by too much knowledge, should get harm, and hurt, and injury! You may dismiss your fears; learning only spoils fools, and pedants, and smatterers—the creatures who can easily pick up tools, but know not how to use them—who pride themselves more upon the *show* of tools than men of common sense upon the skilful handling of them. Your true scholar is not such. *His* learning is his instrument; his knowledge is designed for good and useful ends, not for ornament and display; and whether it be his treasures are from the languages, or the rich revealings of history, or skill in the sciences, or the beautiful creations of art; in all he sees the great and plastic power of man for human well-being and human progress.

With all this mental culture, let it be also remembered, that man has a body, is of a composite nature, has a physical existence, as well as a mind. Forgetfulness of this fact has greatly injured the cause of learning. Men have idly supposed that to cultivate manhood was to cultivate the brain merely. *True*, cultivation of men is the bringing out, harmoniously, *all* their powers—mental, moral, and physical: hence we shall fail in our attempted cultivation of manhood here, if we do not raise up and train useful, practical men. Our youth must be trained to be active, and useful, and enterprising. For of what use, I ask, will they be to the heathen, with all their Latin and Greek, and science and history, if they come up into life and society with hands of baby softness, be-booted and be-strapped, be-muffled and be-scented—so delicate and gentlemanly that they cannot handle a hoe or wield an axe, if needed, and with no heart, if they become missionaries or commissioners, to build a hut in the "*bush*," or to cook, with their own delicate hands, a meal of victuals. Out upon such creatures, I say, in a land like this! They are men-milliners, popinjays, ladies-maids—or, as the poet paints them—

> "The flies of latter spring,
> That lay their eggs, and sting and sing,
> And weave their petty cells, and die."

And these, too, are the men who bring learning and scholarship into ill-repute; not true scholars indeed, not men of erudition, not the men who, by close thought and laborious, painful study, seek the ground of things, but your *dilettante* students, your amateur scholars!

For never, in all the world's broad history, has such ill desert fallen upon learning through the character of those who, in very deed, were true scholars, whether from the schools or self-made men. For all the great generals, the founders of states, the rulers of immortal fame, the men who have inaugurated letters, and learning, and science in commonwealths and empires, the great authors, renowned teachers and philosophers, and immortal philanthropists—yea, all the names of might and power in history, with the rarest, scarcest exceptions, have been ranked in the lofty scroll of scholars. "For," says Lord Bacon, "the conceit that learning should dispose men to leisure and privateness, and make men slothful, it were a strange thing if that which accustometh the mind to perpetual motion and agitation should induce slothfulness, whereas, contrariwise, it may be truly affirmed, that no kind of men love business for itself but those who are learned; for other persons love it for profit, as a hireling that loves work for the wages or for honor, . . . or because it putteth them in mind of their fortune, &c., &c. Only learned men love business as an action according to nature, as agreeable to health of mind as exercise is to health of body, taking pleasure in the action itself and not in the purchase; so that of all men they are the most indefatigable, if it be towards any business which can hold or detain their mind." *

In prudence, with assiduousness, under a deep sense of responsibility to God, and man, and the state, may we all determine to use our influence, and to set the example, which may tend to cultivate men and manhood in our country. Let law and religion,

* Lord Bacon, "Advancement of Learning," b. 1.

learning and scholarship, pure speech, noble ideas, and sacred principles—the order and moral dignity of the family—man's moral strength, woman's winning beauty, her stainless purity, her exalted excellence and piety,—and the simplicity of youth,—let these be the agencies we use in forming and compacting the main and master instrument for the fulfilment of a nation's mission—ITS MIND AND MANHOOD!

The results that will proceed from such high endeavor are clear and certain. We shall raise up on these shores a race of men, a stock of manhood, and a growth of manners, which shall confuse and mystify all the past chronicles of time pertaining to our race. We shall falsify all the lying utterances of the speculative ethnographies and the pseudo-philosophies which have spawned from the press of modern days against us. And we shall bring about such an expansion of mind and such a development of character, that the report thereof shall bring to our shores curious travellers to behold here the mature outgrowth and the grateful vision of a manly, noble, and complete African nationality!

And now, having fit and capable men for the beneficent work of a nation, we may turn to other means and agencies by which it may work out its end and mission. One of these is COMMERCE—perhaps *the* foremost. All men can see at a glance how one nation blesses another by the interchange of commodities: for this is our experience, and in many ways our blessing. And were it not for trade and commerce, how sad and miserable would be the condition of vast masses of the human family—how

4*

civilization would be retarded—how slow would be the progress of brotherhood, humanity, and true religion! In the days previous to the use of the magnet and the successful adventures of Columbus, when non-intercourse seemed the rule of the world, and heavy tariffs kept nations apart, then national strife almost universally prevailed, and the common tie of humanity seemed completely severed. Gradually, during the succeeding centuries, ships have multiplied, tariffs and imposts have been relaxed, and now we have just commenced a new era in the world's history; and "FREE TRADE" seems about inaugurating, under the Divine Providence, a new evangel to men. And what already is the result? Why, in every land the masses of the population are being made more comfortable, and are becoming blessed. Take the single article of tea: there are persons here who have seen the time when tea was a luxury, and now it is a common staple in nearly every civilized land on the globe. Take sugar: why, even after the common use of tea, for a long time, sugar was used by few. And now the poorest laborer in England or Scotland, the backwoodsman far away in the western wilds of America, the emigrant on the coast of New Zealand, or here, on the shores of Africa, can daily at his meals enjoy the pleasurable exhilaration of the—

"Cup which cheers, but not inebriates,"

made still more pleasurable by the sweets of the cane.

Thus it is that commerce, providentially, has become a beneficent agency for the good of man. And thus it should be: what I mean by this is, *not* that this is a genial happening, or an adventitious good; I mean more than this. I mean that there is duty and obligation on the part of nations *thus*, and *in this manner*, to contribute to the well-being of the human race. I want sugar; I want tea; I want cotton fabrics for my family; I want utensils of metal for domestic use; and the luxuries of foreign lands for pleasure and gratification.

But the country in which I live cannot perhaps produce tea; nor supply me with china for my table; nor cotton fabrics for my wear; nor the luxuries I have mentioned for my delight; nor the articles for common need and convenience.

But the Chinese and the English, the Americans and the French, are able to supply me with these articles, for a proper remuneration. Moreover, these people cannot get oils, and dyes, and other articles *we* can command, which they need for constant use; and therefore if they will supply our needs, we, in return, can give them what they seek and desire.

What is duty in this case? Why, most assuredly, that those foreigners are bound by duty to meet my wants, and I am equally bound to meet theirs.

I say, without hesitation, that this is duty; and God teaches this most clearly by his providence. When a nation or a number of nations refuse to do their commercial duties, one to the other, they are punished: the healthful life-blood of the body politic ceases its natural flow, and stagnation ensues, or progress and civilization are retarded, or the nation is either judicially smitten down at once, or a sudden check is given to its free and genial growth, and it stands before us " without fruit, twice dead, plucked up by the roots," * and yet at times with the seeming semblance of vitality.

I cite no evidences; for already in this address I have shown the suicidal and retributive nature of all selfish isolation—of all misanthropic exclusiveness; and, at the same time, I have given the historic proof that there can be no national vitality or progress, without a community of thought and sentiment, and the interchange of products and commodities, between different countries.

And from all this we may learn *our* duty. We have a genial clime, a most productive soil, a population not large, but of peculiar fitness to the capacity and the productions of the soil and to the demands of commerce. We grow here SUGAR and COFFEE; the cane has a richness and endurance in this land, as is acknowledged, beyond that of Cuba or Louisiana; and coffee here gives a larger yield to the tree, and for a longer period, than in most other countries. Other articles arrest our attention: *Indigo*, with a small capital, under the new French process of preparation, can be made to yield at least $400 per acre; for Indigo brings, at Liverpool and New York, nigh three dollars per pound. The *Cinnamon* will grow here; the experiment of its growth has just been proved successful at Cape Coast, and we should have larger groves of it. FLAX and HEMP are both of tropical growth—both in great demand in all the markets of the world, and lucrative in trade. You know the high value of COTTON, and its great demand;

---
* Jude 12.

you know also how important the production of this article has become in the decision of that great moral question of the age—THE DESTRUCTION OF SLAVERY; and I need not pause here to show what a blessing we might become to our race and to the world, by the "disturbing element" of thousands of bales of cotton, competing with the oppressors of our race in the ports of Liverpool and Glasgow, and beating down their ill-gotten gains! It grows all around us here, amid the huts, and villages, and the rice farms of our heathen neighbors, and by the use of bounties we can largely prompt its growth among them, as also by our own labor lead to its extensive and profitable cultivation in our own fields.

To the query put, "How can we as a nation bless mankind, and contribute to their well-being and civilization?" I answer, that our farmers, by their toil and energy, can lessen the needs of distant men, break down the barbarism of unrequited toil, and give cheer, by their production, to foreign lands.

The annual demand for sugar, for coffee, for cotton, has never yet been fully met in any of their great markets. Within a few recent years, the East Indies, Algiers, Egypt, and the Fantees, below us on this coast, have been increasing the quantity of cotton sent to England; while there has been no sensible diminution of the large masses shipped from America; and yet to the "Board of Commerce" in Manchester there are few, if any, questions more puzzling than this—that is, "*Whence* they can secure new and larger supplies?

It is the same with sugar: Cuba, India, Singapore, do not furnish a sufficient supply, and Louisiana is falling off. And you all know that there is a market everywhere for our coffee as soon as we are ready to meet the demand. And thus we see the ability God has given us to serve men in the broad field of the civilized world before us, and we should meet that duty at the earliest day that thrift and enterprise will enable us.

Another duty germane to this devolves upon us. There are plants, barks, dyes, and woods all around us, and still more in the interior, which the commercial and scientific world needs and asks for. The further we push into the interior, the more abundant and the more valuable do these gifts of nature become. Moreover, the learned and the Christian world want *now*, at once, if God so permits it, the solution of the great inner mysteries of this continent. To this end expeditions on all sides are investing the continent. Now we hear of one in the East, on the White Nile; then of another, through Nubia, across the desert, to lake Tschad. Now they run up the Quorra, or some other branch of the Niger; and again we hear of one from the Cape, by land, across to Zanzibar.

Are *we* to have nothing to do in this great scrutiny? Look at the map of Africa! See how all along this coast, from Goree downwards, travellers have furnished the geographical world with such an amount of information that it has been enabled to dot the map of Africa with the towns, and villages, and rivers, and marked localities of neighborhoods some hundreds of miles interiorwards; but take *our* vicinage, with Monrovia for a centre, and you can make a semi-circle, its back circumference the Kong Mountains, its ends touching the coast, of nearly all which the scentific world knows nothing!

I am aware of our slender resources and our thinly-scattered population, and no wise man expects an infant to do a giant's work. But we can do something. Let us systematically, year by year, push more and more into the country, if it be but ten, or even five miles a year; open gradually a highway into the interior; * look out the goodly land beyond us, "well watered everywhere as the garden of the Lord," † and appropriate it; press onward a highway for the tribes far back, nigh the mountains, to come unmolested hitherward by open roads; and so by and by we may get large herds of cattle from the interior, and instead of sending some $60,000 or $100,000 out of the Republic for the single article of meats, we may have "our oxen around us strong to labor," and "our sheep may bring forth thousands and tens of thousands in our streets." ‡

---

* This subject of *roads* is one of the most important that can be pondered and acted upon by the people of Liberia. Our independence of the foreign market, the cessation of our biennial and exhausting wars, the promotion of industrial habits among the natives, the opening of larger farms among ourselves, the wide promotion of civilization, and the extension of the gospel in the interior, are all connected with *road-making*. With regard to *belligerent* natives, no better plan could be adopted than that of obliging them to keep wide roads open wherever they live nigh our settlements; and whenever a war occurs they should be forced, as one of the terms of treaty, to open a road some thirty or forty miles into the heart of their country. Trade would then keep it open, and they cannot fight in an open country.

† Gen. xiii. 10. ‡ Ps. cxliv. 13, 14.

Of course, we could not do such a work as this in a brief period, but we could agree upon a system, and system seems the main thing in all great projects; and such a system would give our merchants plenteous HIDES from the interior for shipment; vast quantities of OIL, which would be their own, without foreign competition, as on the coast; new discoveries of WOODS and DYES, and especially would it lead to the settling of civilized men in the interior, and the wide cultivation of great staples; and all the while important revelations would come through us to the world, as we pressed further into the heart of the continent, of the tribes near the mountains of the Kong, if not, indeed, of the dwellers at the sources and along the valleys of the Niger.

And in this way we should be meeting the demands of science, aiding in the work of civilization, extending Christianity, and doing our work as a Christian state.

But there are *two* great works which are our special duty and mission, and which we should never lose sight of :—

First, We should be opening a highway for the gospel of Christ Jesus into the far interior, and thereby competing with the missionaries of England and America in the gracious rivalry as to who shall first reach the needy tribes living under the shadow of the Kong Mountains, and make more musical than ever, by the voice of salvation, the sweetly flowing streams from those mountains, which are, doubtless, the tiny sources of the Niger.

Next, A matter of highest import: by these internal ventures we should be achieving the commercial independence of Liberia, or, at least, giving it mastery and might.

I am no merchant, and I have in no way whatever, a direct interest in the mercantile affairs of Liberia; but as a citizen I do endeavor to study the best interests of our Commonwealth, and to scan closely all that affects her fortunes.

We are all descendants of Africa, and hence we claim a special interest in, and a peculiar right to, her fruits, her offerings, and her gifts. But after all, how very limited is our participation therein! I hear of ivory, and oils, and dyes, and precious woods, and gold; flowing from all parts of this western coast to foreign lands, to enrich their princely merchants, and to build up their great houses. We all see here that fine line of steamers, which, according to her wont, shows that England knows how to appropriate with skill and effect the resources of foreign lands to her own good; and we hear, likewise, of projected "Ebony lines," for the increase of *foreign* wealth and luxury. And to all this I have no objection whatever, because it is the legitimate and the healthful process and result of commerce.

It may be that such a one as I,—a man more busied with books, and papers, and sermons, than with ledgers, accounts, and prices current,—should not venture to speak upon these matters. But I must say, nevertheless, that I should like to see some of these great houses here; and to recognize, as some of these princely merchants, the merchants of our own town and country, citizens of this Republic! I am not satisfied,—I tell you the truth,—that the wealth of this, our Africa, should make *other* men wealthy and not ourselves. It troubles me in the night, and in the day it vexes me, that of all the moneys poured out here for fish, and meats, and shoes, and merchandise, so little stays at our own water-side.

The policy which shall modify this state of things is not, I know, to be demanded altogether of the merchants. The whole country, by management and legislation, is to aid in bringing about this result. And it seems to me that, by increase of agricultural activity, by the opening of roads, by a more extensive system of farming, by a proper attention to our great tropical staples, we may at one and the same time increase the comfort and well-being of our communities in general, give importance to the agricultural interest of the land, assist that strong arm of the nation, mercantile enterprise, and thus aggrandize the country!

And now, before I close, allow me briefly to say, that, as a new Christian state, there is *one* MORAL good we can do the world : *we can strive after a lofty style of government, and the lustration of law and order.*

I see the seeming vanity of such an aspiration. But I have neither time nor inclination to bestow thought upon what merely *seems* to be presumptuous, when I have a real truth and a possible reality to suggest.

The world *needs* a higher type of true nationality than it now has: why should not we furnish it? I know the wont to regard precedent in fashioning and compacting the fabric of government. And it is, to a great degree, a wise tendency; for it is a perilous sea on which to embark,—that of nationality; and all along its course one sees strewn, everywhere, the wrecks of nations. And, therefore, an infant state needs, and should seek light as

"It goes sounding
On its dim and perilous way."

And this light comes, to a great degree, from the past,—the light of national experience. Hence we must read history, and the philosophy of history, and laws, and the genius and spirit of laws. But are we ever to be bound by these? Are they ever to hold the spirit, and the brain, and the healthful instincts of cultivated and civilized humanity, in this day of the world's high advancement,—hold them ever in check and close restraint? Must we, in order to be a nation, imitate all the crudities and blunders which statesmanship has gravely handed down in history as rule and authority? I trust not; for no thoughtful man can look into the history of states without perceiving many national forms and established customs which even now have mastery, but which are nothing more nor less than empty gewgaws. I do not lack, by any means, reverence for the sage wisdom of ages; neither do I despise the ancient forms of older states, which often are the clothes-garments of noble truths. But he must be blind who does not see that the formal precedents and the hollow forms which, for ages, have held and bound the souls of vast empires and mighty kingdoms, are now vanishing before the clear brain and the cool common sense of mankind.

> "Even now we hear, with inward strife,
>   A motion toiling in the gloom,—
>   The spirit of the years to come
> Yearning to mix himself with life.
>
> "A slow developed strength awaits
>   Completion in a painful school,—
>   Phantoms of other forms of rule,
> New majesties of mighty states."

Why should we haste, with foolish, blind zeal, to pick up the chaff, and rust, and offal, which wise nations are throwing away? Why not seize upon their cautious, prudent eclecticism, now, in our masculine youth, instead of going the round of a stale, perhaps a foul, experience? Why not make OURSELVES a precedent? Why should we not profit by the centuries of governmental history, if even we should appear venturesome?

> "The noble soul by age grows lustier,
>   Her appetite and her digestion mend;
>   We cannot hope to feed and nourish her
>   With woman's milk and pap unto the end:
>   Provide you manlier diet!"

If I mistake not, the great *desideratum* of the nations is, a rigid honesty; a clear, straightforward rectitude; the absence of chicane, of guile, and cunning; the cleaving the meshes of policies and heartless diplomacy; and the constant and happy consciousness of the ideas of God, of truth, and of duty. We see it now nowhere among the nations; in some there is an approach, a desire, an aspiration,—so strong, in some cases, as to threaten great men,—and ancient houses, and aristocracies. But how sickening to read the memoirs of Prime Ministers and State Secretaries in times past,—ah! and, alas! to read them in our own day, at times, with our own open eyes!

How proud a thing for this young nation, if, from the start, she sends out the reputation that eschews all this; that the simple instincts of morality, the plain dictates of honesty and honor, should be the rule of *our* governmental polity at home and abroad, AND GOD OUR GOVERNOR!

For this the people are chiefly responsible; for, in a representative government, the moral purity of the masses produces its reflex in their rulers; and, therefore, parents and guardians, and teachers and ministers, should endeavor to train the popular mind to right habits of thought, to just notions of government, and of citizenship, to high principles of self-respect, and to prompt instincts of obedience and subjection to rule. If, in the quiet walks of life, in the family, the workshop, and the school, we can but secure the true sentiments of honesty, sobriety, self-control, and manly dignity, conjoined with legal obedience, then we are safe; for the influence thereof will ascend to the higher spheres of life with a controlling power, and we shall have a government here, the reflex of a pure, honest, healthful public sentiment, manifesting, in the arena of political life, the rigid honesty and the simple purity which characterize the dealings of plain, honest men. As a consequence, intrigue, corruption, subornation, could never find here sanction, vantage-ground, or undisturbed and settled rule.

For this end we must turn our attention to public men and to public transactions, with a large open eye, and with a discriminating spirit; otherwise, we can never reach the ideal of a high, noble commonwealth. And here we catch a glimpse of duty to governors. And here I would say, most seriously, that we, who are private citizens, should learn ourselves, and teach our children, to respect all constituted authority, to reverence the laws, and to fear our rulers. The fact that this is a republic, voids not the remembrance of the sacred Word, that "the powers that be are ordained of God."* If, therefore, we would more and more approach ideal governmental superiority,— while, indeed, studying our rights, jealously watching the safeguards of liberty, in a free state like this,—we should always maintain a manly forbearance, and that generous balance of thought and inclination which eschews the blustering demagogueism, whose tendency is to make rulers insecure in their high places, and cause weak minds in authority to cater to public prejudice and passion. Rulers should never fear the people; and it is the depth of meanness in a man, or a number of men, who would create a public sentiment, which would so relax rule and authority, that it should fall away to magisterial sycophancy and official mean-spiritedness.

As the people, so also their rulers, are bound to give their free gifts for the high ends we have pointed out in civil government. And here two things stand out prominently, and can never be forgotten by rulers without treason to God and recreancy to the state.

* Rom. xiii. 1.

The *first*, that, if the just powers of government come from the *people*, so, also, do they come from God; and, therefore, that in all legislation in a Christian state, the introduction, for any purpose of expediency, or in compliance with blind popular passion, of that which opposes morality and the Divine law, is obnoxious to the Divine Governor, and must eventually bring down upon it the repugnance of thinking men. The ruler, therefore, who would give dignity to the governmental regimen of his country, must, like such a man as Sir Matthew Hale, remember that nations are governed by those bright statutes which are inscribed upon the broad bosom of Jehovah, as well as by the codes and constitutions of states. So, also, the *other* larger truth is to be remembered by rulers and officers, and especially by those who take here, on earth, the " mimic seat " of " awful justice throned on high,"—the truth, contained in the majestic words of Hooker,—that " Of law there can be no less acknowledged than that her seat is the bosom of God, her voice the harmony of the world: all things in heaven and earth do her homage, the very least as feeling her care, and the greatest as not exempted from her power. Both angels, and men, and creatures, of what condition soever, though each in different sort and manner, yet all with uniform consent, admiring her as the mother of their peace and joy."*

These remembrances on the part of people and rulers will ever give the check, on the one hand, to wild Radicalism, to which, as one of the trials of states, all Governments are called; and, on the other,

* Ec. Polity, B. 3.

will protect us from the iron bond of tyranny forever. They are the conserving elements, the saline qualities —if I may so term them—which retain the healthful energies and the youthful life of nations. And, without these, the people, in a popular government, while retaining the forms of freedom, are nothing more than a band of idiots, shouting, with insane frenzy, around the cap of liberty; and the rulers of such a people stand before men and the world pretenders, impostors, and shams!

May the might of manhood, the healthful, quickening, vital influences of honest commerce, and national intercommunication, with the force of law and the Divine Providence, ever preserve this rising commonwealth from these disastrous happenings and these deadly results.

The aim and intent of the words I have spoken this day, fellow-citizens, have been, I trust, made clear and plain. I have endeavored to show that we, as a nation, ought to render our contribution of good and blessing to mankind; and I have aimed to point out some of the means by which we may meet this duty. *Two* things, I think, may be seen through all this subject with clearness and distinctness,—that is, that energy and self-reliance are two prime, most important agencies in working out and fulfilling a nation's work and mission. For it is with the nation as with the man: when the materials are at hand, the *individual* must employ his own hands and use them. No one else but himself can do it for the man, none else for the nation. All the instrumentalities for large development and a great national work are furnished us, as a new Christian state. We have soil, and sky, and bright heavens, and a luxuriant clime, and the broad, strong hands of hardy men, and civilization and histories, and the high inner instincts of true men, if we will but listen at times to our own hearts, and also the sight of numerous nationalities. These are the materials Providence has placed within our reach. Now, what we have to do is to show a quick, keen brain, and strong practicalness. We should throw ourselves, under God, upon our own powers and our own abilities. No other people are to come here and work for us; *we* have got to work for ourselves. And it is only by clearly, wisely, seeing this, that we shall be able to secure to ourselves the appliances of high culture, the fruits of hardy effort, the gifts of science and of art, the happiness of superior men, the respect and confidence of mankind, and the Divine benignity.

For now it comes about in the world's civilization that *help, aid, support*, are words that have a low significance. The Christianity of 2,000 years has not educated the world up to consideration for the weak, nor respect for the lowly and the feeble. *That* is to be left for a higher stage of human culture and the golden age beyond. The civility of the world has still a pagan element; it loves hardihood, robustness, strength, and mightiness. Even in its moods of benevolence, and in its fits of charity, it shows this peculiarity. The Christian merchants of London or New York dole out a partial, limited liberality to aid the heathen; they send golden masses of capital to the strong and enterprising young nations of America and Europe, where they see activity and growing wealth. And thus, simply by the world's mercantile polity, we can see that

"To be weak is to be miserable."

I do not blame the Christian world,—I merely point out the significance of a fact. For the truth thus revealed is, that nothing but earnestness, reality, and vigorous manly effort, can gain for us respect, consideration, and the available resources of a thriving nation. The world, in these our days, can waste no thought upon mendicity, nor ragged, imbecile beggarism. It looks for WORK; and when it sees that, it graciously pauses and bestows a smile. And so powerful, so deep-seated, is this idea and word in the mind of the age, that it is not confined to mere contemplation; it makes the wide atmosphere of the universe resound with it.

For the land, everywhere, in the bounds of civilization, echoes and re-echoes with it; and ocean winds are vocal with its utterance on every side, from steamboats and clippers, and ships, and the fleets of commerce, and the spreading wings of trade. Yea, the civilized world now rises up with an irresistible audacity and demands, "What right have *you* to live, ye lethargic do-nothings? And then, in its own bold, free utterance, declares, "We respect nought but the productive agencies of time."

Into our listening ears come these clear, audible words, on this natal day of our country: "The productive agencies of time, and they only, get respect, and notice, and advantage; all the rest is odious beggarism and contempt." If we wish to rise as a nation, and to be *felt* as an influencing agency in the world, we must make the ideas of labor and achievement master ideas in our communities, and cause the principles of self-reliance and manly energy to become vital and energetic in our midst.

And surely no man here need search for incentive to all this. Here, all around and beyond us, on every side, in ourselves and children, are spur, and stimulus, and high incitement, to every noble work and lofty desire that has circled the brain of the greatest men earth ever saw in all her histories. This ocean, in majesty and magnificence, seems inviting argosies of sail from our ports and harbors, laden with tropical products for foreign lands. This vast and wild Africa, to indefinite depths, seems now yearning to throw off the forest, the jungle, and the bush, and to open a pathway for the spade, the hoe, the plough, and the scythe; so that all the world, ere the coming of its last days, may delight itself with its prolific fulness and its vast and inexhaustible riches. Tribe after tribe, far inward, through marsh, over mountain, down beyond the broad valleys, clear off to the large central lakes of the continent, start up, and seem listening to the faint music of the distant Gospel sweetly sounding on this coast, and crave its blessings and its gifts. The vast rivers and the broad streams, struggling for centuries with the tangled roots, the giant trunks, and the broken branches of the falling forest, would fain burst forth from all their hindrances, and marry themselves a thousand times over to the graceful forms of ships and steamers, which never yet, with gliding keel, have kissed their golden faces, nor ever embraced their sweet and liquid forms.

To make all this reality, seems the plain duty and the manifest destiny of LIBERIA. This is our work, and we must do it or must die. For when God gives a man, or a number of men,—a nation, place, circumstance, opportunity, advantage, and appliance, with

"Ample room and verge enough,"

thereunto added, for a great and noble work; such as the deliverance of a people, or the freedom of a race, or the laying the foundations of a new state, or the building up of a great commonwealth, or the development of civilization in a new sphere, or introducing the kingdom of Christ into very domain of Satan; and they have neither sight to see, nor judgment to gauge, nor brains to understand, nor hardihood of soul to endure and to achieve, nor manly honor to meet their duty and to fulfil their work and mission; then the avenging angel of God stands in the way of such a people, and Jehovah's glittering sword cuts the cumberers down to the ground.

There are some fears; but far more and higher are the hopes, that such blindness to duty, and such fearfulness of penalty, will never fall upon this nation; for nigh at hand, and within our reach, are keen and quickening incentives, and the instruments that are mighty and commanding. Our religion is the *Christian religion*,—PROTESTANT, God be praised, in its main characteristics; and it is harmonious, in all its utterances, as the music of the spheres. Our civilization, in its elements, is that of the world's Christendom; and it springs upward, in all its legitimate tendencies, unerringly as the rustling pinions of a returning angel to the skies. Our language is that of the foremost men of all the earth; and it makes as *our* inheritance, although of other blood and race than theirs, the large common sense, the strong practicalness, the pure and lofty morals, the genuine philanthropy, the noble wisdom, and all the treasures of thought and genius, with which ENGLAND has blessed the world:—

> "We speak the language
> Shakspeare spake; the faith and morals hold
> Which Milton held!"

The workings of our political institutions here, and the movements of society, may, and must be, made to be, as exact and as beautiful as the ways of nature, if we retain hearts and wills in unison with that ONE great heart and will which equally guides a planet and starts the pulsations of our veins. If God gives us strength, we will employ the great aids and the noble availabilities granted us, for a larger development of manhood, a fine expression of rule and government, and for the Divine glory. And then, with the Divine benignity resting upon us, with high aims and pure intents prompting our life and being, we shall be enabled to manifest here human duty, the loftiest ways of manhood, worthy character and true Christian excellence,—all mingled with, and controlled by, law and noble government.

And so, from this point boldly jutting out into the glad free sea,—this spot, dedicated to nationality, consecrated to freedom, and sacred to religion,—from this spot shall be heard, through all the coming times, the full, clear tones of justice, the grateful symphonies of truth, the silvery voices of piety and virtue, mingling ever harmoniously with the choral echoes of the ocean!

THE
PROGRESS OF CIVILIZATION ALONG THE WEST COAST OF AFRICA.

Delivered in St. Peter's Church, Salem, Mass.; Grace Church, Providence, R. I.; St. James's, Bristol, R. I.; Church of the Epiphany, Philadelphia; Christ Church, Hartford, Conn.; Christ Church, Brooklyn, N. Y., &c., &c., during the year 1861.

"The ways of Providence are not confined within narrow limits; he hurries not himself to display to-day the consequences of the principle that he yesterday laid down; he will draw it out in the lapse of ages when the hour is come."—Guizot's "*General History of Civilization,*" *Lecture I.*

"Is it not apparent that civilization is the main fact, the general and definite fact, in which all others terminate, and are included? * * * * This is so true, that, with respect to facts, *which are from their nature detestable, disastrous, a painful weight upon nations, as despotism and anarchy, for example,* if they have contributed in some degree to civilization, if they have given it a considerable impetus, up to a certain point *we excuse and pardon their injuries and their evil nature;* insomuch, that wherever we discover civilization, and the facts which have tended to enrich it, *we are tempted to forget the price it has cost.*"—Guizot's *General History of Civilization,*" *Lecture I.*

"In all things, Providence, to accomplish its designs, lavishes courage, virtues, *sacrifices man himself!*"—Guizot's *General History of Civilization,*" *Lecture VII.*

ADDRESS.

THREE hundred years of misery have made West Africa the synonyme of every thing painful and horrible. So generally, nay, so universally, has this been the case, that it is difficult for us to connect ideas grateful and gracious with even *any* part of that continent. It seems to have an enstamped character which cannot admit of mitigating lights or relieving shades. Fact, and incident, and memory, and imagination, all serve but to breed suggestions that are distressful and agonizing.

The principle of association, moreover, is so tenacious and persistent a faculty that it is almost impossible, at times, to turn it from the channels in which it has been wont to flow, for generations or for ages. And the story of anguish, and rapine, and murder, which is the story of Africa for 300 years,—which has been so prolonged that it has seemed to be *destiny;* which has been so aggravated and intense that it has seemed to be *organic,*—it seems almost impossible to change this story into a cheering episode of blessedness and mercy.

It is not so, however. The great poet of our language tells us that

"The night is long that never sees the day."

Still more pertinent to my subject is the declaration of the Psalmist, "Though ye have lain among the pots, yet shall ye be as the wings of a dove covered with silver, and her feathers with yellow gold." A contrast as broad, and marked, and gracious as this, is now manifesting itself through the vast extents of that continent, and I desire to use my opportunity to set before you a few of its prominent characteristics.

Doubtless all intelligent persons have contemplated the fact of the long-continued and unbroken benightedness of the continent of Africa; but perhaps they have not had their attention called to the recent transitional state into which that continent is passing, on the way to enlightenment and salvation.

The facts pertaining to this subject are so distinct, so prominent, and so interesting, that I may be pardoned if I pause here, for a few moments, and endeavor to present them more minutely.

1. And here, *first* of all, we have to observe the sad and startling fact, that mental and moral benightedness has enshrouded the whole of the vast continent of Africa, through all the periods of time, far back to the earliest records of history. We know that since the Advent of our Lord Jesus Christ, although both civilization and Christianity have streamed out, with the Gospel, from the Holy Land, through all Europe, to various parts of Asia, across the Atlantic

to America, and, at length, from both Europe and America, to the islands of the sea; yet Africa has remained, during the whole of the Christian era, almost entirely unvisited by the benignant rays, and the genial influences of our Holy Faith.

And then, standing at the very start of the Christian era, if we strive to penetrate the long lapse of ages, which anticipated the coming of the Lord, we meet vista upon vista of the deepest darkness, stretching out to the earliest dawn of the world's being. So far as *Western* Africa is concerned, there is no history. The long, long centuries of human existence, there, give us no intelligent disclosures. "Darkness covered the land, and gross darkness the people."

And, indeed, if you will examine the case, you will find no cause for wonder at this universal prevalence of benightedness through all Africa. I know, indeed, that the fact is often contrasted with the advance of both Europe and Asia in enlightenment; and the inference drawn, that is, of negro inferiority, as the cause of the seeming organic wretchedness of that vast continent. But you will remember that the civilization of all races has been conditioned on contact. It is the remark of a great German historian—perhaps the greatest historian of modern times: "There is not in history the record of a single indigenous civilization; there is nowhere, in any reliable document, the report of any people lifting themselves up out of barbarism. The historic civilizations are all exotic. The torches that blaze along the line of centuries were kindled, each by the one behind."*

* Niebuhr.

Where peoples and nations have been so situated that they could be touched by influence and power, there men have gone upward and onward. And this accounts for the fact that newly-discovered islands in the seas have almost always been found low, degraded, and bestial; while, on the other hand, the peoples and races living on continents, generally exhibit the evidences of progress and improvement. But so far as contact with the elements of civilization is concerned, so far as the possibility of being touched by the mental and moral influences of superior and elevating forces is implied, Africa might as well have been an island as a continent. The Desert of Sahara has served as effectually to cut off Africa from the ancient civilizations, as the ocean, for long centuries, separated the Sandwich Islands from the world's enlightenment. Here is the solvement of Africa's benightedness. Physical causes have divorced her from the world's cultivation and improvement. A great ocean of sand has shut her off from that law of both national and individual growth, namely, that culture and enlightenment have got to be *brought* to all new peoples, and made indigenous among them.

Thrown thus back upon herself, unvisited by either the mission of letters, or of grace, poor Africa, all the ages through, has been generating, and then reproducing, the whole brood and progeny of superstitions, idolatries, and paganisms, through all her quarters. And hence the most pitiful, the most abject of all human conditions! And hence the most sorrowful of all histories! The most miserable, even now, of all spectacles!

2. But, as I have remarked, the Christian and civilized world, within a more recent period, has become both assured and hopeful by the fact of an evident transitional state, in Africa, from her night and gloom, to blessedness and glory. The long night of her darkness and misery has been broken in upon, during a little more than a half century, by the opening light of a brighter day of blessedness. Among the several causes which have contributed to these hopes for Africa, have been the following:—

First among these, was the Abolition of the slave-trade, by this country, and then by the leading powers of Europe. Auxiliary to this was the noble effort to rescue the numerous victims of this murderous traffic, by the active fleets, sent by generous nations, on this errand of humanity. Merciful feeling, and humane effort for Africa, served to interest the Christian world in her interests and her well-being. Just in proportion as the nations were prompted to heal the wounds of this afflicted continent, just so have they been scattering darkness from her agonized brow, and hastening the day of her final relief and regeneration.

But *secondly*, in addition to these distinctive philanthropic efforts, I must needs mention here the earnest missionary endeavors which, within the last 70 years, have helped to change to hopefulness the condition of Africa. These streams of saving influence have flowed out from every powerful Protestant State in the world. The whole world's enlightened and reformed religion, has striven for the regeneration of Africa. Missionaries have gone thither from England and Germany, from America and France, from Switzerland and Holland. Their stations are scattered all along the coast of Africa, from the south border of the desert to the Cape of Good Hope.

3. I have described all this as transitional—but it is more than this. The transitional aspects were confined to a preceding period of some 40 or 50 years, dating from about 1790; but these have now passed away. The *remedial*, the *regenerative* state of the Negro race and the continent of Africa, has now assumed a positive form, and reached a normal, and in some spots, an organic state; with both Christian and civilizing features. And these forms of fixed, and abiding, civilization are growing stronger and stronger every day, and taking deeper and deeper root. And there is an almost certain prospect, that a yet more thorough and radical growth will be theirs; as year by year, the work of grace, and the power of government and civilization go on, in the divers settlements of western Africa. All the auxiliaries fitted to these ends are now in use there, under the control of a most favoring providence. I beg to present here, in detail, these formative and creative agencies. (a) First of all *there is the beneficent operation of legitimate Commerce.* For nigh 3 centuries, commerce, on the coast of Africa, was divested of every feature, humane, generous, and gracious. Commerce then was a robber; commerce was a marauder; commerce was a devastator; a thief; a murderer! But commerce, now, under the beneficent influence of Christianity, has become the handmaid of religion; and all along the coast of Africa

she aids in the development of the resources of that continent; and conveys to its rude inhabitants the aids and instruments to civilization, to active industry, to domestic comfort, and to a budding social refinement. Without attempting any elaborate verification of these general statements, relative to West African commerce; I will merely present a few items which will show the progressive expansion and the real importance of African trade. I shall merely speak of two prime articles of that trade, namely *Cotton* and *Palm Oil.*

(1) COTTON. It is not very generally known that West Africa, that is, that section of the continent of Africa which is called *Negroland;* is a vast cotton growing country. The cotton that is grown there is manufactured on simple native looms, into cotton cloths; and these cloths enter into an extensive *home* barter, as also into the *foreign* trade, for the supply of the Brazilian slaves. Upwards of 200,000 of these manufactured cloths, weighing on the average $2\frac{1}{2}$ lbs. apiece, pass out of the port of Lagos. Their value is stated by Mr. Consul Campbell, late consul at Lagos, at £250,000.

About 30,000 find their way from the interior to Monrovia, and the other ports of Liberia A like number are brought and sold at Therbro.

The fact of this great growth of cotton in interior Africa, has not escaped the anxious eye of commerce; and within a few years efforts have been made by English houses, through missionaries and traders, to secure the *raw* material. The signal success of this movement is seen in the Abbeokutan country; where, from an exportation, 8 *years ago*, of about 235 *lbs.* of raw cotton, it has been increased to 3,447 *bales*, for the year 1859.

(2) Palm Oil. In 1808 the quantity of Palm oil, imported into *England*, was only .200 tons. "The quantity that reached Great Britain during the year 1860 was 804,326 cwt." The estimate of the annual amount, from the whole of West Africa, is 60,000 tons.

This exposition of trade you will observe, has reference to but *two* articles. Its real importance would be greatly exaggerated, if I could give you the items which pertain to the trade in other oils beside the Palm: in Ivory, of which 3,000 cwt. are annually exported; in Teak, Ebony, and Camwood, and in Gum-Arabic.

(3) I venture, however, to call attention to one more commercial fact, which will serve to show the growing value of this West African trade. In a recent number of the "African Times," published in London, I see that " the value of the exports of British produce and manufactures to British possessions on the west coast of Africa, has advanced from £263,725 in 1858 to £340,311 in 1860,"—that is, they have increased in value nigh $400,000 in two years.

I add here that such is the increasing value of the trade that the English steam-line on the West coast, earned the latter part of 1861 a dividend of 7 per cent., in addition to $10,000, which was laid aside as a sinking fund.

(b) Next to this, I may mention *the active spirit of travel and inquiry which marks the age.* Adventurous spirits are starting off from every civilized land for Africa; anxious to dissipate the spell, which for centuries has divorced her crowded populations from the world's brotherhood and enlightenment; and eager to guarantee them the advantages of culture, which, during the ages, has raised *them* from rudeness and degradation, and carried them up to the heights of grace and refinement.

Fifty years ago Africa was but little better known than it was in the days of Herodotus. Even the adventures of Bruce were regarded as splendid fictions; and he himself was often refused the courtesies due of society, from the supposed mendacity of his narrative. But the travels of Park and Clapperton, of Ledyard and the Landers, of Richardson and Barth, of Kraft and Livingston; have rectified the geographical errors which existed concerning the Nile and its several branches; have unfolded to the greedy gaze of commerce a vast interior route for trade and barter, by the river Niger, more than rivalling your own Mississippi, in its tropical richness and untouched luxuriant resources;—have modified the degrading prejudices concerning the negro, by contrasting him as free, dignified, powerful, and ingenious, in his native superiority, with the miserable caricature of him, shorn of his manhood, ludicrous, and benighted, in chains and slavery; and have led to the discovery of superior peoples, mighty nations, vast kingdoms, and populous cities with from 50 to 100,000 inhabitants in the interior, subject to law and authority, given to enterprise, and engaged in manufactures, agriculture, and extensive commerce.

And thus, by these adventures, vast millions of that continent have been brought into contact with civilized men; with the fabrics of civilized nations; with the quickening ideas of superior men; and the whole continent itself, save a slight belt on either side of the Equator, has been opened to the scrutiny of travellers; and even this has been recently trenched upon by Burton and Speke in the East, directly upon the Equator.

(c.) Another effective agency now in use in West Africa for a permanent work of regeneration, *is the missions and missionary schools scattered along some* 2,000 *miles and more of that coast, and which are giving, mostly, English instruction to many thousands of native African children.* These mission stations are those of the Church of England and the Wesleyans, both north and south of Liberia; and which form a complete cordon of spiritual posts from about the fifteenth degree of north latitude to Liberia; and from the southern limits of Liberia to ten degrees of south latitude. The most *northern* mission station is that of Gambia.

Here the English Church and the Wesleyans have important stations, with several ministers and catechists; stations on the coast, and *interior* stations some 600 miles up the river Gambia.

About 400 miles lower down the coast, the English Church commenced, in 1856, a mission on the Pongas River, among both pagans and Mohammedans; which has had such real success that it may now be regarded as established.

At about the eighth degree of north latitude is the

great missionary stronghold Sierra Leone. The English Church here has a Bishop, and the Church Missionary Society of England conduct, from that point, their extensive operations in Western Africa. Between 30 and 40 clergymen, the majority of whom are native-born Africans, and upwards of 60 lay agents, are employed in their different stations, whether at Sierra Leone, or Lagos, or Abbeokuta, or on the Niger.

In Freetown, the capital, is a cathedral, and all through the colony are numerous, capacious stone churches and chapels. Two high schools, in connection with the Church of England, are in existence, one in Freetown and the other at Lagos, where, besides the ordinary branches of education, instruction is also given in elementary mathematics, and in Latin and Greek.

Upwards of 20 common schools are connected with their stations. Over 5,000 are on the roll of their churches. Upwards of 20 native young men, natives of the land, are being prepared, some while in active duty, for Holy Orders.

At a recent ordination the Bishop of Sierra Leone ordained, at one ordination, 12 or 14 deacons.

The importance of the great missionary station may be gathered from the fact that Sierra Leone has already become the mother of missions; for from this place have gone out the teachers and catechists, the farmers and traders, the missionaries and civilizers,—men of the negro race,—who have already introduced both the Gospel and civilized institutions at Lagos, made Abbeokuta a stronghold of missions, and churches, yea, and have carried schools and the Gospel to Rabba, 400 miles up the Niger.

This representation of the missionary character of Sierra Leone is incomplete, without a reference to the labors of the Wesleyans and the Lady Huntington connection; which two bodies maintain many ministers and catechists, have built several chapels, and have succeeded in converting to the faith near as large a body of members as the Church of England.

The WESLEYANS have 19 missionaries and assistants in all their stations, including Sierra Leone, Lagos, Abbeokuta, &c.; about 300 lay agents, 54 chapels, 45 day schools, and near 9,000 church members.

At the distance of about 60 miles below Sierra Leone the American Missionary Association have important stations, in the Mendi country, which have already been fruitful in converts, have tended to the suppression of native wars, have prompted native industry, and have originated an active commercial spirit. Some idea of the extent of their operations may be gathered from the fact, that the expenditure for the Mendi mission for 1861 amounted to $16,000.

Lower down the coast, that is, from Sierra Leone to lat. 4°, is the territory of Liberia, where American Christians—Baptists, Methodists, Presbyterians and Episcopalians—have been maintaining their missions nigh 40 years, both among natives and colonists.

The result of these efforts is, that the METHODIST, the leading denomination of Christians, is now organized as a national church, with a bishop, a colored citizen, and 18 preachers, members of conference, and several local preachers; 19 week-day schools are maintained, for both natives and colonists; and *two* High Schools are in operation, where classical education is given to both boys and girls. This body of Christians has several missionary stations among the heathen; several native preachers, and has 32 *native* boys, who are placed in equal numbers in the families of its ministers " for instruction in letters and in home and industrial affairs."

The PRESBYTERIAN body is formed into a synod, with some 8 or 10 ministers. It maintains some 4 or 5 mission stations among the heathen; but is specially noted for the most important educational establishment in the Republic—THE ALEXANDER HIGH SCHOOL, in Monrovia; where a number of youth have received a superior education; and now some of them are holding most responsible positions in the government, as well as in the churches, and in mercantile life.

The BAPTISTS have some 12 chapels and ministers; and a large membership throughout the Republic. In Monrovia they maintain an important High School, where both boys and girls receive a good and thorough English education, with mathematical training. They are united in a CONFERENCE, which meets annually in different parts of the Republic.

The EPISCOPALIANS are a missionary body, under the direction of the Board of Missions of the Protestant Episcopal Church of the United States.

The following will exhibit the agency and the work of this Mission:—

Missionaries, Foreign, (including the Bishop,) 3
" Colonist, 6 ; Native, 1 . . . . } Total 10
Assistant Missionaries : 1 Physician, (colored,) 3 White
    Ladies, 11 Colonist, 19 Native 34
Candidates for orders : Colonist, 3 ; Native, 3 6
Confirmations : Colonist, 53 ; Native, 21 74
Communicants (returns imperfect) : Colonist, 175 ; Native,
    143 ; Foreign, 14 ; total 332
Scholars : Colonist Boarding, 45 ; Day, 223 }
" Native, " 130 ; " 208 } 606
1 High School.

In connection with the Mission are 6 organized Colonist congregations, six principal Native stations, and seven out-stations.

The gospel is preached with more or less regularity, to over 100,000 people.

(d) *Another most powerful auxiliary to the work of African regeneration, is the formation of important Christian colonies on that coast.* The history and the importance of these germs of civilization, on the African coast, are but little known in this country. Let me dwell upon this particular item for a few moments.

The traveller sailing down the coast of Africa, and visiting its various settlements, meets, first of all, with the French settlement of Goree, and then with a few Portuguese ports in the same neighborhood, that is, from the 14th to the 17th degree of north latitude; but after that, Anglo-Saxon authority, whether English or American, sways the coast for nigh 2,000 miles.

The English colony of Gambia is the next point of importance. This settlement comprises a well-built town on the coast, with schools, good churches and chapels, and several ambitious European houses;

and another colony, several hundred miles up the Gambia river, in the interior, at McCarthy's island; which is reached by steamers and large sailing vessels, and which yields an important trade. A day's sail brings the traveller to Sierra Leone, the capital of West Africa, the settlement of recaptured Africans, with a population of over 60,000 inhabitants: its chief town, Freetown, with over 20,000 inhabitants —a capacious city, with numerous fine and even elegant houses; with a cathedral and many stone churches; large shipping, many merchants, and considerable wealth. Here is the Governor's residence, a substantial and capacious building; and here is to be seen, on an elevated site, the barracks for the several regiments of native African troops enrolled in the British army.

Just below Sierra Leone is the REPUBLIC of LIBERIA, founded by the American Colonization Society, with great sacrifice of precious life, and by the expenditure of large means and treasure. I cannot enter into minute statements concerning this young nation. But I beg to say that here is what I claim to be a most singular and striking phenomenon; of 15,000 simple and unlettered men, descendants of slaves, exiles from hereditary wrong and oppression, who, with, indeed, the aid of a large Christian philanthropy, have swept the slave-trade from 700 miles of the coast; have assimilated nigh 20,000 native Africans to them, to their own civilization and religion; have brought into the Christian faith, by baptism, several hundreds of their neighboring heathen; have built some 20 different towns and settlements, with brick, and stone, and frame dwellings; have cleared thousands of acres of lands, and are exporting, as the produce thereof, sugar and coffee to foreign lands; whose merchants are the owners of 40 vessels, engaged in commerce, manned and officered by their own citizens; and who have demonstrated their moral strength and the political capacity of the nation, by the reception in less than 18 months—and that without any disturbance, without any disorganization, but by the turning it into an element of strength and advantage—by the reception, into the bosom of the State, of 5,000 heathen captives rescued, in nakedness and barbarism, by the cruisers of your own nation, from cruel slavers! I do not think I can exaggerate the importance of the Republic of Liberia. There are two or three facts of special importance, which I feel I cannot do otherwise than present in bold relief. *One* of these is, the fact that this little nation, of only 15,000 civilized black Americans has, during some 20 or 30 years, held under control nigh a half a million of bold and warlike heathen, and completely interdicted their participation in the slave-trade. *Second*, that although Liberia is one of the smallest of West African colonies, and its settlements are scattered along some 600 miles of coast; yet we are the *only* manufacturers of sugar and of bricks; we are the only ones who have saw-mills, and cut large quantities of lumber. And we present the singular fact, that is, that although we are the *least* of all the colonies on the coast in numbers; yet from the borders of the desert, to the Cape of Good Hope,

Liberia is the only settlement which can meet demands for sugar, bricks, and lumber; and we can humbly claim, that for nigh 4,000 miles on that coast, we are the foremost of all people in enterprise, and that we own more vessels than all the sons of Africa, in all their settlements, along the whole line of the coast.

And now, through the munificence of citizens of Massachusetts and other states, a COLLEGE has been given to the Republic of Liberia; the college building, nobly situated on the heights of Montserrada, can be seen far distant on the ocean. The establishment of this college forms an epoch, not only in the history of Liberia, but also of West Africa; for already numbers of African children, the sons of native chiefs, and kings, and merchants, are sent to England and Scotland for education. I have myself seen 12 native African children in one school in England; and I have no doubt that at the present time there are fully 50 or 60 of such children in British schools: but alas, many die from the severity of the climate. The favorable position of Liberia College will, I have no doubt, give us advantage in this respect; and ere long, numbers of these children, from beyond our territory, as well as within, will be sent to us for instruction: and thus from Liberia, as a fountain-head, shall flow culture, learning, science, and enlightenment to many of the tribes of Africa, all along the coast, and up its rivers, to its most distant inland quarters!

Below the Republic of Liberia are the several forts, settlements, and colonies of the English; lying some two or three hundred miles apart; namely, Cape Coast Castle, Accra, Badagy, and the important town of Lagos, which bids fair to be the New York of West Africa. At all these places the English have chaplains; missions are planted by the Church of England and the Wesleyans; schools are sustained, and the whole work of evangelization is vigorously prosecuted.

I close this part of my subject with this brief summary of the results of labor, on the West coast of Africa, during the last 40 or 50 years; the several items of which I have gathered from divers sources.

Over 150 churches have been erected; nearly 200 schools are in operation; 20,000 children have been instructed in English; nigh 20,000 baptized persons are members of different bodies of Christians; 25 dialects have been reduced to writing; between 60 and 70 settlements have been formed—the centres of civilization, English-speaking our tongue, with schools, and churches, agricultural operations, and commerce.

The facts I have stated serve to bring before us a few marked principles and conclusions:

1. The *whole of Negroland seems, without doubt, to be given up to the English language, and hence to the influence of Anglo-Saxon life and civilization.* It is a most singular providence that that very people, who have most largely participated in the slave-trade, should have been brought, by the power of God's dealings, and in the workings of His plans, to bear the weighty burden of lifting up this large

section of humanity to manhood, and of illuminating them with Christian light and knowledge. Does any one here doubt this providence? Do any of you question the obligation? Just look then at that large portion of Africa which is bounded on the north by the desert, on the west and south by the Atlantic, and on the east by the river Niger; that immense territory which probably contains a population of from 30 to 50,000,000 of people, and which has been the seat of the slave-trade nigh three centuries; and then notice the other fact, that almost the only forts, settlements, colonies, and missions, along the whole line of its coast, are ENGLISH-SPEAKING, namely Gambia, Pongas, Sierra Leone, Mendi, Liberia, Accra, and Lagos. Can any one doubt that God has thrown the responsibility of evangelizing this people upon the Anglo-Saxon race? Does it not seem manifest that God has laid this people's spiritual burden upon the sensitive Christian heart of England and America? What if this grand cause should prove the agency for neutralizing their national prejudices; or for producing a union, for love and human well-being, such as the world has never before witnessed?

2. Again, I would add, that *the evangelization of Africa is manifestly to be effected contemporaneously with its civilization.* Unlike most of the missionary and evangelizing movements of modern times, God evidently purposes the redemption of *Africa*, in connection with the use of all the appliances of culture, learning, trade, industry, and commerce. All these *are* already being used, in West Africa, as hand-

maids of religion. Civilization is to be a most marked agent in the process of evangelization, among the million masses of that vast continent. We shall see, in West Africa, in these our own days, and on a large scale, that primitive mode of propagating Christianity over a whole continent, which characterized the rapid progress of the faith in Apostolic times; when the Spirit of God seized upon an actual, though pagan civilization; and ran, with an almost electric speed, through Palestine, through Asia Minor, through Greece, through the Roman provinces, through the Roman Empire; until, in less than three centuries, the Christian faith became the master influence of the world; and the diadem of the Cæsars had to bow in submission to the cross of Christ!

So, most probably, will it be in West Africa. The day of Africa's agony is being closed up by the simultaneous entrance of Christian churches and civilized colonies, all along her coasts, and through all her interior quarters!

3. You see here also the important fact that *the main agency God is employing for the ends I have pointed out, is black men themselves.* It is, indeed, in West Africa, as everywhere else in all history, namely, that the primal training, the early preparation come from advanced and superior people. *They always plant the germs of a new faith, or are the pioneers of a new civilization. But the work itself is always effected by indigenous agencies.* So in Africa, the work of these settlements, colonies, and mission, is being done by Negroes. Some of these came from the British West Indies: numbers of them

are recaptured Africans, trained in English schools: thousands of them are *American* black men, educated in the missions of Liberia, or amid the institutions and in the schools of this country : and all of whom, thus enlightened, are Presidents, Judges, Senators, Merchants, Civilians, Planters, and a host of Priests, and Deacons, and Catechists—sons of Africa! How mighty is the hand of God in the affairs of earth! How wonderful is His providence amid the disastrous and destructive doings of men! The slave-trade has been carried on for centuries by cruel, ruthless men, without a thought of mercy. The system of slavery, in the lands of the black man's thraldom, has been a system of greed, and overwork, and lust, and premature decay, and death, with but slight and incidental alleviations. And yet there *have been* alleviations. God never allows any evils on earth to be entirely aggregations of evil, without their incidents of good. So here, in this matter, God has raised up, even in their lands of servitude, a class of black men who have already gone from America, from the British West Indies, and from Sierra Leone ; the pioneers of civilization and Christianity, to the land of their fathers. Thus God overrules the wrath of man. Thus from blasting, deadly evil, is He ever educing good. Thus does He pluck the sting of malignant intent out of the disastrous histories of men ; and transforms those histories into benignant providences.

I know full well how wickedly, how blasphemously, all this story has been used to justify the wrongs of the Negro, and to fasten it all upon the will of God. But when Joseph told his brethren—

"it was not you that sent me hither, but God," he did not mean that they had not acted brutally toward him; but only that, in all the dark deeds of men, there is a higher, mightier, more masterful hand than theirs, although unseen;—distracting their evil counsels, and directing them to goodly issues. God, although not the author of sin, is, nevertheless, the omnipotent and gracious disposer of it. Let us bless God for that master hand of His, which checks, and rules, and guides the policies and histories of men! "Alleluia! for the Lord God, omnipotent reigneth."

And here we may see, in *two* special points, how God shows himself Sovereign and Governor in this world, amid the sore vicissitudes and the bitter trials of men. For *first*, we have disclosed herein the workings of that great law of God, that is, the *call to suffering and endurance, to the end of greatness and noble duty*, in any race or people whom He has elected to greatness, and might, and future empire. For without doubt, the black man, in the lands of his thraldom, has been in the school of suffering; yea, tried in the fiery furnace, that being tried, he might secure therefrom the strength, the character, and the ability which might fit him for a civilizer and a teacher. Not for death, as the Indian, not for destruction, as the Sandwich islander, has the Negro been placed in juxtaposition with the Caucasian; but rather that he might seize upon civilization; that he might obtain hardiment of soul; that he might develop those singular vital forces, both of the living spirit and the hardy frame, in which I claim the Negro is unrivalled; and thus, himself, be enabled to go forth, the creator of new civilizations in distant quarters, and the founder, for Christ, of new churches!

And *next*, we may see in all this *that law of compensation which God vouchsafes the wronged and suffering, for all their woes and suffering.* After being afflicted, by nigh three centuries of servitude, God calls chosen men of this race, from all the lands of their thraldom—men laden with gifts, and intelligence, and piety—to the grand and noble mission, which they only can fulfil, even to plant colonies, establish Churches, found Missions, and lay the foundations of Universities along the shores, and beside the banks of the great rivers of Africa. He lifts up this people from lowly degradation, to the great work of evangelizing the vast continent of Africa, so that the grandeur and dignity of their duties may neutralize all the long, sad, memories of their servitude and sorrows.

4th, and lastly: I remark that the facts I have referred to *are full of promise of that future glory in Christ which is promised, and which will surely be given to Africa.* She has passed, sadly, wearily, through long ages of agony and woe; but the end is approaching. "The night is far spent: the day is at hand." The day when civilization and true religion shall make triumphal march through all her quarters, is rapidly drawing nigh. Yea, the time has already come when rudeness and barbarism shall be replaced by culture and refinement. Schools shall be filled by ten thousands of joyous children ; Trades shall be pursued by her crowded populations ; Agriculture shall pour forth its gifts and offerings for distant marts; Commerce shall bear multitudinous treasures to foreign climes; and Art shall multiply its blandishments, to

> "Soften the rude and calm the boisterous mind."

It was a remark of the great William Pitt: "We may live to behold the nations of Africa engaged in the calm occupations of industry, and in the pursuit of a just and legitimate commerce; we may behold the beams of science and philosophy breaking in upon their land, which at some happier period, in still later times, may blaze with full lustre, and joining their influence to that of PURE RELIGION, may illuminate and invigorate the most distant extremities of that immense continent."

And already have these noble words been somewhat realized. I myself, with my own eyes, have seen the fulfilment, in partial degrees, of this grand prediction. Large masses of native children are now being trained in Christian schools. A great company of native catechists have gone forth from their homes to train and evangelize their heathen kin. A host of native priests and deacons have been commissioned to go forth as missionaries, in divers tongues to preach the gospel: already have they penetrated the wilds of the interior; already have they reached the banks of the Niger; and soon the full picture painted by the great orator, shall assume the features of grand reality, "and science and philosophy, with pure religion, illuminate and invigorate extremities of that immense continent."

But nobler words and a more glorious prediction

have been uttered concerning Africa, than even the glowing words of the great British orator: for the words I now utter are the words of inspiration, they come from God Himself: "Ethiopia"—from the Atlantic Ocean to the Indian—from the Mediterranean to the Cape, "shall soon stretch out her hands unto God!"

THE

PROGRESS AND PROSPECTS OF THE REPUBLIC OF LIBERIA.

Delivered at the Annual Meeting of the New York State Colonization Society, New York, May 9th, 1861.

"The Americans are successfully planting free Negroes on the coast of Africa: a greater event, probably, in its consequences than any that has occurred since Columbus set sail for the New World."

—*Westminster Review.*

SPEECH.*

I have been requested, sir, by your Secretary, Rev. Dr. Pinney, to offer this resolution, and to make a few remarks upon it: and I have felt it a duty to comply with his request, and to come here to tell how great a work this Society is doing on the west coast of Africa, that is, in the Republic of Liberia. I shall speak of what I have witnessed with my own eyes; I shall detail the facts which are matters of experience; and I shall mention some of the blessings and advantages of social and political society there, in which I have participated. For, sir, I have been a citizen of the Republic some eight years, and a residence in Africa such a period affords one sufficient

---

* The reader of this speech will find considerable variation, in some of its statements, from the original publication of it. The reason is briefly this, namely, that on the delivery of it, in the Author's great anxiety to avoid exaggeration, he *understated* various items herein mentioned. More careful inquiry and investigation enable him to give the statistics, now brought forward; which will be found to accord with official documents.

experience to speak from. When I went to Liberia my views and purposes were almost entirely missionary in their character, and very much alien from any thing civil or national; but I had not been in the country three days when such was the manliness I saw exhibited, so great was the capacity I saw developed, and so many were the signs of thrift, energy, and national life which showed themselves, that all my governmental indifference at once vanished; aspirations after citizenship and nationality rose in my bosom, and I was impelled to go to a magistrate, take the oath of allegiance, and thus become a citizen of Liberia. And I then decided for myself and for my children, so far as a parent can determine the future of his line, that Liberia should be our country and our home forever. Nor have I repented this election. As denizens of *all* new countries, so we have been called to the trials and some of the sufferings of emigrants; and sickness in my family has caused us to seek restoration in the land of our birth; yet, if it pleases God to open to me my field of labor, I shall soon be wending my way back to my home again.

The resolution in my hand expresses gratification at the signs of industrial, moral, and intellectual progress in Liberia. And this, sir, is the assertion of fact. In every department of life and labor in Liberia there are unmistakable evidences of growth. I feel the assurance to affirm here that in every quarter the most casual observer can perceive strength, confidence, self-reliance, development, increase of wealth, manliness, and greater hardiment of character. A glance at any of the facts indicative of national growth serves to show this. *Take the item of Agriculture.* When I went to Liberia the farming and husbandry of the country pertained chiefly to the home supply. But the case is somewhat different now, and the change, considering the small civilized population, is indeed wonderful. The productive capacity of the republic warrants this assertion. Look at our coffee-fields. It is, indeed, not generally known, but, indeed, I make a *moderate* statement when I say, that our citizens have planted, and have now in full growth, not less than 1,000,000 coffee trees. It is true that we are not telling as much upon the market as we are able to in this particular. Various reasons can be given for this, some arising from the state of the country; some from the condition and character of the people; especially from the fact that the acquisitive principle is latent, reserved, and sluggish in many men in the land; but the main reason is, that we have lacked suitable machinery for cleaning our coffee.*

But there are signs that even now serve to show that we are yet to have a large participation in the coffee trade of the world, and this is seen, especially in the interest exhibited in this trade by the citizens of Bassa, and in the important and increasing exports which are annually made from that county.

* I am happy to say that this last difficulty will soon be overcome. Through the warm interest and enterprise of Edward S. Morris, Esq., of Philadelphia, Liberia is likely to be supplied, this year, with "COFFEE-CLEANING MACHINES," capable of hulling over 1000 lbs. of coffee a-day, with ordinary hand power.

Look next at the facts relating to our production of sugar. When I landed on the shores of Liberia, eight years ago, not a pound of sugar was exported from the land; I doubt whether as much as a pound was then made for home consumption. But, sir, since those days life, and energy, and power have been thrown into this branch of industry. The forest has been levelled; broad fields have been cleared; and hundreds of acres of sugar-cane have been planted, cut down, manufactured into sugar, and replanted again, and again, and again. Taking the Republic in the aggregate, we have between five and six hundred acres of land appropriated to the growth of cane. Some of the farmers on the St. Paul's River have thirty acres under cultivation, some forty, some sixty. This year there is unusual activity among the planters. Sugar-making is no longer an experiment among them; they have put forth their effort and it has succeeded; the market has welcomed their contribution, and *they have made money*. *This* stimulant has incited them to nobler efforts, and I have no doubt that some half-dozen men on the St. Paul's will, this year, enlarge their respective farms to one hundred acres each. At the last grinding season, some of these men manufactured and shipped to foreign ports, some thirty thousand pounds, some forty thousand pounds, and in one instance fifty-five thousand pounds of sugar, with a proportional quantity of molasses and syrup. These facts, with the strong current of industrial interest now flowing in this particular channel, warrant the belief that Liberia bids fair to become one of the greatest sugar-producing countries in the world.

These two staples, that is, sugar and coffee, are the chief staples produced by us; and having referred to them, I need not detain you by any special reference to cocoa, cotton, and other articles which have not as yet entered largely into the calculations and efforts of our farmers as sources of gain.

Take the item of Trade. All along the coast and in the interior, from Sherbro River to Cape Lahou, our merchants have set up their trading factories among the natives. This trade is a trade in CAMWOOD, IVORY, GOLD, COUNTRY CLOTHS, and especially in PALM OIL. In order to carry on this trade our citizens need the service, *coastwise,* of sloops and schooners, and those whose ambition has stretched beyond the home trade, have bought for themselves brigs and barks for foreign trade. And thus the merchants of Liberia are owners of quite a respectable commercial fleet. The number of vessels, small and large, owned by Liberia, and engaged in trade, is forty.

What the correct statement is of exports and imports, I can only say proximately. The imports at the single port of Monrovia, for the year 1860, amounted to near $150,000; but as there are *five* other ports in the Republic, and two of them of great importance, that is, with respect to native trade, I have no doubt that our imports exceeded $300,000. I am happy to say that our exports exceed our imports; we are factors and producers over and above our consumption of foreign products; and thus we are enabled to show signs of thrift and progress, and indicate increasing wealth. The report of exports from the port of Monrovia is about $192,000 in 1860, and I presume that the sum of $400,000 is no exaggeration of the amount for the whole republic.

Take next those items which pertain to the best and most abiding interests of man, those which pertain to civilization—I mean schools and religion. Through the provident care of the several denominations of Christians in the United States, all our settlements are provided with schools, and opportunity for securing a common education is afforded to a goodly portion of our population. The Methodist, Baptist, Presbyterian, and Episcopal missions have each their schools in all of our larger towns. In these schools are gathered together, under teachers of, in the main, respectable acquirements, our civilized children. But they are not exclusive. Numbers of native children, servants on the farms and in the families of our citizens, are also received in these schools. The Sunday-schools receive a much larger number of natives and Congoes for instruction, and the churches are ofttimes filled with them. I have seen, in some Sunday-schools, with our own children, thirty, forty, and fifty native children, under instruction in English and the Christian religion. Added to this, are the schools, exclusively for natives, under missionary direction, all which agencies are bringing forward a large class of natives of the soil, English-speaking in tongue, and civilized in habits and manners. Some of these already approach our own civilization. Many of them are respectable citizens in our towns and neighborhoods; men who not long since were heathen, but having been brought up in American families, are now civilized men. They live in our towns and villages; they go to our schools; they visit our families; they pay taxes; and they marry among our people. Some of them are teachers; a few have become ministers of the Gospel. One case of this civilized transformation is worthy of notice. It is the case of a native young man, who was brought up in a mission-school at Bassa; subsequently he was brought to *this* city, and went to the second colored public school in this city, and afterwards returned to Africa. On a recent occasion, a vacancy having occurred in the representation to the Legislature in that county, this young man was pitched upon by the Bassa people as the proper person to be sent. I believe, however, that the purpose of his fellow-citizens was frustrated by some missionary arrangements; but from the way I have heard responsible citizens speak of him, I feel quite certain that the people of Bassa regard Mr. Pitman as one of their foremost men for character and ability.

I am endeavoring to show how in various ways Liberia gives evidences of moral, industrial, and intellectual progress, and I think the statements I have brought before you evince energy and progress among my fellow-citizens; but perhaps a more life-like representation of activity in Liberia may be gathered from a brief account of a recent journey along our coast. I left Cape Palmas, a few weeks ago, on my return to America, and on our journey we stopped at every settlement on the way to the capital. When we reached Sinou we found there the bark E. B. Roye, the property of a most enterprising fellow-citizen, Mr. E. J. Roye, merchant of Monrovia. In a day or two we reached the settlement at Bassa, and there we found a small craft trading, owned by another fellow-citizen. We went to Junk, and there we saw the fine steam saw-mill of Payne and Yates, their yard filled with plank, and a long distance along the banks multitudes of logs, which are furnished them by the enterprising natives there, for their mill. Off from the town we found there, lying in the harbor, two vessels, the property of Payne and Yates, Liberians, loading with lime and plank. We went on to Monrovia, and, as we turned the noble projection which makes Cape Montserrada, we found in the roads *six* vessels and the steamer Seth Grosvenor, all the property of our own citizens, and floating the Liberian flag. We went ashore and entered the streets of our capital; a city regularly planned and gradually filling up with brick and stone edifices. The next morning we were woke up with the early sound of martial music, and, hastening into the streets, saw a fine body of troops gathered from several settlements, and led by the Secretaries of State, and of the Treasury, on their march to the beach to embark for the southern section of the country, to put down a pestilent set of natives, who, for the last three years, have been giving us much trouble and defying our authority.

A few days afterward, I took a journey to the new interior settlement, Careysburg. I sailed up the St. Paul's and found everywhere the signs of progress. I had been nigh three years away from Montserrada County; and great was my surprise to see large and extensive fields cleared, and planted with sugar-cane, which, when I went to Palmas, were a dense wilderness; new brick and frame-houses recently erected; brick-kilns at divers places, containing from fifty to one hundred and fifty thousand bricks. Great was my delight, as we sailed up the river, to behold widespread sugar-fields; the brick mansions of the farmers, ranged upon the banks of the river; and to see in the distance, the curling smoke ascending, and the floating steam from the sugar-mills, at several points, where the grinding of the cane had commenced, and sugar was in the process of making. Stopping a few hours at the farm of an old friend and schoolmate, who plies two noble packets on the St. Paul's; has a large sugar-cane farm; and at the same time is making, this year, one hundred thousand bricks, I mean Mr. Augustus Washington; I started thence, through the wilderness, for Careysburg. After a few hours' travel, we came first to a solitary log-house of a new settler; soon after we reached a group of good, substantial dwellings, forming a little village, surrounded by acres of recently cleared land. After a while we arrived at the neighborhood where large preparations are being made for the interior road. There I saw, at different places, the banks of some four different streams secured by neat, solid masonry of our own laborers, in preparation for the bridges, projected for the cart-road. In two places, fine bridges, symmetrical and substantial, had been thrown across these streams. At another spot I saw a company of twenty odd men, in busy activities, preparing a new bridge, and grading the road; and all this work was being done by workmen, emigrants from this country, citizens of Liberia and under the direction of Liberian officers and superintendents. Five hours brought me to Careysburg; and as I ascended the main street to a lofty elevation, I saw, on every side, the town laid out before me, with the precision of a multiplication-table. All around were visible more than a hundred mansions of the emigrants, surrounded by largely cleared patches of vegetables; their humble chapels in elevated positions; a large reserve in the heart of the settlement for a public park; not far in the distance were the larger farms of the settlers, while the air was filled with the cheerful sounds of labor, of conversation, of hilarity; and peace and happiness seemed to rest upon man and beast and nature!

I have presented these incidents to you, sir, as evidence of life and activity in Liberia. They show, I think, that men are alive in that country, and are moving the arms of industry. There are, you know, sir, incidental, but significant things, in all lands and among all men, which serve to show more clearly than more marked demonstrations, that society, in its different departments, is instinct with productive energy. So these facts which met me a few weeks ago, in Liberia, evince that an industrial impulse prompts the people of that country. They show, in fine, that the springs of action are at work in our communities, and give the promise of a not distant state of aggrandizement, of greater political importance, of commerce, and wealth and refinement.

I have been speaking thus far, sir, with reference to that part of the resolution which relates to the industrial, moral, and intellectual progress of Liberia. I wish now to show, in as brief a manner as possible, that as the Republic is growing in itself, so likewise it is telling upon the interests of the aboriginal population. I have already referred, incidentally, to this topic. I wish, however, to call attention more distinctly to one or two facts which will show more strikingly the work we are doing among our uncivilized kin in Africa. *Our diffusion of the English language illustrates this point.* A mighty number of native children have been brought up in our colonist families and in mission-schools. Many of these, it is true, on reaching their majority, return to country homes; but they carry with them good English utterance; in many cases capacity to read and write; in *all* cases many of the elements of civilization. I have had native boys working for me, who when they wished any article from their distant towns, would write an English note, in as good style as myself; and yet they dressed and were living in native style. Their habits, civilized necessities, and acquired wants assimilate to ours. Vessels sailing from American ports loaded with provisions, on reaching our coast, find a ready market in native towns, as well as among our civilized settlers. They buy meat, and fish, and sugar, and molasses, as well as cloth, tobacco, and beads. And thus, in these and various other ways, our different settlements are diffusing a civilizing influence among our native population, and gradually bringing them up to our standard of civility. There is also another large class of natives who live among us constantly: the youth who have been apprenticed to our families, have grown up in our midst, and who have been brought, more or less thoroughly, into civilized habits. These form an important and valuable accession to our population. You know, sir, that our population is often set down at 15,000 persons; but this by no means does us justice. *That* is very likely our *emigrant* population: but for every *American* citizen, you may safely put down another, either *native* or *Congo*, who has been trained in our families or schools, and who form, in the aggregate, an equal population to our own. They are indeed the *lower crust* of our civilized population; but we should have the full benefit of their enumeration, and we should be thus reckoned fully at 30,000 civilized people.

Let me now advert briefly to one more evidence of our influence among the natives, and the regenerating power of our people and polity: *I refer now to the civil and political influence of our government upon the natives around us, especially as it respects their rights, freedom, and civil elevation.*

You know, sir, that slavery is indigenous to the soil of Africa. Indeed, sir, it is indigenous to all soils on the globe, and is the cause of misery and distress wherever it exists. It is thus in Africa. But the hopes of freedom, the aspiration for liberty, work as strongly in the bosom of the native African as in any other man on the globe. The servile population of our surrounding tribes, even to the far interior, know where safety can be found from the oppressor. Hence, this class, when they find the yoke intolerable, seek the protection of our flag. Runaway boys and fugitive slaves come to us from the Bassas, the Queahs, the Veys, the Deys, and especially the Pessahs, who are the hereditary slaves of the interior. All along the banks of the St. Paul's, in the rear of our new settlements, are to be found a heterogeneous compound of people of all these tribes, living in small towns, enjoying the protection of our laws. I remember the case of two boys who escaped the slavery of their tribe, by coming to my own neighborhood; they were pursued by their native master. They were taken before a magistrate, who refused to return them to their master. The ground assumed was, that slavery was not recognized by our laws, and that fugitives from slavery could not be sent back to bondage. Thus, sir, our Republic is already a refuge of the oppressed. Thus, sir, are we demonstrating to the heathen tribes of Africa the highest laws of freedom, and the beneficent operation of Christian government. And thus likewise are we realizing on the soil of Africa, the words of one of your own poets:

"No slave-hunt in our borders, no pirate on our strand,
No fetters in Liberia, no slave upon our land!"

It is these realities, which I have witnessed, experienced, participated in, which have led me to commend the Republic of Liberia to those of my friends in this country, who, either from enterprise or the spirit of emigration, feel disposed to look to other lands. For a number of years past, a goodly number of American colored men have left this country, in order to better their fortunes. Some have gone to California, some to Australia; and, after accumulating wealth, returned again to their homes. A like feeling now influences many in these States, save that they are seeking *permanent* homes abroad. Some are going to Hayti; some have their attention turned to the West coast of Africa, especially to the Yoruba country, and the locality of Abbeokuta. And this latter class interest me a deal more, I confess, than those who are going to the West Indies. And this chiefly because the *need* of Africa—*her need of civilized emigrants*—is great, and because educated free colored men are *the* fit agents to effect the regeneration of Africa. We cannot, it is true, make great pretensions; our training and culture have been exceedingly imperfect. We have been deprived of many of our rights in this country. We have been debarred from many of those privileges and prerogatives which develop character into manhood, and mastery, and greatness. Still we have not been divorced from your civilization. We have not been cut off from the lofty ideas and the great principles which are the seeds of your growth and greatness, political, intellectual, and ecclesiastical.

On the contrary, we too have learned clearly and distinctly the theory of free speech and of constitutional government. We too have participated somewhat in all the vast wealth, both religious and civil, of your Anglo-Saxon literature. We too have learned the advantage, and have risen to the elevation of all those great legal charters which interest men in government, and which make government subserve the best interests and desires of its citizens. And these kindly though incidental providences have placed us in governmental capacity, and in fitness for the prerogatives of government, in advance of many peoples, who in other respects are above us. The freed black man of America is, I feel assured, a superior man, in the points I have mentioned, to the Russian, to the Polander, to the Hungarian, to the Italian. Notwithstanding our trials and burdens, we have been enabled to reach a clearer knowledge of free government than they, and to secure a nobler fitness for its requirements, duties, and guarantees. I speak from the facts which have fallen under my observation, among my brethren in Africa. And hence I feel desirous that those enterprising and Christian men here, who are looking abroad for new homes, and other fields of labor, should join us in Africa, for the regeneration of that continent. My own desire, moreover, is that instead of scattering ourselves thousands of miles apart along the coast, we should rather concentrate our parties and our powers. Of course, I cannot say a word in the abstract, against the mission which draws many men, and some of my own personal friends, to Abbeokuta. But I do regard it a mistake in policy. I have the impression that providence points out all that field to the freed and cultivated men who have been raised up and prepared by the English at Sierra Leone; and who, especially by blood and language, seem to me God's *chosen* messengers to the valley of the Niger and its far interior. And I have the conviction that we of the United States, with our peculiar training, and with our democratic tendencies, will find ourselves out of place, as well as in an uncongenial element, in the strong governments of interior Africa. And therefore I have thought that in every way, it would be far better for men leaving this country for Africa to join their fortunes with us in Liberia. Our training, habits, customs, education, and political experience, have made us—it is not, it is true, a dignified mode of expression, but I have used it in private, and may be pardoned its use here—they have made us "Black Yankees;" and I feel assured that in Liberia, we shall find a more congenial field, better appliances, a government more suitable to our antecedents, better fitted to a youthful nation and an aspiring emigrant population; to achieve *that* which seems to me the master aim of all our colonization to Africa, and the noblest duty of the Republic of Liberia—I mean the evangelization and enlightenment of heathen Africa! But, sir, I fear I tire you, and I close at once.

For three hundred years the European has been traversing the coast of Africa, engaged in trade and barter. But the history of his presence and his influence there, is a history of rapine and murder, and wide-spread devastation to the families and the homes of its rude and simple inhabitants. The whole coast, sir, has been ravaged wherever his footstep has fallen; and he has left little behind him but exaggerated barbarism, and a deeper depth of moral ruin.

Now, sir, we are there: we black men of America—we who have been trained in the severe school of trial and affliction—we who have been educated amid the free institutions of this country; and, sir, I pledge you in behalf of that able man, our national chieftain, and all the other leading men of Liberia, that we will endeavor to fulfil the duties which devolve upon men laying the first foundations of new empire; and to meet in a proper manner, the obligations which Divine Providence has brought upon us.

GOD AND THE NATION.

Preached before Trinity Church, Monrovia, July 30th, 1854.

"We know, and indeed, what is better, we feel inwardly that religion is the basis of all civil society, and the source of all good and of all comfort."—BURKE.

"Religion is the foundation and cement of all human societies."
HOOKER.

A SERMON.

PSALM xxxiii. 12.—"Blessed is the nation whose God is the Lord; and the people whom he hath chosen for his own inheritance."

LAST Wednesday was the anniversary of our national independence: and I feel that, as a Christian pastor, I should not let this event pass by, without calling special attention to it from the pulpit. For I am not one of those in whose mind religion is so far divorced from national and governmental affairs, that it becomes wrong for a minister to speak about any thing that is political in its bearings. On the contrary, my belief is that Christianity should permeate all the relations, and all the institutions of society; and hence that there is no true, faithful, exercise of the Christian ministry, unless that ministry causes the faith to touch everywhere with an illuminating, life-giving energy. Political partisanship in the ministry is unseemly, distracting, and unspiritualizing in its influences and tendencies: but that there is any thing in the State, or in the general principles or policy of government, which is without its moral character, or, which is *entirely* unrelated to Christianity and the Church, is a grievous error. For every thing in this world tells some way upon religion, however merely material or secular it may be; and from the mysterious woof of Divine Providence are brought out, in the end, those complete and masterly events, which at once scatter the mists of human doubtfulness—

"And justify the ways of God to man."

And therefore I say that a spirituality in ministers, which pretends to such loftiness and elevation that it cannot attend to the affairs of earth, and cannot see the bearing of Christianity upon government, and laws, and policy, is vain and illusory. There *is* a relation of the pulpit to the commonwealth. Religion *does* take cognizance of all national affairs. Christianity does maintain its ascendency on the State, and all its concernments: for one of the prime ideas of the Word of God is, the fact of Divine Sovereignty over all the nations of the earth; and the magnificent idea of the Scripture is, that the Lord Jesus Christ is of right "King of kings"—the Great Spiritual Potentate over all the EMPIRES OF CREATION; and that all of them are yet to be brought into subjection to His rule and under the authority of His laws! As an officer in the Kingdom of His grace, that Kingdom which He has established in this world;—a Kingdom which is yet to rule over *this* and all other nations; and, as a citizen of this country, I deem it fit, and meet, that while the ideas of freedom, nationality, and independence, are fresh and lively in your minds, to bring before you the *relation of Christianity to our country :*—or, GOD IN A NATION ; with the moral and spiritual lessons connected therewith.

There are *three* principles pertaining to this subject, to which I desire to call your attention :

First, that national greatness is always correlative with the ideas of God and religion.

Second, that the true ideas of God and religion, if maintained in purity by a nation, will make that nation immortal.

Thirdly, that the greatness and renown generated by these ideas, depend upon the *individual* character, spirit, and enterprise of the people.

FIRST. I am to show that national greatness is always correlative with the ideas of God and religion. By this I mean that a nation is great just in proportion to the clearness of its idea of God. If a people think that God is a Spirit, that idea raises, or will raise them among the first of nations. If, on the other hand, they think that God is a stone, or a carved image, or a reptile, they will assuredly be low and rude. A nation that worships stocks, or ugly idols, can never, while maintaining such a style of worship, become a great nation. In ancient times, it is true, there were great nations that were idolatrous, but their infancy was religiously simple ; and it was only as they increased in power, dominion, and military renown, that they receded from the simple, natural forms and rites of their fathers ; and fashioned, by their gross imaginations, or brought home from their conquests, the hideous idolatries which ruined them.

While yet fresh and young, with the mighty power of natural religion in their souls, they were strong, mighty, and prosperous. When luxury and affluence were secured, idolatry arose; and they gradually failed, and at last perished! No nation that we know of ever became great whose origin was *coeval* with a worship of stocks and stones. And however mighty a nation, that *is* idolatrous, is, if it clings to idolatry, it must fall! Should England, or Holland, or Prussia, or the United States, renounce reverence of the true God of heaven, and determine, that henceforth they would worship some noble animal or some carved image; they would at once bid " a long farewell to all their greatness." And not only because God would frown upon them for such base apostasy; but, as I think I may state it—on the abstract principle that the idea of God contains, inherently, such transforming power in a nation, that it makes or unmakes, according as it is clear, and right, and grand; or, on the other hand, is low, and rude, and sensual.

This is what I mean by the statement, that national greatness is correlative with the ideas of God and religion.

And now, for a few moments, let us think upon this subject, and endeavor to see what measure of truth it contains, and how we may appropriate that truth to our own profit, to the good of our neighbors and country, and to the glory of God.

Now, if you take up the speeches or treatises which explain such national or economical questions as I have referred to, you will find much said concerning the source and origin of the greatness of nations. We shall find sage and weighty observations concerning trade and commerce; industry and manufactures; agriculture and production; wealth and luxury; science and art. As a general thing, these are considered the fountain-heads, whence have arisen the mighty streams of national greatness in the different ages of the world.

There can be no doubt whatever that commerce has a vast deal to do with increasing the might and power of nations: and so has agriculture; and so manufactures; and so likewise science, in its various departments.

But then the question arises, what leads to commerce? to agriculture? to manufactures? to wealth? to art? I am speaking now, understand, not of the mere supply of natural wants, by fitful activity, as in the savage state—I refer to SOCIETY, if you please, in the early buddings of civilization. What leads, I ask, to these developments of organized society? Why, the enterprise of men! But what is the main spring of human enterprise? Thought. But then, again, what is the generative principle of the mind's active power and activity? THE IDEA OF GOD!

Let me present a few facts, which I think will neither be doubted nor denied. Look around you among the nations, and notice for a moment their characteristics. There is England, and Holland, and Prussia, the United States, and France, and Belgium. They are the greatest nations on the face of the earth. In their religious ideas they entertain the true and pure idea that God is a Spirit. But the time has been when their ancestors were barbarians; without commerce or enlightenment; and then they worshipped dumb idols, and bowed down in fear and awe to graven images. Christianity was introduced among them a few centuries since, and the night of ancestral darkness departed; and it is a fact that this idea, that is, of the oneness and essential spirituality of the Divine Being, has been unfolding and developing itself; that has caused their rise, gradually, and in proportion as they received it with more and more clearness and distinctness, to their present commanding power and influence in the world: for *as* Pagans they could never have *originated* nor retained commerce and civilization.

But perhaps some one here will want to know whether these principles pertain to those ancient States, whose names are associated with so much grandeur and magnificence. There were Nineveh, and Babylon, and Egypt, among the first empires of the world. He may ask, "Was it the idea of God which carried them up to the height of their glory?" This, without doubt, was the case. When our first parents left their Paradisiacal home they carried with them, though tarnished, those pristine ideas of God and His attributes, which had been their crown and glory in Eden. And there is evidence in the Bible and in profane history, that the enlightenment of our first parents was transmitted, for centuries, to their descendants; and was the cause of all that wondrous refinement and civilization, the fragments of which have been disentombed from the sands,—the obelisks and the pyramids of Egypt; and the monuments are now being dug up from beneath the banks of the Euphrates; and which, transmitted to England and to France, adorn the Tuileries and the British Museum. It is a wrong idea to suppose that the first ages of the world were blind and uncultivated; and equally wrong is it to suppose that man *advanced* from barbarism to civilization, instead of that he fell from it. Adam was doubtless a most complete and proper man; and his descendants, although they carried with them for many hundred years, some of his high enlightenment and rare capability, still must have greatly deteriorated from the high pattern of their great progenitor. But still, though fallen, they did carry with them, as they spread abroad in the earth, those lofty ideas of the great God, with whom their Father talked in Paradise: and those ideas made them great, started thought, kept up the consciousness of a high manhood, led to enterprise, originated large ideas and grand purposes, prompted them to build great cities, and to lay the foundations of magnificent empires. But, alas! so soon as they lost those lofty principles, then commenced the facile process of sure decline. As they became idolatrous, weakness advanced, and ruin ensued. This was doubtless the downward course of the first *five empires of the world.* By the inspiriting force of simple, natural religion, they were raised to power, majesty, and culture. But when they became deceived and seduced by the idolatries of their neighbors; or allowed a loose authority to a corrupt imagination; and fashioned the forms of a Divine Power to themselves; then, not all their intellectual greatness, nor the vastness of their imperial power, could preserve them from decay and ruin. The whole process is detailed by St. Paul, in his epistle to the Romans—" Because that when they knew God, they glorified Him not as God, neither were thankful; but became vain in their imaginations, and their foolish heart was darkened. Professing themselves to be wise, they became fools, and changed the glory of the uncorruptible God into an image made like to corruptible man, and to birds, and four-footed beasts, and creeping things." And when they took birds, and beasts, and creeping things as their deities, God brought them down to the level of beasts and creeping things! and laid Nineveh, and Babylon, and Egypt, low in the dust! And where, I ask, on the face of the earth, can you find a nation that worships birds, and beasts, and creeping things, that is great, powerful, and free? Where? Not one! A people are always as high as their idea of God. If their idea of God is a reptile or a worm, they must grovel, they cannot rise; they cannot be great; no commerce, laws, nationality, art, or manhood can proceed from such a people. The ideas of God and religion rule the human being; and if, in a nation, those ideas are low, then the heads and souls of that people are bowed down, and know no elevation. But, on the other hand, the true idea of God magnifies a nation's mind, and leads to development in every mode and direction: for it lifts up man to every thing great and noble; and so enlarges his soul that the depths of the earth are not deep enough for his penetrating gaze; and the boundless seas not grand and majestic enough for his swelling thought; nor the illimitable spheres above vast and extensive enough for excursive reason; and so, after all adventurous daring, and grand endeavor, and ennobling effort, his soul is forced back to the Great Being, the idea of whom, within his soul, originated all his thought and action; to seek satisfaction in the Infinite and the Eternal! But the soul that worships things low and grovelling, clings to the dust; and is not only divorced from all spiritual greatness, but knows not even the simplest beauty of nature, nor yet the excellence of its own being!

SECOND. I advance now to the second point which I was to speak of, that is, that the true ideas of God and religion, if maintained in purity by a nation, will make that nation immortal.

I present this consideration because every thoughtful man desires that his country may live; and hence it is a matter of importance to all such, to learn and know what will prolong, and hand down to the future that nation's life, with which he is connected, and which he loves. There are various causes which cause this solicitude in the breast of a good citizen: the great poet of our language says that "man is a creature who looks both before and after;" and among his many cherished sentiments, are hope for his children and love of his country. And I have no doubt that, to a great extent, it is because reason and manly feeling thus act in man, that, besides anxiety for a pure *past* history, a Christian patriot ponders deeply upon the interests of the *future*. It is the wont of most men, in the ordinary current of life, to think but little whether they shall live *very* long in this world: they know they must die; they know the allotted period of man's life, and they look for the bound of their earthly existence at no very remote period. But no good citizen, no true patriot, wants his country ever to die; but wishes rather that, when buried and cold in the tomb, his country may live on, and be immortal! But here the question arises—" *Is* immortal life a possible element in a nation's being? Such a thing has never been. Man has never witnessed vitality of this kind and of such a measure in history. China, though dating back, it is said, to the time of Noah—China, whose age numbers thousands of years—China, the oldest of all governments, is going to ruin! And when we read the history of mankind, we see nothing but the rise and fall of nations; but *permanent*, national existence —nowhere. Even Macaulay looks forward to the time when some civilized New Zealander shall come across the wide Ocean; and standing on London bridge, look around upon the ruins of St. Paul, and the fragmentary and columnar remains of the fallen Metropolis of Britain.

But though this *has* been the fashion of past national existence, yet I must confess, that I cannot approve the reasoning, which would necessarily make it the certain destiny of all *future* nationalities. For one thing seems quite clear, that the promises of perpetual endurance of divine favor, for " thousand generations," were made to the Hebrews in their *corporate* capacity; and imply also, that if that people had been true on their part, to the covenant made with them; God, on His part, would have been faithful *forever to them.* Moreover, there are causes which now affect the fate of nations, which never did before in all ancient history; and it is only, by parity of reasoning, that is, that like causes produce like effects, that we can conclude that, because past nations have all perished, therefore all modern nations *must* perish. The reason why the great nations of antiquity perished, was because they lacked some strong preserving element, an unrelaxing conservatism; which could redeem them from the shock of adverse circumstance or ruinous influence, and yet live; they had it not, and they died! Their commerce, letters, laws, luxury, could not preserve them; for there is no inherent life in commerce, letters, laws, and luxury. Their religions did not, for they were false, and all error is full of death; and therefore these nations died. But now an element *has been* brought into modern civilization, which was never known before, and which makes it a question, whether all nations must go down into decay and ruin. Since the coming of Christ, a new principle has been introduced into this world of ours, and into national life, which can become part of a nation's existence, and thus preserve, intact, its vitality! I know the objection:—" Man dies, and he is necessarily mortal. *What is a nation but the aggregate of the individual men it contains?* Therefore a nation is necessarily mortal and decaying." But I doubt much the correctness of this mode of thought. I cannot think that the assertion that " a nation is *but* the aggregate of the individual men within it," contains the full and the complete idea of national being. A nation is SOCIETY, in an organized state, under the influence and control of broad principles and superior ideas. *This* does not define man, the individual: neither can any single incident or accident of the one or the other, be presented as representing the proper idea of either. The necessary mortality of man, therefore, cannot imply the necessary decay and ruin of the State, for the man dies; nay, whole generations of men die; but the State lives and flourishes; and it is my belief, that now, under the vital influences of the pure religion of our Lord Jesus Christ, the nation that recognizes the God of heaven as its supreme Governor, and places itself ever under the sanction of His laws and governance, may look for the infusion of a higher life than has been the usual wont of nationalities, and may run along the pathway of a glorious immortality. And here the Christian patriot of Liberia can see whence *this* nation, though young, weak, without resources, and yet in feeble infancy, can lift up its head, and look down calmly, and with assurance, through the deep vistas of the future; and purpose in God, to have for her children, in ages yet to come, a national life; and live on forever, mindless of decay, and fearless of ruin! We know that there is no trust in wealth; for Babylon was wealthy, and she is gone. We know there is no reliance to be placed in power and luxury; for Rome had these, and they could not save her. We know that great commerce and extensive trade can give no security; for the Phœnicians were thus distinguished, and they went down. We see that national life and perpetuity do not spring from learning and wisdom; for old, cultivated, and elegant Greece is now a "base kingdom." But independently of all this, we also know that if the light of letters grows dim; if the power of commerce and of wealth relaxes; if luxury cloys and enervates; and the might of arms becomes nerveless and fails; we know, I say, a power which knows no decay and which repels all weakness; which is all-vital and energic; which, amid the transitoriness of all temporal things, retains the fixed reality of heaven; and which, here, amid the things of time, shows even now the might and endurance of eternity:—I mean the religion of Jesus.

THIRDLY. But these various suggestions I have made are not alien from duty, but rather have a weight of individual responsibility connected with them; and hence I have joined with my two former propositions, the principle, namely—"That the greatness and renown which the ideas of God and religion generate, depend for their vitality, in a nation, upon the individual character, spirit, and enterprise of the people in that nation." I beg to call your attention to this point, and I desire to impress it most strongly upon your minds. We talk of a nation, but too often forget that a nation is made up of the aggregate of the individuals that live in that nation. We speak of our country, but should never fail to remember that this, our country, is composed of all the integral persons who are citizens of this country; that you and I, and your neighbor beside you on your seat, and my neighbor by me here, and all the other men, women, and children in the land, make up our country and compose this nation. And hence, whatever greatness or renown a country may have, it flows in from the *individual*, personal contributions of this, and that, and the other man, and of *all* our fellow-citizens; who, either by industry, enterprise, skill, talent, statesmanship, learning, or, far above all, by character and goodness, give the country a name, and add to its greatness and renown. For you should remember that no one man can make a country. We say that Peter the Great made Russia, that William Pitt saved England. But these expressions are only figurative. What we mean by them is, that these master minds directed the spirit of their respective nations; and, by their talent and character, led the people to do those things which, in the one case, raised Russia from barbarism, and in the other kept England out of the greedy grasp of Napoleon. For any one can see that neither the monarch nor the statesman could do these things alone. There is every probability, moreover, that there were as great men in Russia and in England as these men, only that they were not in the position to lead the national mind; and, still further, that these other great men, in their several positions, were large contributors to the whole mighty mass of virtue, enterprise, and character, which swelled up the honor and the fame of their respective countries. And herein we have *our* individual teachings, each and every one of us, as Christian patriots of Liberia. Whatever Liberia be *now*, or may become in the future, depends upon the aggregate character of her citizens. No one man can make Liberia a great nation. Her greatness, which is all in the distant future, if, indeed, she ever attain it, can never come from any single individual, be he who he may. But if you and I, and all our compatriots, " quit ourselves like men," for the glory of God in this land, and for the honor of our country; and transmit a pure piety and masculine virtues to our children; then the name and the institutions of Liberia shall be perpetual, and she herself immortal! But you will notice the condition I introduce, that is, that we quit ourselves like men—like *godly* men— each and every one of us, in our respective spheres. To this end the scholar must bring his lore; the merchant his enterprise and wealth; the man of letters his refinement; the artizan his skill; the mechanic his plodding energy; the agriculturalist his industry. Every effort must be made to deepen the tone of morals among us; to increase a sense of personal honor and manly integrity; to make the attainment of mere self-ends to be regarded as low and vulgar; to create a public sentiment in which the baseness of men, and womanly shame, shall, perforce, seek obscurity instead of exhibiting a brazen front; and, in fine, to give such an ascendency to Christian truth and principle, as may strengthen and encourage good men, and delight the heart of our God. Our children must be trained up in intelligence, manners, and virtue, and our wives and daughters must present to the world an unstained chastity, a purity and simplicity of manners, at once pleasing and attractive, and a womanly dignity and self-respect, which shall both demand respect and excite admiration.

A spirit of vigorous enterprise must be at once originated by government as well as individuals: bold, but judicious ventures must be made in every direction—in farming, in trade, in commerce—to give importance to the nation in foreign lands, and to increase the individual wealth of our merchants and citizens. I speak of wealth as a desirable acquisition; and, as a Christian minister, I have no hesitation in doing so: for with proper aims and purposes before him, any man may as properly be ambitious of riches as of health, or shelter, or mental growth, or of innocent recreations. For although *godless* riches and unsanctified wealth " make themselves wings and fly away," and " perish by evil travail," and are filled with " deceitfulness," and are spoken of as " corrupted ;" yet we see, both in sacred writ and in God's providence, that He gives riches, and wealth, and affluence, as precious gifts and favors, to the chosen ones whom He wills. For " Abraham was very rich " through His favor; and David had earthly prosperity in his day, and " died full of riches and honor ;" and to Solomon the Lord declared—" I will give thee both riches and honor." Moreover, we find the record that " the Lord maketh poor and maketh rich "—that " the blessing of the Lord, it maketh rich "—in the blessing of Solomon—" both riches and honor come of God," and that " by the fear of the Lord are riches and honor." When I speak of wealth, however, I do not refer to the pitiful sums, which some minds of narrow scope aim after, for mere personal pride and luxurious content; but rather to the solid accumulations—to the grand acquisitions which may *approximate*, in our humble circumstances, to the great capital of merchants, and traders, and landed proprietors, in great lands abroad.

And this, not that it should make men foolish—priding themselves on the perishing things they may amass; which is the most ludicrous thing the angels look down upon;—but wealth to do good, to glorify God, to add to the nation's importance, to push forward civilization through Africa, to promote science, to found virtuous families, to increase comfort, and to provide for those, for whose existence and well-being we as parents are responsible. And thus, by industry, by enterprise, by skill, by learning, all colored and characterized by genuine piety; let us each and all, in our several positions in life, and in the fear of God, make a new start for the upbuilding of the Republic and the glory of the land!

In conclusion, let me make a few suggestions, which, I think, are in their nature calculated to give encouragement, self-reliance, and incentive to the manifestation of high and manly citizenship.

1. First, then, let me say that the fact, that we belong to *that* race of which we are members, is incentive to earnest endeavor for the Commonwealth. A prime consideration here, is the fact that we are members of a but rising race, whose greatness is yet to be achieved—a race which has been spoiled and degraded for centuries, and in consequence of which has been despised. For the name, and fame, and character, and well-being of this race, in every quarter of the globe, let us, as we are in duty bound, strive, by the means of this our nationality, to afford them cheer, by the sight of manhood and of progress here, and give them

> "Secret refreshings that repair the strength,
> And fainting spirits uphold."

In another respect, moreover, we are stirred to energy and activity. We belong to a race possessed of the qualities of hope and endurance, equal at least, to any class of men in the world. The mid passage alone was enough to exterminate any people; but we, in large remnants, have survived it, both in body and soul! We have lived through all the lacerations and soul-crushings of the deadly system of slavery, and the miserable influences of caste. Not merely the life of the *body*, but the moral being, the SOUL of this poor race, has stood the shock of mental pain, and anguish, and sorest desolation, and yet come forth at last triumphant! Signal examples are vouchsafed us for courage and for hope. Bear witness, departed shades, who attest the moral strength and endurance of this race! Thou immortal Toussaint! Statesman, General, Ruler! Thou generous Eustace! Christian and Philanthropist! and all the other unnumbered hearts who have struggled, alas! in vain for freedom! Or ye, who on many a plantation have calmly, quietly died, rather than submit to the yoke! Or, ye other children of faith, who, under the saddest of all earthly ills, have manifested the wondrous power of grace, by the wisdom of patience and the calm dignity of hope!

2. I remark, *secondly*, that we have a further inducement to pious patriotism, from the fact that God's gracious favor is evidently manifested to our race. For three centuries we have been passing through the ordeal of trial and suffering, in the

severe school of slavery: and yet in all these days God has been with our fathers, upholding and sustaining them. Other races have been swept out of existence, but God has preserved *our* life; and, in the lands of our captivity, has given our brethren freedom from the yoke, the light of Christianity, and some of the enjoyments of intelligence and culture. And now, wherever we look, the acknowledged manhood of the race has been won, and the race is going upward and onward to high intelligence and increased power. Not only are they emancipate and freed in the British and French West Indies, but, in the changes which emancipation has caused, the children of the former oppressors of our race are being reduced; and the blacks are rising to influence, and are fast coming into the possession of the property of their former masters. The whole of the British West Indies are yet to form, under English authority, one large black empire. In Brazil the same genial process is being eliminated out of all the dark obscurities of slavery. In Hayti there exist undoubted evidences of a growing civilization, refinement, intellectual culture, and commercial expansion, and clearly showing, that, were it not for the incubus of Romanism, Haytian civilization would fast run up to its culminating point. In the United States the free black men of the North, by the encouragement of friends, by the formation of High Schools and the opening of Colleges, are making rapid progress in the acquisition of learning and in strength of character.

Now, with these evidences of God's favor upon

our race, can we do otherwise than hold up our heads and press on with vigor. Sixty years ago the savans of Europe and America were debating the question —" Whether the Negro is a man ? " and now there is no moral interest in the world which commands so much attention and regard as that of the black man; agitating even disinterested but generous Europe, from Britain to the domains of the Czar; and shaking, from centre to circumference, the fabric of American nationality. And with all the prerogatives and advantages of our own nationality and Protestantism—the latter of which is not possessed either by our French West Indian brethren or by Hayti— shall we not strive to take the lead, ere long, of the entire black race, and by our pure example, by the manifestation of thrift and high endeavor, cheer them on their way, and give them full demonstration of the real though latent capacity we possess? Let us accept with gratefulness the indications of God's gracious favor to us, and tread with firmness the open pathway of science, letters, religion, and civilization!

And now I close as I began, holding up before you, in conjunction, the ideas of "GOD AND OUR COUNTRY." It is a matter of the primest import that we keep ever fresh and lively in our minds this grand relation: "GOD AND OUR COUNTRY." Not God alone, regardless of human relations, for that is nothing but fanaticism: as if there could be a healthy piety indifferent to the family or the nation! Nor yet, on the other hand,—" OUR COUNTRY "—mindless of God and regardless of the sanctions of religion, for that is Atheism; and in the end, in its effects, confusion and ruin. Our only safety under the moral government of this world is in fastening our country upon the throne of God. For without Him there is no life, in the body nor in our souls; in states nor in institutions; in nature, in plants, nor in trees; in the depths of the seas; amid the whirling hosts of the heavens. And so there is no life in a nation without God. "In Him is life," and there is none besides. All growth proceeds from Him, whether it be the tiny plant " beneath a mossy stone," or the spiritual vitality of the grandest Archangel in the eternal heavens! All fixedness, all endurance depend on Him, whether it be the firm seating of the hills around us, or the everlasting permanency of the eternal throne! Ay, brethren, God is every thing; and all of high, and great, and noble, depends on Him. In the idea of God, in the evolvement of the religious idea, in the pure, and strengthening, and gracious principles of Jesus, is a nation's only sure and real hope for growth and permanency. And therefore I say again— "GOD AND OUR COUNTRY"—for if this idea, in all its true relations, governs the minds of this people, then shall our country be unto God for ever, for a people, and for a name, and for a praise, and for a glory. "For happy is the people that is in such a case; yea, blessed are the people who have the Lord for their God."

THE
FITNESS OF THE GOSPEL FOR ITS OWN WORK.

Preached at St. Mark's Church, Harper, before the Christmas Convocation of Cape Palmas, Christmas Day, 1859.

"For as the rain cometh down and the snow from heaven, and returneth not thither, but watereth the earth, and maketh it bring forth and bud, that it may give seed to the sower and bread to the eater; so shall my word be that goeth forth out of my mouth: it shall not return unto me void, but it shall accomplish that which I please, and it shall prosper in the thing whereto I sent it."—ISAIAH lv. 10, 11.

A SERMON.

Romans i. 14.—"I am debtor both to the Greeks and to the Barbarians."

This style of expression, wherein St. Paul mingles *personal* references with Gospel teachings, is common in his epistles. Of all the several writers of Scripture, none speaks so much and so often of himself as this Apostle; not one who uses so frequently the personal pronoun "I." In the verse which follows my text we see the same peculiarity: "I am not ashamed of the Gospel of Christ." In the 11th chapter,—"I also am an Israelite, of the seed of Abraham, of the tribe of Benjamin;" and, again,—"For I speak unto you Gentiles, inasmuch as I am the Apostle of the Gentiles." And so likewise in chapter ix. 16-20. But though this is, indeed, common with the Apostle, it is a great mistake to suppose that he is egotistical. Never was there a man, in all the world's history, in whom selfishness was so thoroughly mortified. So entirely conformed had he been made by the Spirit, to the Lord Jesus his Master, that his whole life, after his conversion, presents the rarest, most exquisite spectacle of self-forgetfulness and self-sacrifice that the world has ever witnessed.

It is therefore no absorbing thought of self, no exaggeration of personal pride or self-importance, which led the Apostle to speak of himself, and to make so many personal allusions. It has a far different origin. It proceeds from a deep mastery of the Gospel over his soul, and from the most solemn convictions of personal duty connected therewith. Underlying all this frequent and multiform egoism, there is a most painful sense of man's spiritual needs, and a most yearning desire to meet and supply them. The two feelings seem to mingle and unite in his soul, to so overpower all other feelings, to so intensify all other sentiments and emotions, that the Gospel and himself become, as it were, identical in his soul: this is his life; aside from this he has no being; and hence he ever speaks as though *he* bore the whole burden of the Gospel—as though he, Paul, alone was set for the defence and confirmation of the Gospel. And therefore he pours forth his ardor, his burning desire, his zealous flame, in a continual strain of egoisms, through the whole of his *thirteen* epistles; the significance of which may be best comprehended by that one singular, personal expression—"I am crucified with Christ; yet not I, but Christ liveth in me; and the life which I now live in the flesh, I live by the faith of the Son of God, who loved me and gave himself for me."

We are not, therefore, to concern ourselves so much with the Apostle himself, as with the burden of his heart—*the Gospel of Christ, in its adaptation to the needs of men.* This idea so fills his soul that it overcomes him. "Here is man's safety," seems to be his feeling. "Here is man's hope; there is no salvation without this. Here is balm, and here is the physician."

These few words of explanation open the way for me to introduce to your consideration the topic, that is—" The fitness of the Gospel to the great needs of humanity, and the great work it contemplates with respect to those needs "—to which I desire to call the attention of this Convocation this morning.

1. With respect to these spiritual needs of men, we have no great difficulty in apprehending them. Our human miseries are so common and so personal that no one can miss them. They lie at every man's door. They press heavily upon every man's soul. *There are the common miseries of life,* which bring their measure of soul-sickness, and plead for healing. This earth is a charnel-house, filled with the diseased and suffering. The griefs and the pangs of the wretched issue forth continually from palaces, and huts, and alms-houses, and hospitals, in all the lands of earth. Cold, and hunger, and famine, lade the air with the plaints and the murmurings of their multitudinous victims. Injustice and oppression crush out the hearts of millions. War, intemperance, and lust, destroy the hearts of nations, sweep millions into untimely graves, carry desolation and sorrows into innumerable families. And passion, hate, and

jealousy, poison the well-springs of life at their highest sources.

But besides these, *there are the deeper, more secret, and sorer miseries, which afflict the universal heart of man.* As there is a wretchedness which is originated in physical ill, which comes out of the bodily afflictions of men, so there is an anguish which has the soul itself as its fountain-head, and preys upon its own vitals. "The heart knoweth its own bitterness." There is an *inward* agony and desolation, the torture of which is felt by mortals, but which they cannot, at times, find words to tell each other. The pains and the sorrows which disappointments, and failures, and jealousy, and care, and treachery, and malice, gender in the souls of men, who can estimate? Then there are the lacerations of bereavements, the sorrows and the desolations which death entails. Deeper yet are the gnawings and the pangs of wounded consciences; the stings of felt but unrepented iniquity; the shame of exposed baseness; the fear or the hardihood of blackened guilt; the convulsive agonies or damning yet determined remorse; the terrible apprehensions of death!

These are what may be regarded as the great spiritual miseries of man, and they are common to mankind everywhere, whether on Christian or on heathen ground. They are those ills and sufferings which assail our human nature, irrespective of circumstance or condition. No one will deny their presence in the better states of society; and if any one doubt their existence among such rude and benighted fellow-creatures as the heathen around us, we can refer, without the shadow of a doubt, to the FACTS which meet us on every side in this benighted land. Are not tears, and shrieks, and heart-breaking moanings the heritage of these poor people, as well as of us who are civilized? Do not sorrows press heavily upon their spirits, and woful agonies eat into their hearts? Does not grief furrow their brows, and the cancer eat away their soul? Are there not miseries so brimful and multitudinous that the spirit ofttimes gives way, and the poor victim seeks willingly the sod, saying to corruption, "Thou art my father; and to the worm, thou art my mother and my sister?" Are they not bruised, and wounded, and lacerated, all their life long, by all the divers thrusts of deadly sin? And does not death come here to *them*, with all its doubt, and desolation, and agony? The groans of infants, the shrieks of convulsed children, the despair of men and women, passing, in darkness, from time into eternity, come wafted on the breeze from these crowded towns, at times, every morn and eve. And then, when death has done its doleful work, and carried grief and wretchedness into their sad homes, do we not see the deeper traces of his mischief and malignity in the wretched rites and the miserable ceremonies which attend the passage of the dead from the hut to the grave? A whole populace carried away in a frenzy by the absurd notions of the after-life which they cherish among them; the exhibition of debasing superstitions over the dead bodies and the open graves of the departed; the abject subjection of these poor creatures to the power of the devil, to whom they cringe and degrade themselves lower than the beasts of the field; and then, at times, that which cannot but touch any feeling heart, the convulsive sobs, the bitter moanings, the mournful weepings over the departed—stout men made weak as water over the lifeless remains of children; heart-broken mothers lifting up their voices in despairing tones, reminding one of the words of Scripture: "Rachel weeping for her children, and would not be comforted, because they are not!"

2. Now, with respect to this universal phenomenon thus presented, the declaration of St. Paul is equivalent to this: *that the Gospel is the complement to man's universal needs and miseries.* He says, in effect, these words: "I know that men have intense spiritual ailments; I am aware of man's inward needs and miseries; I see clearly the fact of soul-sickness, and God has made me an instrument for man's cure and man's relief. Hence I have announced this sacred medicine among my own kith and kin—the Jews; but do not think for a moment that this medicine is for them only. The day of differences and distinctions has passed away. The blood of Jesus Christ is for all men. It is indeed my duty to preach this to the Jews; but Jesus is your Saviour as much as theirs; and it is as much my duty to preach it to Gentiles as to them. Yea, I am debtor both to the Greeks and to the Barbarians, to the wise and to the unwise!"

And this explanation shows most clearly how the personality and egoism of St. Paul fade and vanish before the glory and the power of the Cross. It does this other service also—it furnishes the great truth, that is, *the fitness of the Gospel for all men.* The Gospel, and the Gospel alone, is healing and restoration. No idea is comparable with this in importance to man. There is, indeed, a seeming indifference to religious subjects among men; but he who looks narrowly into things will clearly see that of all subjects that appeal to men and influence them, religion, all over the globe, is the deepest, most powerful, most absorbing. But all the other anxieties of men upon this subject have been fruitless. At length the redemption of Jesus is announced to the nations; and at once all the needs and the painful necessities of the case are met.

This exclusive claim of the Gospel to be the medicine for the deep and otherwise incurable diseases of the soul is visible in two distinct points, which I will briefly point out:

(a) We know from experience and from observation that the disease which is destroying souls is *one;* and, as all men are alike in constitution, it follows that the cure must be one which will affect all alike. Now, many of the ills of men are local; they pertain to particular nations, zones, and hemispheres, and hence the cures of certain ailments in one quarter could not benefit men with dissimilar ailments in other quarters of the globe. Now, the peculiarity of the Gospel is, that the remedy for the great evil which underlies all human woe is both fitted and designed for all men. It is world-wide in its adaptedness, and universal in its efficacy.

If you go to China, the disease which is the fruitful source of all her multiplied miseries—social, civil, religious, and political—is sin. If you come to Africa, you find the fruitful source of her heterogeneous ills and sufferings is sin. If you visit the islands of the sea, sin there is the parent of pains and agonies.. If you turn to India, sin, among her many millions of idolaters, is the desolator. And so, if you traverse the provinces of enlightenment, whether in Europe or America, everywhere you will see the deadly spots of the same loathsome leprosy, which from the infant days of the world has been eating out the vitals of humanity.

Now, whatever may be the development of this virus, if you do not attack it itself your labor is in vain. You may cure this evil; you may get rid of that ailment; you may lop off this withered limb; and cut off that cancered excrescence; and yet, after all, if you do not go directly to the seat of the disease which is ruining man, your labor is vain and profitless.

Sin in the heart, that is, selfishness, alienation from God, perfect absorption in self, *that* is the disease in every man and nation on earth which must be cured; and whatever other alterations, changes, and apparent good may be done, if that is not effected, then nothing has been done. And *that* the Gospel alone can do. It can do it anywhere and everywhere. Its power is not confined nor limited. It is fitted to men of every clime and nation. It is the only remedy, the only agency on earth, which has such power and ability. The Lord Jesus Christ is the only physician of souls who stands up amid the million masses of men, capable of turning and touching any one of the crowd surrounding, and by touching curing, and sending them away healed and whole, for time and for eternity.

There is another point in which we may see the fitness of the Gospel for all men. I have been showing, objectively, how the Gospel is adapted to us; (*b*) but now I wish to point out its fitness, in that *God has made us in such a way, that we are fitted to it*. And this is seen in the fact that wherever the Gospel is proclaimed as the healing agency for sinners, and the terms are announced by which its saving power may be obtained, all men can understand and appropriate it. If the Gospel demanded *money* as its terms, if it demanded *learning*, if it demanded *power*, if it demanded *wisdom*, if it demanded *skill*, few of the wretched sons of men could secure its blessings and its gifts. They could not meet its terms, they could not come up to the demand, they could not answer the requirements. As a consequence, the Gospel would not be fitted for all men, nor be adapted to the whole race. But see how, in its terms and requirements, the Gospel proves its universal fitness. The grand terms of the Gospel are repentance and faith. And never have there lived a people on earth, however lowly and debased, who have not had regret; none who have not exercised, in some way, the quality of faith. All men have been sorry about something in their lives, and so when they are convinced of the error of sin against God, they can be sorry for sin. All men have believed in something around them, and therefore when Jesus is pointed out to them, they can believe in the "Lamb of God, who taketh away the sins of the world."

Here, then, is a new principle introduced into this world, which comes to us with the claim that it can heal all the wounds and bruises and lacerations which sin has bred in this world for the ruin of the souls and bodies of men; and, on examination, we find that its great Author adapted it exactly to our nature, and, conversely, fitted the nature of man everywhere to it; and this, we cannot but feel, is "the tree, the leaves whereof are for the healing of the nation."

3. All this, however, is but a theory of the fitness of the Gospel. The *facts* of Church history and missionary enterprise give full confirmation of it. The past, at least, is certain. Everywhere in the world where the Gospel has secured permanent residence, it has worked a marvellous transformation; and often, where it has but in passing been casually proclaimed, it has left behind a lingering odor, at once healing and sanctifying. We sit down and brood over the evils of Christian countries, forgetful that those evils are in no way whatever the fault or fruit of Christianity, but only show the quarters where devils have not been cast out, where evil spirits still linger, and show the needed power of Christ's Church. By this short-sightedness, moreover, we lose the full impression of the wonderful work the Gospel has done, and fail to see the conquering might inherent in the religion of Jesus. It was four thousand years before Jesus came into the world; but the nineteen hundred years of the Christian era are more than a match for those old four thousand years in beneficence, in brotherhood, in love, and in purity. What great

work of goodness was ever done under the Old Covenant which can compare with what the Gospel is doing every day in our time, both on Christian and on heathen soil? What large and extended blessedness was ever carried through all the earth, to all the sons of men, by any religion before Jesus came? There was no such universal agency in being; no such world-wide influence existed anywhere. But when the angels of Bethlehem proclaimed on the mild airs of Palestine, "Peace on earth, good-will to men!" then a new order of things was heralded to all the sons of men—to every quarter of the globe. The Gospel then began its work, and ever since has been pushing its way through the giant hindrances of sin, and proving in innumerable ways its adaptedness to all the conditions of life, to all the nations of the earth, to all the sons of men.

The phenomenon is before us in the history of man, and its details are manifest. Look now among men for any thing high, noble, manly, brave, generous, beautiful, large-hearted, expansive, and where do you find it? Nowhere else but among Christians! The bravery of arms; the security of freedom; the order of states; the manliness of nationality; the purity and excellence of woman; the expansion of colonies; the beauty of art; the assiduities of philanthropy: what are these but the gracious fruits of Christianity? Aye, and wherever Christianity goes she produces these fruits. See how, in a single generation, our Holy Faith has brought forth the first beautiful blossoms of these excellencies from the dark and chaotic disorder of the Pacific isles, New

Zealand, Sierra Leone. Should we have doubt that yet nobler triumphs await her progress in new and opening fields among more susceptible and anxious people? I know that we often get discouraging words from the wise men of the world as to the prospective results of missionary labors. They look back with an inquisitorial eye, a carping mind, and a doubtful and denying spirit, at the long years of Christian zeal and energy from the time of Christ. They see the larger quarters of the globe under the rule of Satan, and presumptuously demand, " Where is the promise of His coming? *We* do not see the signs of the earth's conversion. Heathenism still rules the masses of men. Even where your missionaries have been sent, and your mission schools and churches have been built, we can see no signs of the superior power of the faith you are preaching."

And yet it is a singular and striking fact that, with regard to those particular fields at which the sneers of doubters have been aimed, God there, on those very spots, has demonstrated the foolishness of man and the power of His Gospel, by the abundant ingathering of souls from among the heathen. Who is there here who does not remember the bitter, biting wit and the keen sarcasm with which a humorous priest in England once ridiculed the missionary zeal of CAREY? And yet Sidney Smith lived to hear and know of the triumphs of the faith in India, of the strong and permanent establishment of Christ's Church amid the splendid monuments of Hindooism. So, only a year or two ago, a leading English review brought all the power of a proud intellect, all the keen force of a bitter, savage pen into play, to demonstrate the folly of attempting to change the hearts and to save the souls of the heathen. And before the ink was well dry upon their blasphemous pages, the news came careering by wind and sail of that recent singular spiritual upheaving in India, which for months has been bringing multitudes to prayer, to submission, to baptism. Here on this coast, where heathenism is rampant, English and American civilians and traders sit down at table with us missionaries, and assure us that the natives of this coast can never be converted to Christianity. And at once up rise Samuel Crowther, J. C. Taylor, our own Jones, and Kinkle and Harris, and Pitman, and a host of other native-born negroes, all along this coast, from Sierra Leone to Abbeoukuta, and in the name of God cast back the infidel imputation, and declare in their lives and utterance that the Gospel is the "power of God to salvation, to every one that believeth"; to the Jew, the Greek, and the barbarian alike. And it is these, and such like facts as these, from every quarter of the globe, which demonstrate by FACT that the Gospel claim is true in its results as well as in theory; namely, that it is the one only remedy for that which, without it, is the incurable disease of all human souls, the leprosy of sin!

Since the Gospel is thus proven, both by theory and fact, to be the only remedy for the ills of life, the only hope for eternity, we have (*a*) ground for faith in all our work and labor in this field in which God has placed us. It is God's scheme, and it is designed by Him for the salvation of the nations. You may be assured, therefore, that it shall not fail in the work to which He hath appointed it. Here, then, we have the character of God pledged to the completion of His own work. We have His promises, too, that His Gospel shall prevail, and He has given vouchers for the triumph of the Gospel, in the glorious facts which the work of missions presents in every quarter of the globe, and among the most debased of human tribes, "turned from dumb idols to serve the living God." There is a certainty about our work, then, which anticipates our labors, and which has never been realized before, in any of all the endeavors of men. Here is ground for faith and assurance which men in no other undertaking could possibly experience. We do not merely trust in and hope for the triumphs of the Gospel; we KNOW that all the rudeness and barbarism of surrounding heathenism shall vanish from this neighborhood; that the Church of God shall supplant the disorganized paganism of this people; and that here, where now indifference, obstinacy, sickness, death, and discouraging weakness seem to baffle all missionary zeal, the Cross of Jesus Christ shall shine with a burning lustre, on hilltop and in the valley—the symbol of an o'ermastering and victorious faith!

(b) We have, moreover, every incentive to renewed exertion in all our labors; for we see that a great feature in the economy, that is, the workings, of this gracious scheme for man is, *God's use of human agencies for the ends he purposes.* We are the present agents He employs for the grand objects we have been considering. And as God has always blessed the wise efforts of faithful men and holy women striving to save souls and to glorify Christ, so we have every spur and incitement to press on in our work, looking for and expecting gracious results to follow faithful labors. With all our hopes and encouragements, however, we must remember that the Divine blessing waits chiefly upon those efforts of His people that are in accordance with the universal law of fitness. Random zeal and injudicious energy accord with no law of His government, and, as a consequence, bring forth but few of the fruits which are the result of His perfect system. The kingdom of God, in all relations, is marked by the presence and the power of this great principle, that is, *the adaptation of means to ends.* The law of order rules and reigns under the highest spirituality and the most exuberant grace. The Holy Spirit breathes, and vivifies, and enlightens, in strict accordance with the most rigid system. There is nothing erratic in the kingdom of grace. All the facts of Scripture, though at times seemingly confused and disarranged, have, nevertheless, underlying them great laws of regulation. There is a science of Scripture; so, likewise, there is a science of the application of Scripture. So far as the facts which may serve for precedents are concerned, God has given us but few in the Bible. The Acts of the Apostles seems to be the history mainly of missions among civilized people. What was the course of the immediate followers of the Apostles, in their work among the rude and barbarous pagans of old, we know but little of. We have, however, the whole broad field of modern missions for nigh three hundred years before us. God thus by His providence teaches us the details of our work and labor, points out to us the mode and manner in which sacred truth may be savingly applied to the souls of the heathen, and also how His servants may conduct missions among barbarous people. We must fall back, then, upon these facts for instruction and direction as to the regimen and rule of our work here. We know already *what* we have to teach souls. But we need, *all* missionaries need, skill and discretion as to the modes of carrying on their work. Let us observe the wise steps of our predecessors here. Let us seek out and examine the lives of the noble spirits who have spent their lives in Gospel labors on heathen soil. No one can estimate fully the riches of missionary biographies or the value of missionary journals. There are the records of the mother Church of England, the narratives of the successful ventures of the godly of the different denominations; and, not seldom, of even pious Romanists. Everywhere we may learn wisdom and pick up instruction. Culling advice from this field, learning discretion from another, extracting skill from a third, we shall, with a prayerful spirit and with the Divine blessing, become master workmen for Christ in the household of faith.

But there is this great favor vouchsafed *all* the true disciples of Christ laboring for Him, that, whatever may be their mistakes, their ignorance, their blindness, and their unskilfulness, *He* abideth faithful; "He cannot deny Himself;" that "the word of God abideth for ever;" and that, though even our labors may be crude and ill-designed, yet we can speak the pure words of salvation to needy souls, and they shall bear fruit, despite our weakness and infirmities, to the praise and glory of His grace, if we only stand aright in our place: "holding the Head, from whom all the body by joints and bands having nourishment ministered, and knit together, increaseth with the increase of God."

ADDRESS ON LAYING THE CORNER-STONE OF ST. MARK'S HOSPITAL.

Delivered at Harper, Cape Palmas, Liberia, April 24th, 1859.

"And they brought unto him all sick people that were taken with divers diseases and torments, and those which were possessed with devils, and those which were lunatic, and those that had the palsy; and he healed them."—MATT. iv. 24.

"Jesus of Nazareth . . . . who went about doing good, and healing all that were oppressed of the devil."—ACTS x. 38.

ADDRESS.

It is a work of mercy which has brought us here to-day; a work of mercy which is required by the needs of man, and which is certainly congenial with the spirit of Heaven. We have divine assurance that such a work as this is acceptable to God; for, without a multiplicity of texts, we may refer to the words which our Lord himself repeated from the Old Testament: "I will have mercy, and not sacrifice"; and to those other precious words which fell from his own gracious lips: "Blessed are the merciful, for they shall obtain mercy." We have just had additional testimony to the same effect, in the graphic description of the judgment, which has been read as the lesson for the day; and which shows us the satisfaction of a gracious judge, in the beneficence of the righteous.* And these are sufficient, without any other evidences, that God, in his word, approves those gra-

---

* The 25th chapter of St. Matthew, from the 31st verse, had just been read.

cious saving efforts, which are designed to lessen the miseries of earth, to mitigate the pains and sufferings of men, to assuage the griefs of wretched humanity, and, at the same time, to increase the sum of human happiness, and to give comfort, well-being, and satisfaction to our fellow-creatures. Such words, from Scripture, warrant, too, our joy in an occasion of this kind, and justify a proper pride and satisfaction on the part of the projector of, and the co-workers in, this labor of love. Every consideration suggests these happy feelings, and prompts such pleasurable emotions. There is no jar here, to-day, of selfish pride, or dissonance of injurious and boisterous passions. We are not a crew of base malignants; nor are we the agents of dark disaster to our fellow-men.

We have met with no sinister purposes before us; nor do we aim at objects that are to bring woe and anguish to any portion of our kind. On the contrary, every thing here designed, contemplated and expected in this undertaking, is for good and blessedness. We would lessen pain. We would end suffering. We wish to neutralize bodily anguish; to arrest the deadly progress of disease; to mitigate inevitable decay, and, where the grave lies surely before him, and death is certain, to pave the way of the sufferer to the tomb, with as much of quiet, comfort, and ease, as skill and benevolence can possibly effect.

Nor are the aims here contemplated, those only which are bodily or medicinal. The body is but the machinery and instrument of the immaterial essence which inhabits it; and while, indeed, desirous, both by skill and kindness, to adjust and restore this machinery, when fractured, or disarranged, or lacerated, or under decay; yet, by so much as the soul is superior to the body, so do we estimate its superior value, and aim the more, directly and indirectly, to seek its good. Spiritual, as well as bodily good, is one of our aims and objects in this blessed project. We cannot, if we would, escape the notice of *soul-suffering* in this world. We have to recognize the presence of spiritual as well as bodily disease among our fellow-creatures. By sense, and thought, and reason, and observation, and experience, by each and all, we have had forced upon our attention those internal disarrangements, those mental fractures, and those spiritual lacerations, which are wasting away the better portion of man's being, and of which, indeed, physical ailments and bodily pain are but the outward signs and symbols. And, for both the one and the other, the disease of the soul, as well as that of the body, human beings need medicines, skill, and the Physician. Here, as everywhere else in the world, poor human nature must needs have the medical man and the minister. And this is to be a Hospital for diseased bodies and for maimed and wounded souls.

2. It is this intrusion of human misery which lessens all our joys through life, and makes brief-born and transient our brightest pleasures. All our delights are mingled with pain in this world, all our happiness is clouded with sadness. Even the satisfaction of this gracious work, which we inaugurate to-day, is neutralized by the contemplation of disease, which it forces upon us, and by the knowledge of

loathsomeness, of agony, and of sickening decay, which it is designed to neutralize. While our minds would fain dwell upon mercy and benevolence to man, bruised bodies and aching limbs force themselves upon our imagination or our sight. While we would delight ourselves in the harmonious tones of human joy, our ears are filled with the sighs and groans of men's misery. Indeed, this world of ours, ever since the fall of Adam, has been a scene of suffering and woe. Bodily distress and physical anguish have ever been the common portion of man all over the globe. The condition of man may but too justly be characterized as a condition of suffering. With respect to the body as well as to the sensitive soul, the words of Scripture are equally true, that " man is born to trouble, as the sparks fly upward." The frames of but few, born into this world, are whole, and strong, and healthy. Somewhere, in every one's system, there is a tender point, or an infirm organ, or a weakened nerve, or a fractured limb, or a heart not altogether sound, or a lingering cancer, or just the taint of corruption, which will cause a diseased lung, and in the end produce consumption. And thus disease, everywhere, produces sorrow and wretchedness. The air is filled with the shrieks and groans of the suffering. The very sounds of nature are plaintive and mournful. Every breeze that sweeps over the plains, has its tale of pain and anguish. Every wind, in melancholy tones, wails out its agonizing report of disaster and of death. Even in the gentlest gales, we may hear the groans of infants, the shrieks of convulsed children, the moans of agonized men, the throes of distressed and dying woman, and all the various notes of misery with which earth is filled.

3. Into this region of distress and death—this world of suffering and of woe, Jesus Christ appeared. He came on a lofty mission to earth, in order to see what were the pains and pangs of wretched humanity; and to exert a divine power, capable of arresting the deadly tide of disease, in human frames and human hearts. He came in his own distinct and peculiar manifestation—"the PRINCE of life," for the purpose of scattering disease and of destroying death and its powers. He was the reality of that incident in the life of the High Priest, when we read that "He stood between the dead and the living, and the plague was stayed." Aaron was but the type, but Christ is the reality of that wondrous healing power. And when He came, the world experienced an efficacy of actual curative might, which it had never before known in all its histories.

Here, now, was the great Physician. Here was "Balm of Gilead." He went about everywhere, doing good. He spent a life of generous and saving restorative power, healing all manner of disease and sickness. He fed the hungry. He comforted the widow. He raised the dead. The deaf had their hearing restored. The blind were reclaimed from darkness, to look forth in joy upon the brightness of clear skies and "the lilies of the field." The paralytic regained lost vital power to disabled limbs. The withered hand was made whole, and became once more pliant and elastic. Lunacy was changed to calm rationality and clear sense. Indeed, all manner of sickness gave way, at once, at His presence. The fiery heat of consuming fevers, and the malignity of noxious ailments, were conquered at His approach; for even leprosy, which is death, seated triumphant amid vitality, yielded at His touch; and life and vigorous health ran suddenly, and with alacrity, through the stagnant veins of its despairing victim.

4. I am told that these were miracles; and so, indeed, they were. They were mighty works; "great and astounding marvels;" wondrous and amazing powers. They were facts and occurrences which startled the senses, and overcame all the deductions of reason, and outran the flights of imagination. But they were something more than this. They were mercies as well as wonders; grace-tokens as well as demonstrations of God's great power; in fine, manifestations of that gracious and merciful spirit which characterizes the religion of Jesus, as well as mighty miracles which evidence the Faith.

Ignorance of this is blindness to the spirit of the New Testament, and of the acts of Jesus. For, without doubt, no man has even seen the deep reality and the wondrous significance of our Lord's miracles, who has only regarded them as wondrous marvels, and hence, has failed to notice the Divine Love, the genial and genuine humanity, the large-hearted philanthropy, and the tender, melting sympathy, which they everywhere so savingly signify. The Lord Jesus, never be it forgotten, was not only a wonder-worker among men, but He was, and pre-eminently so even in them, a compassionate Saviour, a sympathizing friend, a brother, "touched with a sense of our infirmities," touching men ever with the subduing touch of kindness, and with a healing power.

5. And this feature of Christ's miraculous power, it should be remembered, is the one which all the ages through, and now, in our own day, still remains an unfailing inheritance in Christ's church and to Christ's people, aye, and even to a heedless world. The age of miracles has gone; but it may well be doubted whether, since Jesus came into this world, any distinct power or influence He once exerted, has ever departed, entirely and in every way, from among men. After the birth in Bethlehem, Jesus is ever present in this world;—His presence is never again to depart from it, until the consummation of all things. His glorified body is indeed in Heaven; but He is with His Church always, even unto the end of the world. And, being present, those wondrous powers, and that mighty energy, which He wrought among men, in the days of His manifestation, are likewise ever present, and never shall depart. There is not one of us here to-day, but who believes in Jesus' personal presence in this church. We all have a firm faith that He is really and undoubtedly with his ministry and people, in all their work and service in His behalf on earth. We are fully convinced, that in prayers, and preaching, and sacraments, He is not a far-off, but an ever-present Lord. But where is the warrant for the dubitating thought, that this presence is vouchsafed only to those offices which are called distinctively religious, and which pertain exclusively to the soul? Where is the ground for supposing that

the Lord's presence is confined to those things alone which we specially entitle spiritual.

There is, indeed, no such ground. This sceptical persuasion is, in some, the fruit of a mere surface thought upon the high prerogative of Christ's Church; in another class, it is the offspring of a halting unbelief; in others, again, it proceeds from unworthy and unwarranted notions of the inferiority of matter, in general, and of the body in particular; forgetful that *all* things, since Christ's coming, are sanctified to the loftiest purposes.

"For the base world, now Christ hath died,
 Ennobled is, and glorified."

In truth, brethren, to deny, or even doubt, Jesus' presence, as pertaining to the body as well as spirit of man, *to the whole man*, is to hold a mere brutal theory about man, and to make nugatory the efficacy of our Lord's incarnation. For the terms of the large promises of Jesus justify us in looking for, and assuring ourselves in, the presence and strength of our mighty Lord in all our work and labors, in which we aim at the welfare of the bodies of men. Moreover, the very fact that our Lord went up on high in our flesh, seems to show that that glorified body is still the sympathizing medium between "GOD manifest in the flesh," and frail humanity, in pains and misery.

The form and mode in which power goes out from Jesus, is different now from what it was when men approached, and saw, and felt, and handled that awful person; but the essence and the energy are the same.

Our Lord, at the beginning of his ministry, declared: "The spirit of the Lord is upon me, because He has anointed me to preach the Gospel to the poor; he hath sent me to heal the broken-hearted; to preach deliverance to the captives, and recovery of sight to the blind; to set at liberty them that are bruised.

And ever since, not only until the Ascension, but all these two thousand years of the Christian era, Jesus has been preaching the Gospel to the poor; it is He who, on Christian and on heathen ground, has been healing the broken-hearted; He it is who has broken the fetter from the limbs of the captive and the slave, and proclaimed emancipation; and it has been JESUS who, in multitudinous almshouses, asylums, infirmaries, and hospitals all over the globe, has healed the bruises, sores, and lacerations of men; enabled physicians to give sight to the blind, and hearing to the ear; made the lame to walk, and cured the dropsical and the paralytic. The *bodily* presence of Jesus has not been here on earth; but all curative influence, this restorative and healing power, came from the religion of Jesus, and is verily and indeed the work of our own gracious Lord.

Thus again, the Redeemer after His Resurrection, when taking leave of His Apostles, declared: "All these signs shall follow them that believe: in my name shall they cast out devils; they shall speak with new tongues; they shall take up serpents; and if they drink any deadly thing, it shall not hurt them; they shall lay hands on the sick, and they shall recover." Is there nothing in it for us in our work here save as reminiscence? Are men to receive these words in no other way than the literal? Do you so magnify these undoubted miracles that when their distinct and characteristic marks vanish, the Church of God sinks to a lower and utterly diverse manifestation of Divine power, so that she is confined to the *outward* signs of miracles for her interpretation of these large and glorious promises? And do their external, visible characteristics, sever us of these modern times entirely from these mighty works of our Lord? Or do you suppose that because the outward and visible sign of these wonders is denied us in this age, that therefore Christ is not still fulfilling the very same promise in this naughty world to the discomfiture of sin and Satan? Surely this is the last place in the world for any such unbelief. Here, or indeed anywhere else on heathen ground, where Satan has established his kingdom, but where the Holy Spirit has lifted up " an effectual banner " against him in Christian missions, we do indeed see " devils cast out ; " we see the sick reclaimed from feebleness through the renovating agencies of a new faith ; we see Christian converts outrunning, in all the respects of strength of virtue and intelligence, all their heathen kin ; we see a power scattering the darkness and disseverance of thousands diverse and inferior tongues, and by Christian philosophy, and the energy and diffusion of the Christian English tongue, reverting the confusion of Babel into the harmony of goodly brotherhood and love. If we cannot believe all this, are we prepared to attribute these gracious results to some other influence than Christ Jesus'? Are we willing to believe that there is another power in this world besides that of JESUS to do good to the bodies and souls of men? And is it indeed the case that Christians cannot have the faith that great as were the miracles of Christ, "that greater works than these" were to be done by His people?

Surely none of us are prepared for such a concession as this. While, indeed, granting that the age of miracles has departed, we claim that the gracious and saving power of Jesus is still the heritage of Christ's people. If the wonder-making phase of miracles has gone, their restorative and compassionate features are still continued by our Lord, in this sinful world. For Jesus Christ came upon earth, and took upon Him our flesh, for this very purpose of good and blessedness to man. He came to touch man with a saving power, and therefore He took our bodily nature upon Him, not to touch and heal men for the brief period of His earthly stay among men, but unto the world's end; and therefore, if we would trace to its source the beneficence which we see around us, in the restored bodies of men, we must recognize the healing power of our Lord still exerted for good, although it comes to us by the agency of our fellow-creatures, and is exerted through the art and skill and genius of man. When the woman in the Scriptures took hold of the garment of the Saviour, He instantly declared that "virtue had gone out of Him." The very touch sent forth healing efficacy. So now healing still continues to go out from His body—His touch still works a curative influence. That glorious body on the right hand of the Father still gives forth a power to repair, a health and life-giving energy, a healing influence, to weak and wretched men.

And it is thus, in one view, that Christianity continues, even to our own day, a standing miracle. This miraculous power of the faith may be seen, I know, in other aspects; but I wish now to fasten attention upon this one point, and claim for our blessed Lord a power which is all and peculiarly His own. Christ is the Healer of the nations; *directly*, that is, in saving and sanctifying the sinful souls of men; *indirectly*, in healing and curing and restoring their bodies by the agencies of physicians, medicines, and hospitals. These are His miracles of love, those the miracles of evidence.

6. And all this will appear yet more distinctly if you will notice the fact that such humane efforts as this of ours are specially Christian. It is the genius of Christianity which has produced the philanthropy of civilized countries. It is the spirit of Jesus' religion which has prompted that high art, that marvellous skill, and those humane institutions by which, in all Christian lands, disease is conquered, life is lengthened out, and pain is neutralized. It is thus that Jesus' presence is felt in the world, even in matters physical and temporal. No other religion has ever prompted such generous benevolent skill, or thus provided for the miserable and the outcast. On the banks of the Ganges the maimed and the decrepit are cast into the river as food for crocodiles. Pagan and Mohammedan travellers through the deserts of Africa desert the sick and the diseased, and leave them to the tender mercies of the jackal or the tiger. The Indian in the western wilds of America casts out the emaciated and the helpless to the ravenous wolf

without pity or remorse. We see here among the heathen, at times, the utter absence of sensibility or feeling for those, even relations or parents or children, who are suffering pain and agony, or who are sick unto death. Even in that religion of which Christianity is an offshoot, the religion of the Jews, although mercy and kindness are marked peculiarities, still we discover no special provisions for the sick; no regulations for gathering them into lazar-houses and receptacles. Indeed, the history of mankind shows that there is no *natural* tendency to humane and charitable deeds. The human heart, of itself, never originates efforts and institutions of the kind we are originating this day. It is not of man to assuage suffering, to heal the sick, to save the miserable. It was left to the sublime and humane spirit of Christianity to start such works of mercy and such works of love. Jesus had to come into the world, and since His advent the poor, the maimed, the wretched, the blind, and the deaf have been cared for. Wherever His holy religion has been established, there hospitals, almshouses, and reformatory institutions have sprung up all over Christendom; and the woes, and agonies, and wails of poor distressed humanity have been cared for. We claim, as we have the right to claim, that this is the work of our Lord. No matter what may be the agencies used in the conversion of men, or who may have been the ministers or teachers who led them to Christ, we deny the glory to these agents; we claim that Jesus worked their spiritual restoration. So, in like manner with regard to all eleemosynary works and houses, though we recognize the zeal of warm-hearted men and gentle women, the large charities and the heroic self-sacrifice of fearless nurses and physicians, yet we claim all for Christ. This stream of pitifulness for the suffering has its rise in the merciful bosom of our own risen and glorified Lord. All the philanthropy of this world, whether flowing in legitimate or indirect channels, has been prompted by and caught up from this precious faith of Jesus. Whether men reclaim the drunkard, or free the poor slave, or give sight to the blind or hearing to the deaf, or rectify fractured limbs, they learned it all in the school of Christ. The religion of Jesus is the only one which cares for both body and soul. Wherever, in its practical workings, there is a forgetfulness or neglect of either of these portions of our humanity, there Christianity appears misshapen, one-sided, deformed; neither do her advocates gain any real advantage for her by excessive devotedness to one portion of man which is purchased by neglect of the other; indeed, that is a mere mockery of the spirit of Christ, which, while pretending solicitude for the spirit of man, is at the same time indifferent to his temporal estate. The religion of Jesus is a religion which lays hold of both body and soul for time and for eternity. And though Jesus has gone upon high, still He ever liveth. He is ever present in his Church for good and blessedness for the whole, entire, compact being of man, one and undivided—the undying spirit, and the mortal frame, which at the resurrection is to be clothed upon with immortality.

7. We bless God for the holy religion of Jesus, which He has revealed to man. We bless Him for

all the gracious fruits and the saving influences which proceed from this religion. We bless Him for the new spirit which it has spread abroad in this sinful world, for the lofty principles by which it strengthens the will of man, and for the noble deeds to which it has given birth. We bless Him for all the benevolent institutions which He has started into being, in all the fields of its victory and triumph. We bless Him for all the Christian houses, hospitals, homes for little orphan children, refuges, reformatories, houses of mercy, and asylums, into which have been gathered the sick and the emaciated all over the globe, in all the ages of the Faith. We bless Him for all the generous enterprises which the Christian religion has started into being for the bodily relief and the temporal welfare of our fellow-creature. We bless Him for all the philanthropic schemes by which the drunkard is made sober and saved, the outcast Magdalen is made pure in both body and soul, the poor slave is emancipated and becomes a man, the leper is cared for, and his sorrow and desolation mitigated, the prisoner is blessed, the sailor rescued, and the crippled and the diseased are cured.

And while indeed "holding the Head," even the Lord Jesus, as the fountain of all bodily as well as all spiritual good to man, we bless God, also, for all the noble men and women who in all the ages of Christianity have drank in fully the spirit of our common Master, and have gone about among widows and orphans, among the sick and the diseased, the blind, the lame, and the deaf, imitating the Lord's example, "doing good to men." Blessed and merciful spirits!

ye who are yet on the shores of time, still diligent in saving deeds and holy charities; or, ye more lofty ones, reaping the fruition of your goodly service for men on the far-off shores of blessedness and glory; we hail and salute you as among the best benefactors of your kind, as the faithful ministers of grace and restoration to afflicted men!

With this goodly company we are happy to associate this day our reverend brother* who projected this work, and who, by God's favor and the aid of generous friends, has been enabled to bring it to this favorable point. We thank God for the grace thus freely given him for us; "for He loveth our nation and builds" us an hospital. Other things add to the gladness of this ceremony. We are happy in the occasion which assembles us together. This is St. Mark's day, and our Church calls upon us to commemorate that eminent evangelist and saint, who laid the first foundations of the Church in Africa, and who is believed to have moistened its soil with a martyr's blood. In what more befitting manner could we keep the day than this?

We are happy in the selection of the spot from which, in fair proportions, is to rise this house of healing and of mercy. Here, amid pure, untainted, and healthful breezes, the invalid may gain strength to his body and revive hope to his sinking heart.

---

* St. Mark's Hospital was planned and projected by the Rev. C. C. Hoffman, of New York City, missionary of the Protestant Episcopal Church at Cape Palmas, Liberia, and the building has been carried on, and approaches completion, under his superintendence, and through his zeal and labors.

Here this house will stand a prominent object, and be seen from afar on the ocean, greeting the eye of the sick sailor or the timid, tremulous emigrant, assuring both that, although they approach the shores of Africa, yet the religion of Jesus here, as everywhere else, mitigates the pestilence, heals the sick and the diseased, comforts the miserable and the outcast, and is full of healing, consolation, and of love! "May the beauty of the Lord our God be upon us, and establish Thou the work of our hands upon us; yea, the work of our hands establish Thou it!"

THE
RELATIONS AND DUTIES OF FREE COLORED MEN IN AMERICA TO AFRICA.

Addressed to Mr. Charles B. Dunbar, M. D., formerly of New York City, but now a citizen of Liberia.

"It is in Africa that this evil must be rooted out—by African hands and African exertions chiefly that it can be destroyed."
—MCQUEEN—*View of Northern Central Africa.*

"We may live to behold the nations of Africa engaged in the calm occupations of industry, and in the pursuit of a just and legitimate commerce; we may behold the beams of science and philosophy breaking in upon their land, which at some happier period, in still later times, may blaze with full lustre, and joining their influence to that of PURE RELIGION, may illuminate and invigorate the most distant extremities of that immense continent."—WM. PITT.

LETTER.

HIGH SCHOOL, MT. VAUGHAN, CAPE PALMAS,
LIBERIA, 1st Sept., 1860.

MY DEAR SIR: It is now many months since I received a letter from you, just as you were about sailing from our shores for your home. In that note you requested me to address you a letter setting forth my views concerning Liberia, suggesting, at the same time, that such a letter might prove interesting to many of our old friends and schoolmates in New York. I have not forgotten your request, although I have not heretofore complied with it. Though convinced of the need and possible usefulness of such a letter as you asked from me, I have shrunk from a compliance with your request. Not to mention other grounds of reluctance, let me say here that I have felt it a venturesome thing to address four hundred thousand men; albeit it be indirectly through you. Neither my name, position, nor any personal qualities give me authority thus to do. The only excuse I have is the depth and solemnity of all questions connected with Africa. I see that no one else of our race has done it; perhaps I may be pardoned for assuming so great a task.

I may add here that I address the "Free Colored Men of America," because I am identified with them; and not because I feel that *they*, especially, and above all the other sons of Africa, in distant lands, are called upon for zeal and interest in her behalf. It is the exaggeration of the relation of *American* black men to Africa, which has turned the hearts of many of her own children from her. Your duties, in this respect, are no greater than those of our West Indian, Haytian, and eventually our Brazilian brethren. Whatever in this letter applies to our brethren in the United States, applies in an equal degree to them. But I am not the man to address them. I fear I *presume* even in writing this letter to American black men, and have only just now concluded to do so by the encouragement I have received in two pleasant interviews with Mr. Campbell and Dr. Delany.

And even now it is with doubt and diffidence that I conclude to send you this communication. My reluctancy has arisen chiefly from a consideration of the claim put forth by leading colored men in the United States, to the effect "that it is unjust to disturb their residence in the land of their birth by a continual call to go to Africa." This claim is, in my opinion, a most just one. Three centuries' residence in a country seems clearly to give any people a right to their nationality therein without disturbance. Our brethren in America have other claims besides this; they have made large contributions to the clearing of their country; they have contributed by sweat and toil to the wealth thereof; and by their prowess and their blood they have participated in the achievement of its liberties. But their master right lies in the fact that they are Christians; and one will have to find some new page and appendage to the Bible, to get the warrant for Christians to repel and expatriate Christians, on account of blood, or race, or color. In fact, it seems to me a most serious thing to wantonly trench upon rights thus solemnly and providentially guaranteed a people, that is, by a constant, ceaseless, fretting iteration of a repelling sentiment.

Of course I do not intend any thing akin to this in my letter. I would not insult the intellect and conscience of any colored man who thinks it his duty to labor for his race on American soil, by telling him that it is his duty to come to Africa. If he is educated up to the ideas of responsibility and obligation, he knows his duty better than I do. And, indeed, generally, it is best to leave individuals to themselves as to the *details* of obligation and responsibility.

"The primal duties shine aloft like stars";—and it is only when men *will* not see them, that we are bound to repeat and re-utter them, until the souls of men are aroused, and they are moved to moral resolution and to noble actions. But as to the *mode, form*, and *manner* of meeting their duties, let the common sense of every man decide it for himself.

My object in writing this letter is not to vex any of our brethren by the iteration of the falsehood that America is not their home, nor by the misty theory " that they will all yet have to come to Liberia." I

10

do not even intend to invite any one to Liberia, glad as I would be to see around me many of the wise and sterling men I know in the United States, who would be real acquisitions to this nation, and as much as I covet their society. I am not putting in a plea for colonization. My object is quite different; in fact it is not a strict compliance with the terms of your letter, for I shall have but little to say about Liberia. But believing that *all* men hold some relation to the land of their fathers, I wish to call the attention of the sons of Africa in America to their " RELATIONS AND DUTY TO THE LAND OF THEIR FATHERS."

And even on such a theme I know I must prepare myself for the rebuff from many—" Why talk to *us* of fatherland? What have *we* to do with Africa? *We* are not Africans; we are Americans. You ask no peculiar interest on the part of Germans, Englishmen, the Scotch, the Irish, the Dutch, in the land of their fathers, why then do you ask it of us?"

Alas for us, as a race! so deeply harmed have we been by oppression that we have lost the force of strong, native principles, and prime natural affections. Because exaggerated contempt has been poured upon us, we too become apt pupils in the school of scorn and contumely. Because repudiation of the black man has been for centuries the wont of civilized nations, black men themselves get shame at their origin and shrink from the terms which indicate it.

Sad as this is, it is not to be wondered at. "Oppresssion" not only "makes a wise man mad," it robs him also of his self-respect. And this is our loss; but having emerged from slavery, it is our duty to cast off its grave-clothes and resist its deadly influences.

Our ancestors were unfortunate, miserable, and benighted; but nothing more. Their history was a history, not of ignominy and disgrace, but of heathenism and benightedness. And even in that state they exhibited a nobleness of native character, they cherished such virtues, and manifested so much manliness and bravery, that the civilized world is now magnanimous enough to recognize such traits; and its greatest men are free to render their warm eulogies.*

When then colored men question the duty of interest in Africa, because they are not Africans, I beg to remind them of the kindred duty of self-respect. And my reply to such queries as I have mentioned above is this: 1. That there is no need of asking the interest of Englishmen, Germans, Dutchmen and others in the land of their fathers, because they have this interest, and are always proud to cherish it. And 2d. I remark that the abject state of Africa is a most real and touching appeal to *any* heart for sympathy and aid. It is an appeal, however, which comes with a double force to every civilized man who has negro blood flowing in his veins.

Africa lies low and is wretched. She is the maimed and crippled arm of humanity. Her great powers are wasted. Dislocation and anguish have reached every joint. Her condition in every point

* For a most able and discriminating article upon this topic, see "WESTMINSTER REVIEW," January 7, 1842, Art., Dr. Arnold. Also, those humane and truthful Essays of Mr. HEAPS—"FRIENDS IN COUNCIL," vol. 2.

calls for succor—moral, social, domestic, political, commercial, and intellectual. Whence shall flow aid, mercy, advantage to her? Here arises the call of duty and obligation to colored men. Other people may, if they choose, forget the homes of their sires; for almost every European nation is now reaping the fruits of a thousand years' civilization. Every one of them can spare thousands and even millions of their sons to build up civilization in Australia, Canada, New Zealand, South Africa, or Victoria. But Africa is the victim of her heterogeneous idolatries. Africa is wasting away beneath the accretions of civil and moral miseries. Darkness covers the land, and gross darkness the people. Great social evils universally prevail. Confidence and security are destroyed. Licentiousness abounds everywhere. Moloch rules and reigns throughout the whole continent, and by the ordeal of Sassywood, Fetiches, human sacrifices, and devil-worship, is devouring men, women, and little children. They have not the Gospel. They are living without God. The Cross has never met their gaze, and its consolations have never entered their hearts, nor its everlasting truths cheered their deaths.

And all this only epitomizes the miseries of Africa, for it would take a volume to detail and enumerate them. But this is sufficient to convince any son of Africa that the land of our fathers is in great spiritual need, and that those of her sons who haply have ability to aid in her restoration will show mercy to her, and perform an act of filial love and tenderness which is but their "reasonable service."

I have two objects in view in addressing you this

letter: *one* relates to the temporal, material interests of adventurous, enterprising colored men; and the *other* pertains to the best and most abiding interests of the million masses of heathen on this continent—I mean their evangelization.

First, I am to speak with reference to the temporal and material interests of adventurous, enterprising and aspiring men in the United States of America. I wish to bring before such persons reasons why they should feel interest in Africa. These reasons are not, I am free to confess, directly and distinctively philanthropic; although I do, indeed, aim at human well-being through their force and influence. But I appeal now more especially to the hopes, desires, ambition, and aspirations of such men. I am referring to that sentiment of self-regard which prompts to noble exertions for support and superiority. I am aiming at that principle of SELF-LOVE which spurs men on to self-advantage and self-aggrandizement—a principle which, in its normal state and in its due degree, to use the words of BUTLER, "is as just and morally good as any affection whatever." In fine, I address myself to all that class of sentiments in the human heart which creates a thirst for wealth, position, honor, and power. I desire the auxiliary aid of this class of persons, and this class of motives, for it is such influences and agencies which are calculated to advance the material growth of Africa. She needs skill, enterprise, energy, *worldly* talent, to raise her; and these applied here to her needs and circumstances, will prove the handmaid of religion, and will serve the great purposes of civilization and enlightenment through all her borders.

There seems to me to be a natural call upon the children of Africa in foreign lands to come and participate in the opening treasures of the land of their fathers. Though these treasures are the manifest gift of God to the negro race, yet that race reaps but the most partial measure of their good and advantage. It has always been thus in the past, and now as the resources of Africa are being more and more developed, the extent of *our* interest therein is becoming more and more diminutive. The slave-trade is interdicted throughout Christendom; the chief powers of earth have put a lien upon the system of slavery; interest and research in Africa have reached a state of intensity; mystery has been banished from some of her most secret quarters; sunlight, after ages of darkness, has burst in upon the charmed regions of her wealth and value; and yet the negro, on his native soil, is but " a hewer of wood and drawer of water"; and the sons of Africa in foreign lands, inane and blinded, suffer the adventurous foreigner, with greed and glut, to jostle them aside, and to seize with skill and effect upon their own rightful inheritance.

For three centuries and upwards, the civilized nations of the earth have been engaged in African commerce. Traffic on the coast of Africa anticipated the discoveries of Columbus. From Africa the purest gold got its characteristic three hundred years ago. From Africa dyes of the greatest value have been carried to the great manufacturing marts of the world. From Africa palm oil is exported by thousands of tons; and now, as the observant eye of commerce is becoming more and more fastened upon this continent, grain, gums, oils of divers kinds, valuable woods, copper and other ore, are being borne from the soil to meet the clamorous demands of distant marts.

The chief item of commerce in this continent has been the "slave-trade." The coast of Africa has been more noted for this than for any thing else. Ever since 1600, the civilized nations of the earth have been transporting in deadly holds, in poisonous and pestilential cabins, in "perfidious barks," millions of our race to foreign lands. This trade is now almost universally regarded as criminal; but in the light of commercial prudence and pecuniary advantage, the slave-trade was as great a piece of folly as it was a crime; for almost beneath their eyes, yea, doubtless, often immediately in their sight, were lying treasures, rivalling far the market value of the flesh and blood they had been so eager to crowd beneath their hatches.

Africa is as rich in resources as India is; not as yet as valuable in products, because she is more unenlightened and has a less skilful population. But so far as it respects mineral and vegetable capacity, there seems to me but little, if any, doubt that Africa more than rivals the most productive lands on the globe.

Let me set before you, though briefly, some of the valuable articles of West African trade. I must remind you, however, of three things: *First*, that the soil, the rocks, and the flora of Africa have not had the advantage of scientific scrutiny, and as a consequence but little is known as yet of her real worth and wealth in these respects. *Second*, that West African trade is only in a nascent state—that it comes from but a slight fringe of the coast, while the rich interior yields, as yet, but a reluctant hold upon the vast and various treasures it possesses. And *third*, that such is the mysterious secrecy American and English houses retain and *enjoin* upon this subject, that even approximation to the facts of the case is remote and distant.

The following table is an attempt to classify valuable products and articles of present trade. Nearly every article mentioned has come under my own personal inspection; the exceptions are not over a dozen and a half:

Nuts.	Dyes and Dyewood.	Gums and Wax.	Animals.
Palm Nut.	Camwood.	Beeswax.	Oxen.
Ground Nut.	Barwood.	Grove Tree.	Sheep.
Cocoa Nut.	Indigo.	India Rubber.	Hogs.
Cola Nut.	Christmas nut.	Gutta Percha.	Goats.
Castor Nut.	And divers other colors, blue, red, yellow, and brown.	Copal.	Fowls.
		Mastic.	Ducks.
		Senegal.	Pigeons.

Skins.	Grains.	Fruits.	Vegetables.
Bullock.	Rice.	Oranges.	Yams.
Sheep.	Maize.	Lemons.	Cassada.
Deer.	Millet.	Plantains.	Potatoes.
Monkey.		Bananas.	Tan yah.
Leopard.		Citrons.	
Gazelle.		Limes.	
Squirrel.		Guavas.	
Raccoon.		Pineapples.	
Lion.		Papaw.	
		Mango Plums.	
		Alligator Pear.	
		Bread Nut.	
		Tamarind.	

Timber.	Minerals.	Special articles connected with trade and domestic use.	Fish.
Teak.	Iron.	Sugar-Cane.	Mackerel.
Ebony.	Copper.	Coffee.	Mango Perch.
Lignum Vitæ.	Gold.	Cocoa.	Cavalla.
Mahogany.		Pepper.	Gripper.
Brimstone.		Cotton.	Herring.
Rosewood.		Tobacco.	Mullet.
Walnut.			Chub.
Hickory.			Perch.
Oak.			Pike.
Cedar.			Trout.
Unevah.			Cod.
Mangrove.			Skate.
			Eels.
			Oysters.

I cannot dismiss these tables without a few remarks relative to some few prominent items they enumerate; I mean the PALM NUT and OIL, COTTON, INDIAN CORN, and SUGAR-CANE.

PALM OIL.—This article, more than any other West African product, shows the rapidity with which legitimate commerce has sprung up on the coast of Africa. A few years ago palm oil was an insignificant item in the coast trade.* *Now* it is an article which commands whole fleets of sailing vessels, seeks the auxiliary aid of steamers, and affects most powerfully the commerce of England, France, and the United States.

I copy several items pertaining to this export from

---

* In 1808, the quantity imported into England was only 200 (two hundred) tons.

a report of a former acquaintance and correspondent, the late Mr. Consul Campbell, of Lagos. The report, as will be seen, includes several other items besides palm oil, and it refers exclusively to Lagos.

SHIPPED FROM LAGOS DURING 1857.

		Value.
13,097 casks of Palm Oil,	4,942 tons,	£222,390
1,053 Elephant Tusks,	24,118 lbs.,	4,220
868 bales of Cotton,	114,848 lbs.,	3,490
		230,200
50,000 native Cotton Cloths,		25,000
Total value of exports from Lagos,		£255,200

Palm Oil—

From the Benin River,	2,650 tons,
" Palma,	3,250 "
" Badagry,	1,250 "
" Porto Novo, Appi, Vista, &c.,	4,500 "
" Whydah,	2,500 "
" Ahguay and neighboring ports,	2,500 "

16,650 tons, £732,600

150,000 country Cloths of native manufacture from above ports, 75,000

£1,062,800

Of the above productions there was shipped from Lagos in the year—

	1856.	1857.	Increase.
Palm Oil,	3,884 tons.	4,942 tons.	1,058 tons.
Ivory,	16,057 lbs.	24.118 lbs.	8,061 lbs.
Cotton,	34,491 lbs.	114,844 lbs.	81,353 lbs.

Palm Oil from other ports—

	1853.	1857.	Increase.
Benin River,	2,500 tons.	2,650 tons.	150 tons.
Palma,	2,250 "	3,250 "	1,000 "
Badagry,	1,250 "	1,250 "	
Porto Novo, &c.,	4,000 "	4,500 "	500 "
Whydah,	2,500 "	2,500 "	
Ahguay, &c.,	1,800 "	2,500 "	700 "
	14,300 tons.	16,650 tons.	2,350 tons.
From Lagos,	3,884 "	4,942 "	1,058 "
Total shipment in 1857,		21,592 tons.	3,408 tons.

The export of Oil and Nuts from SIERRA LEONE:

PALM OIL EXPORTED FROM SIERRA LEONE DURING THE YEARS

1850,	285,032 gallons,
1851,	212,577 "
1852,	307,988 "
1853,	181,438 "
1854,	304,406 "
1855,	364,414 "
1856,	463,140 "

Total, 2,118,985 gallons, equal to 6,835 tons.
Custom House, Sierra Leone, 18th February, 1857.

PORT OF FREETOWN, SIERRA LEONE.

QUANTITY OF PALM-NUT KERNELS EXPORTED FROM THE COLONY:

1850,	4,096 bushels,
1851,	2,925 "
1852,	46,727 "
1853,	29,699 "
1854,	25,399½ "
1855,	65,388 "
1856,	90,282 "

Total, 264,516½ bushels, equal to 6,612 tons.
Customs, Sierra Leone, 30th January, 1857.

I have no reliable information of the amount of oil exported at the present; but I do not think I shall be far from the point of accuracy, if I put it down at 60,000 tons, which, at the probable value of £45 per ton, equals £2,700,000.

Cotton.—Next to palm oil, cotton is now commanding more attention than any other article. The interesting fact with regard to this staple is that it excites as much interest in Africa as it does in England and America. There are few things in the history of trade more important, more interesting, morally as well as commercially, than the impetus which has recently been given to the growth of cotton.

In 185-, Mr. Consul Campbell made a statement of the probable amount of cotton exported from West Africa. I have to rely upon my memory for the items of that statement; and, if I mistake not, he stated that the people of Abbeokuta exported nigh 200,000 country cloths annually. These cloths are purchased for transportation to Brazil, where there are thousands of African slaves who still dress in the same style as when at their homes. He supposed that full 200,000 country cloths were manufactured for *home* use, which would make the probable number manufactured in Africa, 400,000. And he calculated $2\frac{1}{2}$ lbs. as the average weight of each country cloth;—and $400,000 \times 2\frac{1}{2} = 1,000,000$ lbs. of cotton *manufactured* by the natives of interior Africa, in *one* locality, that is, Yoruba. Doubtless as much more is allowed to grow and run to waste unused.

Now these facts, to a partial extent, were well

known in Liberia, for our merchants are accustomed to purchasing "country cloths," as they are called, and selling them to foreign traders; but Consul Campbell's statements far exceed any realities we have ever thought of, and show that interior Africa is as great a field for the production of cotton as America or India.

SUGAR-CANE.—To what extent West Africa is to become a sugar-producing country it is difficult to conjecture. Many, doubtless, have grave doubts whether this will ever be the case; for my own part I have no misgivings upon the point, that is, its capability of becoming a great sugar-producing country. The natives grow it in all the country about Cape Palmas, and frequently bring cane to the American settlements for sale. With some small encouragement, and a little stimulus, it could easily be made a staple here. My opinions have been strengthened by some observations made in a recent missionary tour. I found cane but little inferior to that grown on the St. Paul's River, growing in nearly all the towns and villages through which I passed, forty, fifty, and sixty miles in the interior. On inquiry, I learned that it is grown by the natives in the interior two hundred miles back. Dr. Livingstone, in his journal, states a like fact concerning the natives in South Africa.*

What a germ have we here for systematic labor,

---

* Dr. Livingstone saw the cane growing, in his tour through South Africa. It is more than probable that that cane is indigenous to both West and South Africa.

plodding industry, the proper direction of the acquisitive principle, and thereby of civilization and Christianity, if only a company of right-minded men were settled on the Cavalla, prepared for the production of sugar, willing to stimulate the native energy, and at the same time to uplift and enlighten the heathen!

MAIZE.—What is the case respecting sugar-cane, equally pertains to corn. It is grown plenteously and extensively in West Africa. On the Cavalla river it is planted with rice, and I am told that in the gathering season hundreds of bushels of corn are left by the natives untouched in their fields. In some cases American colonists have gone and gathered quantities of it without any payment. Here, then, with an enterprising settlement, corn could be obtained as an export. The natives, if encouraged, might easily be made vast and extensive corn-growers. This has already taken place on the Gold Coast. Several cargoes of corn were exported thence in 1859 to England.

As with the palm oil, so with maize, sugar-cane, and cotton; civilized men could, with but little difficulty, increase the cultivation of these articles among the natives, and ship them to traders to their own advantage. And this process is the great secret of West African trade: the foreign merchant, by his goods, excites the cupidity of the simple native, who at Fernando Po brings him barwood; at St. Paul, Loanda, beeswax; at Congo, copal and gutta percha; at Accra, maize; at Calabar, black ebony wood;

at Bonny and Lagos, palm oil; at Bassa, (Liberia,) camwood; at Lagos, cotton; at Tantamquerry and Gambia, ground nuts and pepper; at Sierra Leone, nearly *all* kinds of African produce; at Elmina, Cape Coast, Accra, and Bassam, gold. By this multiform traffic, yet, be it remembered, in its infancy, and capable of being increased a thousand fold, millions of dollars are being made every year on the coast of Africa.

Now all this flows into the coffers of white men. I mean nothing invidious by this. I state a fact, and am utterly unconscious of any unworthy or ungenerous feeling in stating it. "The earth is the Lord's, and the fulness thereof;" and this "fulness" He has given to MAN, irrespective of race or color. The main condition of the obtainment of it is intelligence, forecast, skill, and enterprise. If the black man—the black man, I mean, civilized and enlightened—has lying before him a golden heritage, and fails to seize upon and to appropriate it, Providence none the less intends it to be seized upon and wills it to be used. And if the white man, with a keen eye, a cunning hand, and a wise practicalness, is enabled to appropriate it with skill and effect, it is his; God gives it to him, and he has a right to seek and to search for a multiplication of it, and when he secures it a right to the use of it, responsible, however, both to God and man for the use of right means to the ends he has before him, and for the moral features of his traffic.

But while conceding that the white man has, in the main, fairly won the present trade of Africa, I cannot but lament our non-participation therein; for the larger advantages of it go to Europe and America, and help to swell the broad stream of their wealth, luxury, and refinement. And how deep and broad and mighty is that stream is shown by two facts: 1st, That England, France, and the United States expend annually more than a million and a half of dollars for the *protection of trade* on this coast.* And 2d, That the coast swarms with white men, using all possible means and contrivances *to open trade into the interior*. To this one single end, an immense amount of capital is spent by great mercantile houses, in England, France, and America. One single house in Liverpool employs such a fleet of trading vessels that it is necessitated to keep a resident physician at the mouth of one of our great rivers for the benefit of their captains and sailors. " A single merchant now living, in the course of three or four years, has spent more than $100,000 in exploring the rivers and creeks of Western Africa, merely to ascertain the extent of her commercial relations." † While I am writing these pages, I receive the information that one of the great Liverpool houses has just sent out a small steamer to the bights, to collect the oil for their trading vessels. Simultaneously with this intelligence, I am advised that a number of agents are employed by English capitalists to visit the towns from Lagos to Abbeokuta, and to leave with their chiefs small bags of cotton seed for the growth of cotton. And but a few months ago we

---

* I do not pretend to accuracy in this statement; the expenditure of Great Britain was, in 184–, £231,000.

† Wilson's "Western Africa," p. 521.

hailed in our roads a little fairy craft—the "Sunbeam," steamer sent out by "Laird and Company" for the Niger trade; and since then I have heard of two of her trips, four hundred miles up that mighty river, bringing thence valuable cargoes for the factories which are now established three hundred miles up on its banks.

And now perhaps you ask—"How shall the children of Africa, sojourning in foreign lands, avail themselves of the treasures of this continent?" I answer briefly, "In the same way white men do." *They* have pointed out the way, let us follow in the same track, and in the use of the like (legitimate) agencies by which trade is facilitated and money is made by them.

Perhaps this is too general, let me therefore attempt something more specific and distinctive.

First, then, I remark that if individuals are unable to enter upon a trading system, they can form associations. If *one* has not sufficient capital, four or six united can make a good beginning. If a few persons cannot make the venture, then a company can be formed. It was in this way the first attempts at trading were made by the Dutch and the English, both in India and Africa. A few men associated themselves together, and sent out their agent or agents, and started a factory. And from such humble beginnings, in the 17th century, has arisen that magnificent Indian Empire, which has helped to swell the vast wealth and the cumbrous capital of England, from whose arena have come forth such splendid and colossal characters as Clive, and Wellington, and Metcalf, and the Laurences, and Havelock; and which has furnished the Church of Christ a field on which to display the apostolic virtues and the primitive self-sacrifice of Middleton and Heber, and Wilson, of Henry Martyn, of Fox, and Ragland.

Without doubt God designs as great things as these for Africa, and among the means and agencies He will employ, commercial enterprise is most certainly one. To this end, however, high souls and lofty resolves are necessary, as in any other vocation of life. Of course the timid, the over-cautious, the fearful—men in whose constitution FAITH is a needed quality, are not fitted for this service. If ever the epoch of negro civilization is brought about in Africa, whatever *external* influences may be brought to bear upon this end, whatever foreign agencies and aids, black men themselves are without doubt to be the chief instruments. But they are to be men of force and energy; men who will not suffer themselves to be outrivalled in enterprise and vigor; men who are prepared for pains, and want, and suffering; men of such invincible courage that the spirit cannot be tamed by transient failures, incidental misadventure, or even glaring miscalculations; men who can exaggerate the feeblest resources into potent agencies and fruitful capital. Moreover, these men are to have strong moral proclivities, equal to the deep penetration and the unyielding tenacity of their minds. No greater curse could be entailed upon Africa than the sudden appearance upon her shores of a mighty host of heartless black buccaneers, (for such indeed they would prove themselves,) men sharpened up by letters and training, filled with feverish greed, with hearts utterly alien from moral good and human well-being, and only regarding Africa as a convenient gold-field from which to extract emolument and treasure to carry off to foreign quarters.

Such men would only reproduce the worst evils of the last three sad centuries of Africa's history; and quickly and inevitably so soil their character that the *just* imputation would be fastened upon them of that malignant lie which has recently been spread abroad through Europe and America against us: that is, of complicity with the slave trade.*

---

* Nothing can be more judicious than the following words of Commander Foote:—"Let then the black man be judged fairly, and not presumed to have become all at once and by miracle, of a higher order than old historic nations, through many generations of whom the political organization of the world has been slowly developing itself. There will be among them men who are covetous, or men who are tyrannical, or men who would sacrifice public interests, or any others to their own; men who would now go into the slave trade if they could, or rob hen roosts, or intrigue for office, or pick pockets, rather than trouble their heads or their hands with more honorable occupations. It should be remembered by visitors that such things will be found in Liberia; *not because men are black, but because men are men.*"—AFRICA AND THE AMERICAN FLAG, p. 206.

It is most encouraging to find ever and anon a writer who, in speaking of colored men, avoids the exaggeration of them either into demi-gods or monkeys. Even Commander Foote well nigh loses his balance, on the *same* page whence the above just sentence is taken. In the paragraph which immediately follows this extract, he gives expression to opinions sweepingly disparaging to the negro race, and not of *certain* historical accuracy. Commander Foote says:—"*No negro has done anything to lighten or brighten the links of human policy.*" Such a broad assertion implies that the writer has cleared up all the mysteries of past history; but upon the point, that is, "the relation of Egypt to the negro race," though still a disputed question—yet, with such authorities on our

Happily for Africa, most of the yearnings of her sons towards her are gentle, humane, and generous. When the commercial one shall show itself, it will not differ, I feel assured, from all the others her children have showed. God grant that it may soon burst from many warm and energetic hearts, for the rescue of a continent!

Second. I proceed to show that the whole coast offers facilities for adventurous traders. There are few, if any, localities but where they can set up their factories and commence business. If there are exceptions they are rare; and even then, not really such, but cases where at some previous time the natives have been so basely and knavishly treated, that they themselves have learned to practise the same upon some hapless, unsuspecting captain and his crew. As a general thing, however, native African chiefs court and invite the residence of a trader in their neighborhood, will give him protection, and will strive to secure his permanent stay. On our Liberian coast we see the proof of this in the many factories in existence at divers points. I have myself seen mere boys—young

---

side as Dr. Pritchard, Cardinal Wiseman, and that ripe scholar, the late Alexander H. Everett, one would have supposed Commander Foote would have been a little less venturesome. Moreover, I beg to say that TOUISSANT L'OUVERTURE *is* an historical character. GOODWIN, in his lectures on colonial slavery, says:—" Can the West India Islands, since their first discovery by Columbus, boast a single name which deserves comparison with that of Touissant L'Ouverture?" Read Harriet Martineau's "Hour and the Man"; Wordsworth's fine Sonnet addressed to "Touissant in prison"; and the noble Poem of John G. Whittier, on the same theme; and then compare the opinions of these high names with **Commander Foote's broad assertions.**

Englishmen, not of age—who have come out to this country seeking their fortunes, living on the coast in native towns, without any civilized companionship, and carrying on a thriving trade. The chiefs have an interest in these men, and therefore make their residence safe and comfortable. The trader's presence and barter give the king, or head man, importance, increase his wealth, augment his influence in the neighborhood, swell the population of his town, and thus make it the centre or capital of the surrounding region. But even if it were not thus, the security of traders is insured by the felt power of the three great nations of the civilized world. Such and so great is the naval force of England, France, and America on this coast, that the coast may be regarded as protected. The native chiefs, for many hundred miles, have been taught to fear the destructive instruments of war they carry with them, and nowadays but seldom give occasion for their use.

But aside from all this, I may remark here, 1st, that of all rude and uncivilized men, the native African is the mildest and most gentle; and 2d, that no people in the world are so given to trade and barter as the negroes of the western coast of Africa.

THIRDLY. Let me refer to the means and facilities colored men have for an entrance upon African commerce. And 1st, I would point out the large amount of capital which is lying in their hands, dead and unproductive. There is, as you are doubtless aware, no small amount of wealth possessed by the free colored population of the United States, both North and South. Notwithstanding the multitudinous difficulties which beset them in the way of improvement, our brethren have shown capacity, perseverance, oftentimes thrift and acquisitiveness. As a consequence they are, all over the Union, owners of houses, farms, homesteads, and divers other kinds of property; and, stored away in safe quarters, they have large amounts of gold and silver deep down in large stockings, in the corners of old chests, in dark and undiscoverable nooks and crannies, besides large sums invested in banks, and locked up in the safes of city savings banks.

I have no statistics by me of the population and property of the colored people of Cincinnati, but I am told that their wealth exceeds that of the same class, in any other city in the American Union—that is, according to their numbers. Nashville, Tenn., Charleston, S. C., St. Louis, Mo., Mobile and New Orleans, stand in nearly the same category. Baltimore holds a respectable position. In the "Weekly Anglo-African," (September, 1859), I find that the CHURCH PROPERTY of the colored population in Philadelphia is put down at $231,484. Doubtless their personal real estate must be worth millions. And the same must be true of New York City.

The greater portion of their wealth, however, is unproductive. As a people we have been victimized in a pecuniary point of view, as well as morally and politically; and, as a consequence, there is an almost universal dread of intrusting our moneys in the hands of capitalists, and trading companies, and stock; though in the great cities large sums are put in savings banks. There are few, however, who have the courage to take shares in railroad and similar companies, and in many places it could not be done.

There is *one* most pregnant fact that will serve to show, somewhat, their monetary ability. "THE AFRICAN METHODIST EPISCOPAL CHURCH" is one of the denominations of the United States. It has its own organization, its own bishops, its conferences, its organ or magazine, and these entirely *inter se*—absolutely disconnected with all the white denominations of America. This religious body is spread out in hamlet, village, town, and city, all through the Eastern, Northern, Western, and partly the Southern States. But *the* point to which I desire to direct your attention is the fact that they have built and now own some 300 church edifices, mostly brick; and in the large cities, such as New York, Philadelphia, and Baltimore, they are large, imposing, capacious, and will seat some two or three thousand people. The free black people of the United States built these churches; the funds were gathered from their small and large congregations; and in some cases they have been known to collect, that is, in Philadelphia and Baltimore, at one collection over $1,000. The aggregate value of their property cannot be less than $5,000,000.

Now this, you will notice, is an exhibit of the corporate moneyed power of but *one* class of our brethren. I have said nothing about the Episcopal churches, of the Presbyterians, of the Baptists, nor of the divers sections of the Methodists. But this will suffice. You can easily see from the above, that there must be a large amount of pecuniary means in the hands of the free colored population of the American States.

2d. I turn now to another of their facilities for engaging in African commerce. I refer to NAVIGATION. And here I might rest the case upon the fact that money will purchase vessels, and command seamen and navigators. But you already have *both*. Turn for a moment to New Bedford, Mass. It is now some twenty years since I visited that important seaport. Though but a boy, I kept my eyes open, especially upon the condition of our race there; and I retain still a vivid remembrance of the signs of industry and thrift among them, of the evidences of their unusual wealth, and of their large interest in shipping. I had the names of several parties mentioned to me who were owners of whale craft, and I made the acquaintance of some of them. Among these I remember well some youthful descendants of Paul Cuffee. The same state of things I apprehend exists, though perhaps in a much less degree, in some places in Connecticut; on the Hudson, that is, at Albany and Newburgh, in the State of New York; on the Potomac; at St. Louis, on the Mississippi; and on the Red River. There are scores, if not hundreds of colored men who own schooners and other small craft in these localities; pilots and engineers, captains and seamen, who, if once moved with a generous impulse to redeem the land of their fathers, could, in a brief time, form a vast commercial marine, equal to all the necessities of such a glorious project.

Let me dwell for a moment upon one suggestion, that is, the facilities for securing seamen, and the comparative ease of forming crews. Colored seamen, in large numbers, I apprehend, can easily be obtained. Even in the United States, their numbers are legion; and we may proudly say that, in activity, dutifulness, and skill, they are equal to any sailors on the globe. Nor would there be any great lack of the needed class just above the grade of sailors; that is, a class who would join intelligence and knowledge to practicalness. What a number of men, trained to a late boyhood in the colored schools, do we not know who have sailed for years out of New York as "stewards" in the great "liners." How many of these are there not, who, both at school and by experience, have attained a real scientific acquaintance with navigation. And how many of them, had they been white men, would, long ere this, have risen to the posts of mates and captains! How many of such could you and I point out who were our schoolmates in the old "free school," in Mulberry street? *

Here, then, you have the material and the designated agency for an almost boundless commercial

* In a most elaborate paper, entitled "THE NIGER TRADE," by Sir George Stephen, (Simpkin, Marshall & Co., London, 1849,) the author shows, most clearly, the need and the practicability of employing the agency of black men, for the purpose of African civilization. Sir George suggested the employment of them, in the [British] naval as well as merchant service; in all grades of office, from seamen and marines up to naval officers; and he points to the West India Colonies, and Hayti, remarking, "Hayti has a navy exceeding twenty in number, of which four are steamers; all are, of course, manned and officered by black or colored men." In this paper, Sir George quotes and emphasizes the words of McQueen—"*It is by African hands and African exertions chiefly that the evil must be rooted out.*"

11

staff, for the purposes of trade in West Africa. The facts I have adduced cannot, I think, be disputed. And, on the condition that this machinery is brought into operation, the influences and results are easily anticipated. It must follow, as a necessity, that the trade and commerce of Africa shall fall into the hands of black men. At an early day whole fleets of vessels, manned and officered by black men from the United States and Liberia, would outrival all the other agencies which are now being used for grasping West African commerce. Large and important houses would spring into existence among you all through the States. Wealth would flow into your coffers, and affluence would soon exhibit itself amid all your associations. The reproach of penury and the consciousness of impotency in all your relations would rapidly depart, and as a people you would soon be able to make yourselves a felt element of society in all the relations of life, on the soil where you were born.

These are some of the *material* influences which would result from this movement. The moral and philanthropic results would be equally if not more notable. The kings and tradesmen of Africa, having the *demonstration* of negro capacity before them, would hail the presence of their black kinsmen from America,* and would be stimulated to a generous emulation. To the farthest interior, leagues and combinations would be formed with the men of commerce; and thus civilization, enlightenment, and Christianity would be carried to every state, town,

---

* Just this has been the experience of Dr. Delany, as I hear from valued friends there, at Lagos, and other places.

and village of interior Africa. The galling remembrance of the slave-trade on the coast, and of slavery in America, would quicken the blood and the brain of both parties, and every wretch of a slave-trader who might visit the coast would have to atone for his temerity by submitting to the rigid code framed for piracy. And when *this* disturbing and destructive hindrance to African progress was once put down, noble cities, vast agricultural establishments, the seeds of universities, and groundwork of church organizations, would spring up all along the banks, and up the valley of the Niger.*

There is one certain commercial result—to return to my subject—that would surely grow out of this movement: I mean the flow of large amounts of capital from the moneyed men of America; that is, if black men showed skill, energy, and practicability. Philanthropy would come forward with largess for colored men, thus developing the resources of Africa. Religion would open a large and generous hand in order to hasten the redemption of a continent alien from Christ and His Church. And capital would hasten forward, not only for its wonted reduplication, but also to exemplify the vitality and fruitfulness which it always scatters from golden hands in its open pathway. And when you consider the fact of kinship, on our part, with Africa, the less liability to fever, the incentive to gain, the magnificent objects before us, and the magnificent field on which to

---

* The great hindrance to African evangelization at the present time is the slave-trade. Missionaries feel this all along the coast, from Cape Palmas to Congo.

develop them, and the probable early power of intelligent black men to penetrate, scathless, any neighborhood where they might reside, you can see the likelihood of an early repossession of Africa, in trade, commerce, and moral power, by her now scattered children in distant lands.

For the carrying out such a plan you have, I repeat myself, you have almost, if not quite, all the needed means and agencies even now at hand. You have, all through the States, men who can at once furnish the capital for the commencement of such a venture. You know I am not wont to exaggerate the wealth of colored men. In such matters I prefer fact to conjecture; for certainly among us on this subject imagination has too often proved " a forward and delusive faculty." Yet I do know of some of our brethren in the States who have become moneyed men, not millionaires, indeed, but men worth their thousands. Some of these men are more prominent individuals than others, and as their names are not unfrequently mentioned in such a connection as this, it may not seem invidious in a like mention on these pages. Some of these persons are acquaintances—a few, old friends of former years, but the most are personally unknown to me. There are Rev. Stephen Smith, William Whipper, Esq., of Philadelphia; Messrs. Knight & Smith, of Chicago, Ill.; Messrs. Cook & Moxly, Buffalo, N. Y.; Youngs & Wilcox, of Cincinnati, &c., &c.

It is possible that in a few instances earnest prejudice against every thing African may cause displeasure at this designation. Any one can see that I have intended nothing discourteous; and it should be remembered that commercial enterprise in Africa has no necessary connection with emigration, or colonization. How great soever the diversities of opinion upon these points, on *this* platform, Douglass and Delany can stand beside the foremost citizens and merchants of Liberia. Hence those men whose feelings are the most averse to any thing like colonization, cannot object to the promotion of trade and the acquisition of wealth. Indeed, I have no doubt that there are thousands who would be glad of a safe investment in any thing wherein there is probability of advantage. Moreover, the fretted mind of our brethren needs distraction from griefs and the causes of griefs. Just now, when darkness shrouds their Southern heavens, what could be more opportune, what more desirable, than such a movement? The danger is, that thousands of them in their sorrows, may sit down hopeless, careless, and

"——Nurse despair
And feed the dreadful appetite of death."

Your leading men should strive to occupy the vacant minds of their despairing brethren by the healthful stimulant of duty and enterprise.

Doubtless there are many persons in the States who will view the above suggestions in connection with the Liberian Republic, and in my opinion it will be wise and judicious for them to do so. I have nothing extravagant to say about Liberia. It is a theme upon which I never fall into ecstasies. I cannot find in it as yet place or occasion for violent raptures. I get started a little, at times, from cool equanimity, when

I read the wonderful tales of travellers about the country, or the first letters of enthusiastic settlers. Liberia is a young country, hardly yet "in the gristle," laying, as I dare to affirm, good foundations; but with much pain, great trials, consuming anxieties, and with the price of great tribulation, and much mortality. But is not this the history of all young countries? Has not God married pain, and suffering, and death to the fresh beginnings of all new nationalities? Would it not be marvellous, not to say miraculous, if it were true, that the history of *this* colony—for it is nothing more than a colony as yet—that it had been exempted from these trials? And what right have we to expect that God in these days will work miracles, especially for black men?*

I have never been disappointed in any thing moral, social, or political that I have met with in this land. I came to the country expecting all the peculiarities of struggling colonial life, with the added phase of imported habits, tinctured with the deterioration, the indifference, the unthriftiness, which are gendered by *any* servile system. "All work is badly done by people in despair," says Pliny, the naturalist.† A forty days' passage through the deep sea cannot effect

---

* "No new country can be founded unless under the greatest difficulties. It is the universal law of experience, that however in the late stages of their existence colonies may be prosperous, and to what state soever they may have advanced in the accumulation of wealth, their infant life must always be a life of difficulty and peril."—*Rt. Hon. W. E. Gladstone, Speech before Propagation Soc., Liverpool*, 1858.

† Lord Bacon discourses most pertinently and powerfully to the same effect. See Art. 33 of "*Plantations*," "Bacon's Essays and Wisdom of the Ancients." I regret I cannot copy it here.

such a regenerating influence as to alter character and to implant hope, ambition, thrift, order, and perseverance, where they have never been cultivated.

These anticipations proved correct, save that I found a stronger and a more general disposition to labor than the sad history of our brethren warranted my looking for.* Many things gratified me from the first. Since then Liberia has grown much. Development shows itself on every side. The acquisitive principle manifests itself, and in less than ten years large fortunes will be made, extensive farms spring

---

* The people of Liberia are not lazy, although I am sorry to say, *appearances* are sometimes against them. The case is this:—*Many new men do not know how to labor for* THEMSELVES! They come, at a mature age, when their habits are fixed, into a new school, the operations of which they are unacquainted with. They go into the "bush," and its formidableness overcomes, and crushes them; they sit down in despair and do nothing, and many perish. "Are not such men lazy?" asks some objector. I say no! and my reason for saying so is this: In the year 1856 there were scores of the class above described on the St. Paul's River, doing nothing. Some four or five farmers commenced the cultivation of sugar cane and the manufacture of sugar. This new effort required large numbers of laborers, and as soon as the need was known, the river was alive with men seeking labor. *Who* were these men? The hopeless, the despairing men, who could not see their way through the "bush," and could not improve their own farmsteads. I have seen scores of these men trudging through the rain and mud, in the rainy season, or paddling in fragile canoes, seeking the larger plantations, clamorous for labor; and I have seen the supply so great that a *dozen* men had to be refused at a time. Why was this? These men had been unaccustomed to self-support. Placed under a proprietor, heart and limb were alive with an industrious impulse. Liberia needs CAPITALISTS who can employ this large class of men. Mr. RUFFIN, of Virginia, will perhaps claim this as a proof that black men must have masters. Students of "Political Economy" will put it among the facts which show that where capital languishes, men die, both in body and soul.

up, ships be built on our rivers and sail to Europe and America. There is every sign, too, that the springs of trade will shortly, through our own direct influence, be started through all our native population, for 200 miles in the interior, and that this trade will be our own, and that it will originate a commerce excelling that of Sierra Leone. I believe verily that the great principles of industry, of thrift, and expansion are daily taking root deeper in the soil; and that ultimately they will outgrow and exclude all the weeds of lazy self-content, inflated and exaggerated vanity, unthrift and extravagance. Of course we have here stupid obstructives, men who cling tenaciously to the "dead past"; a few millinered and epauletted gentry,

"——Neat and trimly dressed,
And fresh as bridegrooms,"

who would civilize our heathen neighbors with powder and shot; and a few unthinking, unreasoning men, who verily believe that the foundations of all great states have been laid in barter and pelf. But these are, by no means, the *representative* men of the land. If they were, I should despair of any future for Liberia, and depart.

We have another, a larger class than these; a class which comprises awakened old men and generous and ardent youth; the minds whose great object in life is not mere gain or comfort, but who feel that they have a great work to accomplish for their children, for their race, and for God; who feel that they have been called to this mission, and who wish to spend themselves in the expansion and compacting of this youthful republic, to save bleeding, benighted Africa, and to help redeem the continent. I assure you that there is a school of this character in Liberia; men who feel obligated to philanthropy, who are burdened with a sense of duty, who have the keenest, most sensitive feeling of race, who love Africa, who are anxious for the welfare of the whole negro family, who labor with all their might for the advancement of industry and civilization, who would fain glorify God. When I look upon this class of men, and mark their ways, I feel that the country will yet attain standing and reach some distinction.*

It is these thoughts and observations, and some experiences, which lead me to think that those who look upon Liberia in connection with their commercial desires, are wise. I have no wish to discourage those who are looking to the banks of the Niger. God bless them every way if that is indeed their mission! But, as an individual, I have earnestly

---

* I cannot better illustrate the importance of such a class, as above mentioned, in Liberia, than by referring to a paragraph from a speech recently sent me by a friend: "If the founders of the American Republic had been formed by the same materials as the settlers of California, the genius and liberties of America would have been lost in anarchy or absorbed in an inevitable despotism. It was because, on however small a scale, they were senators and soldiers, impressed with a due sense of the heavy responsibility that rested upon them, and not mere money-getters, that they succeeded in laying the foundations of the greatest republic in the world. They never lost sight of the responsibility of the task they had undertaken,—they felt that they were going for a high position in the eyes of the world, and to set an example for all ages. Feeling this, the early settlers of New England accomplished their mission." JOHN ROBERT GODLY, ESQ.,
before the "Canterbury Association," London.

desired a non-sanguinary evangelization of West Africa. All empire, the world over, in rude countries has been cemented by blood. In Western Africa the tribes universally, save in Liberia, are strong, independent, warlike. Even British prowess, both at Sierra Leone and on the Gold Coast, succumbs at times to their indomitable spirit. And thus you see that, for the establishment of a strong black civilization in Central Africa, a strong and a bloody hand must be used. Color is nothing anywhere. Civilized *condition* differences men all over the globe. Besides this, I have had a prejudice that *that* field God had given to the freed and cultivated men of Sierra Leone—that they were better fitted to the evangelization of the Niger than we; that we, with our peculiarities, bred amid American institutions, might prove a disturbing element to the great work, for which, by blood, training, lingual capacity, and the sympathy of character and habits they were peculiarly fitted; and that our governmental proclivities might jar with what seems a manifest providence; that is, that Christianity is to be engrafted upon such strong states as Dahomey and Ashantee; whose fundamental *governmental* basis it seems to me it is not for the interests of civilization and of Africa to revolutionize or to disturb.

I would not pretend to argue these points, much less to dogmatize upon them; for the need of a civilizing element at LAGOS, especially at Abbeokuta and on the Niger, is so great that I fear even to state the above impressions. And I stand ready to hail, at any time, any nucleus of freedom and enlightenment that may spring up anywhere on the coast of Africa.

In Liberia we have the noblest opportunities and the greatest advantages. We have a rich and varied soil—inferior, I verily believe, to but few, if any, on the globe. We have some of the proofs and many of the indications of varied and vast mineral wealth of the richest qualities. We have a country finely watered in every section by multitudinous brooks and streams and far-reaching rivers. We have a climate which needs but be educated, and civilized, and tempered by the plastic and curative processes of emigration, clearances, and scientific farming, to be made as fine and as temperate as any land in the tropics can be.

On this soil have been laid the foundations of republican institutions. Our religion is Protestant, with its characteristic tendencies to freedom, progress, and human well-being. We are reaching forward, as far as a young and poor nation can, to a system of common schools. Civilization, that is, in its more simple forms, has displaced ancestral paganism in many sections of the land, has taken permanent foothold in our territory, and already extended its roots among our heathen kin. Our heathen population, moreover, in the immediate neighborhood of our settlements, is but small and sparse; thus saving our civilization from too strong an antagonism, and allowing it room, scope, and opportunity for a hardy growth in its more early days. Active industry is now exhibiting unwonted vigor, and begins to tell upon commerce and the foreign market.

Now when you consider that all these elements,

humble, as indeed they are, are our own, that we are the creature and dependent of no foreign government, you will agree with me, I think, that men who have families will act wisely in looking narrowly at our advantages ere they place themselves in circumstances where the moral elements of life and society are more rude, and where the formative agency and influence will belong to some foreign power. That these elements are slow in growth and expansion is true; but this, it will be remembered, furnishes probability of their being sure and permanent.

I have heard the poverty of our particular locality contrasted with the richness of other parts of West Africa. Well, this may be the case; but I think there can be no doubt that there is no nobler, more commanding position in West Africa than that of Liberia. We hold, I think, the key to the vast interior. You have heard it said, and seen it published, that we have no great rivers. But the St. Paul's, the Booma,* the St. John's, and the Cavalla rivers, stretch away into the far interior 300 and 400 miles, with great breadth, and with a vast volume of water. That they come from the same great water-shed from whence, on an opposite side, the Niger drains its mighty waters, seems almost a certainty. And if so, the valley of the Niger, with its wondrous resources and its teeming wealth, will, ultimately, be as available to us as any other people. At present these

---

* The BOOMA is a river at Cape Mt. Settlement. I hear that it is the greatest river in Liberia. I am just informed, as this paper leaves me, that an acquaintance has ascended it, some ninety miles, without any obstruction.

rivers are not navigable any great distance, owing to falls and rapids. But black men in Africa must do what enterprising men do in all other new lands: they must BEND NATURE TO THEIR WANTS AND WISHES. Ship canals are needed twenty miles from the coast, around the rapids of the St. Paul's, and eighty miles from the coast around the falls of the Cavalla, and ship canals must therefore be made. If we have not the *means*, we must go to work and acquire them. If we have not the *science* and the *skill*, we must form our schools and colleges, and put our sons in the way of learning them. And if we have not the men, that is, the *population*, for such a vast and laborious undertaking, we must lift up a loud voice, and call upon hopeful, vigorous, intelligent, and energetic black men, all over the globe, " Ho, to the rescue ! " " Come over and help us ! "

And these are just the great needs of Liberia :— MEN, LEARNING, AND WEALTH. And *wealth* here, as an acquisition, requires the use of the same means and is regulated by the same laws as in any other land. It requires forecast, wakefulness, industry, thrift, probity, and tireless, sweatful toil; as well in tropical Africa as in cold Holland. There is no royal road to it on this soil.

—— " Nil nisi magno
Vita labore dedit mortalibus."

As to *learning*, we have no greater need than this same religion ; and there can be no excess of means, no superabundance of agencies, no delicacy or profundity of culture, unadapted to actual present needs of all this wide region of Liberia. We have our native population, and we have our emigrant youth and children, thousands upon thousands, all around us. And when I look at the quickness, the capacity, and the thirst of the natives for enlightenment, I can see no difference in the needs of the one from the other; I regard them, in the general, as our intellectual equals. If I anticipated for them a merely *secular* training, I should prefer a difference; but feeling, knowing, that the Christian religion is to mould, and fashion, and leaven every thing here in future times, I go for the highest culture that can be given the rising generation, and hail every facility for the furtherance of this end which Providence grants us. In the first passage of the heathen from barbarism it will doubtless be advisable to make much of their training, physical, and to be content with the Bible and moral instruction; but the ultimate aim should be, and most surely will be here, to open to them all the broad avenues of instruction and culture. The great cause of apprehension just now is that the means for supplying general education are but partial, and that the actual need created by our circumstances for the attainment of good literary and scientific training cannot be obtained.

I come to population. We *need* immigration. We are poor in men and women. We do not number over 14,000 emigrant citizens. Numbers of these are crippled, I mean in soul rather than in body, ere they come here. The poverty of emigrants dwarfs the otherwise actual force of the country; and old age, in both sexes, and especially the fact that a large percentage of emigrants are helpless females with children, without husbands, brings out the sad truth that our real available man-force is but small. And yet the moral calls upon us in this new sphere, the intellectual demands, and the physical requirements, with the vastness of territory, and the largeness of providential circumstances around us, while they quicken imagination, fix also the conviction of helpless weakness, and in some men produce indifference or despair; in others, vexation and painful anxiousness. The population question is dwarfing the powers of our strong and earnest leaders. They cannot lift themselves up to grand ideas and large conceptions. In all their efforts they are "cribbed, cabined, and confined."

We need this day for the great work before us, in a region of not less than 500,000 square miles, we need, I say, not less than 50,000 *civilized men*. We ought to be travelling onward through the land, and to appropriate and modify a remark of De Tocqueville's, to be "peopling our vast wilderness at the average rate of at least five miles per annum." And for the work of civilization an enlightenment among our aboriginal population, we should have even now, a mental power and a moral force working through all our territory, fitted for just such a transformation as has been produced in New Zealand and the Sandwich Islands in a period of twenty-five years. The tide of immigration, as it now sets in, promises us no such results. Our ratio of increase, with our present diverse disturbing influences, is but small. Unfortunately, there is no general consciousness of our lack and need in this respect. I have had the fear that some of my fellow-citizens accustomed themselves to look upon Liberia as a "close corporation." The attempt to pass a "naturalization law," in the face of the fact that it takes YEARS to add a thousand living men to our population, chiefly caused that fear. But we in common with you are becoming awake to the conviction that, *as a race*, we have a great work to do. The zeal of England and of America for Africa is opening our eyes. Our own thoughtful men begin to feel the binding tie which joins them in every interest and feeling with the negro race all over the globe. Your "Anglo-African Magazines," "Douglas' Journal," and patriotic addresses begin to tell upon us. And soon there will be a kindled eye, a quickened pulse, a beating heart, and large and generous emotions, for our bruised and wounded brethren everywhere. And when that day comes, the people of Liberia will cry out: "*We* have the largest advantages of all our race. We have the noblest field. Ours is the most signal providence, and our state offers the grandest possibilities of good, the finest opportunities of manly achievement. Why then suffer ourselves to be hindered in working out of 'manifest destinies' of beneficence to suffering Africa by the narrowness of our aims, or the fewness of our numbers and means? It is true we have a wide field to enter, and need more and mightier men to enter it. Let us therefore call our skilful and energetic brethren to come to us and share the suffering and the glory of saving Africa. Let us stand on the beach and on the hill-side, and beckon to them in ALL LANDS to come and participate in lofty duty, in painful but saving labor, and to aid in the restoration and enlightenment of a vast continent!"

I turn now to the *religious* aspect of this subject. In speaking of the religious needs of Africa, it is not necessary I should attempt a picture of her miserable condition, nor enter into the details of her wretchedness. Her very name is suggestive of uttermost spiritual need, of abounding moral desolation, of the deepest, darkest ignorance, of wild and sanguinary superstitions. This whole continent, with its million masses of heathen, presents one broad, almost unbroken, unmitigated view of moral desolation and spiritual ruin. And this fact creates the demand upon the Christian world for ministers and teachers, for the purpose of her evangelization. "The field is the world," and the Church is to occupy it, and she will occupy it.

As members of the Church of Christ, the sons of Africa in foreign lands are called upon to bear their part in the vast and sacred work of her evangelization. I might press this point on the grounds of piety, of compassion, or sympathy, but I choose a higher principle. For next to the grand ideas which pertain to the Infinite, His attributes and perfections, there is none loftier and grander than that of Duty—
"Stern daughter of the voice of God."

It is the duty of black men to feel and labor for the salvation of the mighty millions of their kin all through this continent. I know that there is a class of her children who repudiate any close and peculiar connection with Africa. They and their fathers have been absent from this soil for centuries. In the course of time their blood has been mingled somewhat with that of other peoples and races. They have been brought up and habituated to customs entirely diverse from those of their ancestors in this land; and while the race here are in barbarism, they on the other hand are civilized and enlightened.

But, notwithstanding these pleas, there are other great facts which grapple hold of these men and bind them to this darkened, wretched, negro race by indissoluble bonds. There is the fact of kinship, which a lofty manhood and a proud generosity keep them now, and ever will keep them, from disclaiming. There are the strong currents of kindred blood which neither time nor circumstance can ever entirely wash out. There are the bitter memories of ancestral wrongs, of hereditary servitude, which cannot be forgotten till "the last syllable of recorded time." There is the bitter pressure of legal proscription and of inveterate caste, which will crowd closer and closer their ranks, deepening brotherhood and sympathy, and preserving vital the deep consciousness of distinctive race. There still remains the low imputation of negro inferiority, necessitating a protracted and an earnest battle, creative of a generous pride to vindicate their race, and inciting to noble endeavor to illustrate its virtues and its genius.

How then can these men ever forget Africa? How cut the links which bind them to the land of their fathers? I affirm, therefore, that it is the duty of black men in foreign lands to live and to labor for the evangelization of the land of their fathers : 1st, on the ground of humanity ; 2d, because they themselves are negroes, or the descendants of negroes, and are measurably responsible to God for the salvation of their heathen kin; and 3dly, I press the consideration of duty on the ground that they are Christians. In the good providence of God they have been enabled to pass out of the spiritual benightedness of their fathers into the high table-lands and the divine atmosphere of Christian truth and Christian conviction.

Now I shall not attempt any *formal* argument in proof that black men, or, to use the new term, Anglo-Africans, are in duty bound to extend the Gospel in Africa, for I know enough of human nature to see that such an argument would look like the assumption that our brethren in the States were so ignorant that they did not know their duty as Christians. The very men who, perchance, would contest every other point in this letter, would charge me with insult, if I had just here put forth an *argument to prove* that Christianity requires *black* Christians to be missionaries as well as white ones. They would start up and exclaim : " Do you think that we read our Bibles and yet remain ignorant of the evangelizing spirit of the Bible? Do you think that we are such fools as to suppose that the precepts and commands of Scripture have a *color* on them ? And do you suppose that we are such ignorant creatures that you must needs present an argument to prove to us that we should manifest a missionary heart as well as other Christians? We do not need your teachings, sir. We know something about Christianity as well as you."

I attempt no such argument. It is not to be supposed for a moment that black Christians in New York, Philadelphia, and Baltimore, do not know that there are no distinctions in Christian requirement, that her obligations are as weighty upon them as upon any portion of the Church. I am only endeavoring to show that while that portion of the race that lives in America owes duty in America, it has obligations which likewise pertain to Africa; that devotedness to the cause of the black man in the United States, does not necessarily exclude sympathy for Africa. Let me illustrate this. There is a phase of modern theological writing, which brings out most prominently the fact that our Lord Jesus Christ, though born of a Jewish mother, shows nowhere Jewish idiosyncrasies. You look at the Lord Jesus, you read his life, you study his words, and nowhere can you discover nationality. Men of every clime, and blood, and nation turn to Him, and they find each and all in Him the reflex of one common broad humanity.

The Apostle, St. Paul, more than any other mere man, reached the nearest to this grand and divine Catholicity of the Master. "I am debtor both to the Greeks and to the Barbarians: both to the wise and to the unwise. So, as much as in me is, I am ready to preach the Gospel to you that are at Rome also." Romans, Chapter i. 14, 15.

Nay, he went even beyond this. In his Epistle to the Thessalonians, he speaks of his kinsmen the Jews, in a way which would lead one to suppose that he had become thoroughly denationalized. "For ye also have suffered like things of your own countrymen, even as they have of the Jews: Who both killed the Lord Jesus, and their own prophets, and have persecuted us; and they please not God, and are contrary to all men." 1 Thessalonians ii. 14, 15. So thoroughly had the grace of God eliminated from the soul of St. Paul that withering and malignant principle of caste, which burned more fiercely and intensely in the Jewish mind and blood, than in any other people that ever lived.

And yet, look at this same large-hearted, Catholic-minded Paul; what a patriot he is! what longings he has for his race! How he falls back upon their high and noble prerogatives! Yea, what zeal, what deep desire, what earnest self-sacrifice, he cherishes for them! "What advantage hath the Jew?" he asks, "Or what profit is there of circumcision? Much every way: chiefly because that unto them were committed the oracles of God." Romans iii. 1, 2. The Epistle to the Romans was written after that to the Thessalonians. And again, in the 9th chapter, he says: "I say the truth in Christ, I lie not, my conscience also bearing me witness in the Holy Ghost, that I have great heaviness and continual sorrow in my heart. For I could wish that myself were accursed from Christ for my brethren, my kinsmen according to the flesh: who are Israelites, to whom pertaineth the adoption, and the glory, and the covenants, and the giving of the law, and the service of God, and the promises; whose are the fathers, and of whom, as concerning the flesh, Christ came, who is over all, God blessed for ever. Amen."

To be Catholic-minded, then, does not imply a lack of patriotism. Large, yea cosmopolitan views do not necessarily demand a sacrifice of kinship, a disregard of race, nor a spirit of denationality.

Even so our brethren in the United States, however manfully they claim citizenship in the land of their birth, however valiantly against all odds they stand beside their brethren in bonds, however nobly they may continue to battle for their rights, need not, nevertheless, feel less for the hundreds of millions of their kin " without God and without hope in the world," " in bondage to sin and Satan "; nor yet to put forth less generous effort for their well-being and eternal salvation.

I turn from the point of *duty* to the question of your *ability* and *power* to take part in this great work. I do not know whether or not colored men in the United States would generally acknowledge that they could as a people do something for Africa; I assume, however, as most probable, the affirmative. At the same time, I must say that I do not think there is any deep conviction of either the awful needs of the case, or the solemn obligations connected with it.

I see, however, that this very question of your ability is both questioned and denied in some quarters. I see in the " Spirit of Missions," (October, 1858,) a report of a speech of Rev. Dr. I. Leighton Wilson, Secretary of the Presbyterian Board of Missions, which is of this tenor. He says : " To withdraw our missionaries is virtually to consign those people to perpetual and unmitigated heathenism. The speaker knew of no substitute for the present plan of missionary operation. In the colonization scheme he entertained the liveliest interest. The Liberian Republic offers a comfortable home for those in the United States who choose to go there, but it can never exert an influence which will reach the remote part of the continent. To study out the barbarous languages, prepare dictionaries, to give shape to a community emerging into the light of civilization, we never look to colored men as best adapted to this work. We were shut up to the conclusion that we must pursue this work in the manner already commenced."

I regret exceedingly that one who has done and suffered so much for Africa as Dr. Wilson has, should have ventured such disparaging remarks concerning any of her children as the above.* For if he had put himself to the pains of inquiring into the capacity of the "colored men around him," he would never, I feel convinced, have thus spoken. ′ I am no more disposed to exaggerate the learning or mental ability of our race than their wealth. Indeed, as a race, there is no place for exaggeration. ′ As yet, we are but "parvenus" in the intellectual world. Our greatness lies in the future; as yet we have not secured it. Nevertheless, American black men have done, and are now doing, enough to challenge respect. And even that seems to be withheld by Dr. Wilson; possibly I may mistake him. But when American black

---

* It is hardly necessary for me to tell you that Dr. Wilson has spent the flower of his years on this coast in self-sacrifice for Africa; nor to add that it was *chiefly* through a rigorous and timely pamphlet of his that the British Squadron was not withdrawn from this coast in 1851.

men are ably editing literary journals, publishing respectable newspapers, issuing from the press volumes of sermons, writing scientific disquisitions, venturing abstruse "Theories of Comets," and sending forth profound "vital statistics," vexatious alike to opposing statesmen and divines, they so far vindicate their mental power and ability as to make it manifest that, under better circumstances, in a clear field, they could

—"Move and act
In all the correspondence of nature,"

with force, and skill, and effect.

But Dr. Wilson knows nothing of this particular class of black men. He and hundreds like him know nothing of them. And this is one of the signal signs of the deadly power of caste. It victimizes the white as well as the black man. Here is mind—active, struggling mind—developing itself under most interesting circumstances; rising above the depression of centuries; breaking away from ancestral benightedness and hereditary night; gradually gathering strength, and emerging into light; and at length securing respectability and attracting attention; and yet of this phenomenon, which excited the admiration of Dr. Channing, and arrested the attention of Lord Carlyle and Dr. Playfair, passing travellers, Dr. Wilson apparently knows nothing, but actually speaks slightingly of.

Dr. Wilson rejects the idea of your being capable of exerting a remote and extensive influence. I beg to point out his error by a reference again to the "African Methodist Church," in the United States.

I make this reference on the ground that in the Church of God "there are diversities of gifts, but the same Spirit"; and "there are differences of administrations, but the same Lord"; and "that the manifestation of the Spirit is given to every man to profit withal"; and yet again, that in the great work of Christ for the salvation of the heathen, even *those very "members of the body* [of Christ] *which seem to be more feeble, are necessary."*

And, while fully agreeing to the affirmation, more distinctly stated by Dr. Wilson than I have ever seen it expressed before, that, "the idea of gathering up colored men indiscriminately, and setting them down on the shores of Africa, with the design or expectation that they will take the lead in diffusing a pure Christianity among the natives, deserves to be utterly rejected by every friend of Africa";† still it seems to me that he commits an error similar to that of rejecting the light artillery of an army, because the "cavalry" is a stronger arm of it.

Doubtless *all* the religious societies of colored people in America are humble, that is, as it respects literary and theological qualifications; and the African Methodist Church as much as any other. I do not think they themselves would make any pretensions. *But have they fitness for practical usefulness?*

We can only determine this by facts. Now this denomination has been in existence since 1790. It has gathered into its fold tens of thousands of the sons of Africa on American soil.

---

* 1 Corinthians xii. 5, 6, 7—22.
† Wilson's "Western Africa," p. 507.

"The poor forsaken ones:"

men, however, of earnest mind, who would not sit in the negro pew; men, who but for this society must have been left to indifferentism or infidelity, have had their wounded hearts soothed by the visitations of this society, and their anxious, passionate gaze turned from the trials of caste and slavery, to "the Lamb of God, who taketh away the sin of the world." They have built churches, established schools, founded a college, raised up a ministry of over four hundred men, meet in several conferences, and are governed by their own bishops. Here, then, is a spiritual machinery which has saved the United States the shame of hundred of thousands black heathen. Here is a purely missionary enterprise in the full tide of success, which has been administered by black men over a half century. Stretching from Maine to Louisiana, from Maryland to California; it shows that black men "*can exert an influence which will reach the remote part of the continent*" of America; and why not do the same on the continent of Africa? Operating among negroes, most of whom a century ago were recently from Africa; it shows that American Christians, even *now*, "*can look to colored men as*" [at least, *humbly*] "*adapted to the work*," that is, *to give shape to a community emerging into the light of civilization.*" The disproof of Dr. Wilson's assertion is right before his eyes.

Dr. Wilson's objection, that we are "not best adapted to study out the barbarous languages and prepare dictionaries," I regard as exceedingly unfair. There is not a missionary society in Christendom whose choice of missionaries is conditioned on this single qualification—their "ability to study barbarous languages and prepare dictionaries"! It strikes too as much against *white* missionaries *abroad* as against black men; for are they "BEST ADAPTED," in these respects, compared with such distinguished divines and scholars as Dr. Robinson, Dr. Goodrich, Dr. Turner? Besides, how many dictionaries have the fishermen of Galilee transmitted to modern times? What evidence have we of an eminent scholarship among them like to this demanded of us? Or where is the proof that even the Holy Spirit regarded "the preparation of dictionaries," or a critical lingual capacity as *the* qualifications of missionaries?

We read the history of the Church, and see the conquests of the faith in ancient times in Europe, Asia, and Africa. But how rare a thing is it, to find such preëminent scholarship as, for instance, that of Henry Martyn, Bishop Middleton, and David Tappan Stoddard, the accessories of the devoted missionary spirit, which has converted millions, and brought whole nations into the kingdom of Christ! St. Paul founded the churches of Asia and Greece. But where is the proof that even he was an eminent critical scholar? Christianity was revived and energized in England by Augustine in the 6th century, and then travelled onward with conquering power, until the time of the Reformation; and since then the evangelization of England has been progressing with a resistless march to the present. But the first English dictionary we know of is that of Dr. Johnson.

If I do not mistake the spirit of the New Testament, it requires, I apprehend, in addition to devoted piety, good sterling qualities, and an " aptness to teach," as the ordinary gifts of ministers : [and what are missionaries but ministers ?] It cannot go below this standard ; but it may rise above it to the fiery zeal and wasting labors of St. Paul ; the effective eloquence of Xavier, and Swartz, and Brainerd ; the fine abilities and practical learning of Carey and Medhurst.

If to ordinary gifts, missionaries are able to add these other eminent ones, so much the better fitted will they be to make skilful and effective workers in the Lord's vineyard !

But if not, then missionaries, that is, colored missionaries, to Africa, must be content to labor as effectively as they can, without them ; relying for translations and the superior literary work of missions, upon the occasional white laborers who come from abroad. And with respect to the languages, they must do as two-thirds, not to say three-fourths, of the white missionaries do, that is, work for the heathen through the agency of interpreters. In Liberia, however, more than a *third*, not to say *half*, of the colored ministers speak the respective native tongues in their vicinity, with ease ; and of candidates for the ministry, in the different denominations, I feel well nigh confident that four-fifths of them speak one or two *native* tongues.

You have then humble QUALIFICATIONS fitted to make you, although not learned, yet useful and effective instruments in the salvation of our heathen kin. You can become preachers and teachers ; and the more learned labor can be done by white brethren. As you have fitness, so likewise you have the opportunity to enter upon this glorious and saving work. I wish to show here that if you love Africa, and really possess a missionary spirit, the way is open before you to enter at once among the crowded populations of this continent, and to set up the standard of the Cross. From the port of Lagos, in almost direct line, through a crowded population, and passing by cities containing tens of thousands of people, a highway is now open reaching to RABBA on the banks of the Niger. All through this country the colored churches of America can send their missionaries, build up Christian schools, and lay the foundation of Christian colleges and universities. North of us lies the wide and open field of the Mendians, which is the door to the mighty millions of interior Africa, back to Timbuctoo. Between these two fields of labor is the Republic of Liberia. Our name, our reputation, and our flag will insure you safety two hundred miles from the coast, among large, important, industrious, and active-minded natives. It was only the other day that I made a second visit to an interior station, in company with Dr. Delany, who had been my guest for a few weeks, and became, for the time, my fellow-traveller. We were paddled up the CAVALLA, a fine, broad-flowing river, running through a rich and populous country, with banks rising twenty, thirty, fifty feet, almost perpendicularly from the water's level; its turning points opening ever and anon to our view grand mountain scenery in the distance, with visions of ravishing beauty now and then bursting upon our sight; navigable for sloops and schooners near eighty miles from the coast, and stretching out beyond the falls which here obstruct its passage, some three or four hundred miles in the interior. Everywhere, in every town, we were most cordially received, hospitably entertained, and my teachings eagerly listened to, by whole towns and villages, who invariably turned out in a body to hear the preacher. In most of these towns I had gone preaching before; other missionaries had been there long and often before me; and hence you can see that it was interest that excited them, and not mere novelty.

Now here is a vast, open field ready for the Gospel; but it is but *one* among scores, in the limited territory of Liberia. Saving that the Cavalla can be navigated a further distance inland, there are many other as good opportunities and facilities for the conveyance of the Gospel interiorward, as this.

Now, let me ask, what hinders the colored Christians of America from entering these large, inviting missionary fields, and founding the institutions of Christianity here? Putting aside, altogether, the question of colonization, why can they not as a people come forward to save their race from heathenism, and to give them both the present and the future consolations of religion?

Let me refer in particular to the three classes of religionists among our brethren, with whom I am more especially acquainted: the Methodists, Presbyterians, and Episcopalians.

The colored Episcopalians are a "small folk," I

know, but both of us being churchmen, will make my mention of them excusatory. With three or four of these congregations I am intimately acquainted, and I see no difficulty whatever in the way of their adopting some such plan as this : 1. Preparing, as a commencement, some two or three young men for the ministry, for the special purpose of becoming missionaries to Africa. This, of course, presupposes a regular, systematic effort on the part of the ministers of these churches to interest their people in Africa, and to train them in the *habit* of giving to missions. In this way one young heart and another would ever and anon come forward, anxious to devote himself to the evangelization of Africa. The young men might take theological lessons of the minister, and when prepared, might be placed under the Episcopal authority on this coast, and receive orders. 2. When about sending off the young men, if any pious mechanics, or farmers, or schoolmasters desired to devote themselves to the work, the congregation might extend their interest to them as well as to the candidates for orders, and assure them of continued regard and future zeal and self-sacrifice in their behalf.* 3. A company thus formed, might be placed at the disposal of the mission, with the request, perhaps, that they might be located together, as one party; and the church from whence they came, or

---

* I regret that the theme before me forbids that I should speak of the almost absolute necessity, in any such scheme, of connecting *manual labor* with missionary effort. Indeed no man should become a *colonist* to Africa whose example is likely to encourage the heathen in their irregular, unsystematic, unplodding modes of labor.

some two or three colored churches, might regard *that* station as their own,—supply it with schoolbooks, farming utensils, clothes for missionaries and converts, and provisions to a greater or less extent; might recruit ever and anon with new schoolmasters, or replace decayed or deceased missionaries,—or take charge of their children [in America,] and prepare them for the work of their parents, in the future.

This is only an outline of what the few colored Episcopal churches in the United States could do.* Perhaps you say, "This is a large scheme!" I reply without hesitation that, from my knowledge of the wealth that has been concentrated in it, St. Thomas' Church, Philadephia, could have done all this thirty years ago. The expense of a small mission, thus constituted, would not near equal the lavish expenditure of some city congregation of colored people, in balls, parties, fashionable rivalry, jewelry, pic-nics, and the department which is politely termed *cuisine*.

Without entering into details, I merely remark that from their numbers, and the increasing intelligence and learning of their ministers, the Presbyterians could do a larger work than the Episcopalians. They have so many *white* colleges and seminaries opened to them, so many obstacles have been removed out of the way of their aspiring young men, and so wide and warm and hearty is the desire of all classes of white Presbyterians to build up their de-

---

* There are no less than *three* different fields into which effective laborers would likely be welcomed:—the church in Sierra Leone, in Liberia, and in the projected field in South Africa, where the "Cambridge and Oxford" mission intend to establish a colony.

nomination among the free colored people, that the colored Presbyterian churches could contemplate grand saving schemes for Africa, and undertake at once a large and noble work.

But the "African Methodist Episcopal Church" of the United States has the machinery for a most comprehensive missionary service in Africa. They have a well-tried system; they have experience; they have a large body of ministers; and they have a corresponding body already in existence, under complete organization, in Liberia—I mean the "Liberian Methodist Episcopal Church." If my old friend, Bishop Daniel A. Payne, would only enter into this work with all that warmth of heart, that energy of purpose, and that burning Christian eloquence, which characterize him, what blessedness would he not impart to this land; what spiritual life would he not diffuse among all the churches of his charge in America! His people could start a saving, systematized plan by which health, power, life, and energy would be constantly poured, like a living stream, into the corresponding body in this country, and so be diffused throughout the land, to the villages, the hamlets, and the huts of tens of thousands of our needy heathen kin!

I am not blind to difficulties. I know some of the trials of emigration. I have been called to some of the difficulties, not to say severities, of missionary life. And therefore I shall be free, I trust, from the charge of flippancy. So likewise I am aware of the peculiar obstacles in the way of our brethren in the States. I, too, am an American black man. I, too, have an acquaintance with obstructive idiosyncrasies in them. If you speak of hindrances and difficulties specially theirs, I know all about them.

But I say it deliberately, that the difficulties in the way of our brethren doing a goodly work for Africa, are more subjective than objective. *One of these hindrances is a want of missionary zeal.* This is a marked characteristic of *American* black Christians. I say *American*, for from all I hear, it does not characterize our West Indian brethren; and the infant church of Sierra Leone is already, in sixty years from its birth, a mother of missions. *This* is our radical defect. *Our* religion is not diffusive, but rather introversive. It does not flow out, but rather inward. As a people we like religion—we like religious services. Our people like to go to church, to prayer-meetings, to revivals. But we go to get enjoyment. We like to be made happy by sermons, singing, and pious talk. All this is indeed correct so far as it goes; but it is only *one* side of religion. It shows only that phase of piety which may be termed the "*piety of self-satisfaction.*" But if we are true disciples, we should not only seek a comforting piety, but we should also exhibit an effective and expansive one. We should let our godliness exhale like the odor of flowers. We should live for the good of our kind, and strive for the salvation of the world.

Another of these hindrances is what the phrenologists term "*inhabitativeness*,"—the stolid inhabitativeness of our race. As a people, we cling with an almost deadly fixity to locality. I see this on both sides of the Atlantic. Messrs. Douglass and Watkins assail Messrs. Horace Greeley and Gerrit Smith for pointing out this peculiarity of character in our people. But without doubt they tell the truth of us. We are not "given to change." The death of a master, the break-up of a family, may cast a few black men from the farm to the city, but they go no further. We lack speculation. Man has been called a creature,

"Looking before and after"——

But not so we. We look where we stand, and but few beyond.

So here, on this side of the water. The colonization ship brings a few hundred freed men to this west coast of Africa. They gather together in the city of Monrovia, or the town of Greenville, and there they sit, yea, and would sit forever, if it were not for some strong *external* influence which now and then scatters a few, and a precious few, here and there along the coast.

Here then you see, in this same people, on both sides of the waters, an exaggeration of the "home feeling," which is so exceedingly opposite to Anglo-Saxon influences that I wonder that we, who have been trained for centuries under them, have not ere this outgrown it. Sixteen years from the settlement of Plymouth, sixty families started from Boston and cut their way to Windsor, on the Connecticut.* We in Liberia have never yet had a *spontaneous* movement of old settlers in a body and with a purpose to a new location. The colored people of Rochester, N. Y., in 1853, I hear, were mostly fugitive slaves. The

* Bancroft's History of America, ch. ix.

"Fugitive Slave Law" prompted them to emigrate to Canada; but proximity determined their choice of a home rather than any large principle. We read in the Acts of the Apostles, that when those who at Stephen's death were persecuted, were scattered abroad, "they went everywhere, preaching the word." So when our brethren felt constrained to leave the United States, it was meet, it seems to me, that *some* of them should have thought of Africa and her needs. On the other hand, if Liberians had been duly awake to the welfare of our race, we should have shown our brotherly feeling by inviting the wanderers to our shores.

These *two* hindrances, that is, a lack of missionary zeal and a tenacious hold on locality, will doubtless prevent active efforts for the regeneration of Africa. So, too, they will serve to check commercial enterprise. But as a people, we shall have to rise above these things. The colored churches of America will find, by and by, they can retain no spiritual vitality unless they rise above the range of selfish observation, to broad, general, humane ideas and endeavors. Self-preservation, self-sustentation, are only single items in the large and comprehensive category of human duties and obligations.

"Unless above himself, he can erect himself,
How poor a thing is man."

And this is equally true with regard to Liberian black Christians. Do not think that I pretend to say that we in Africa stand on such a high vantage-ground that we can point invidiously at our brethren in America. I have no hesitation in saying, as my own opinion, that in both the respects referred to above, we are more blameworthy than you.

A *third* hindrance may be mentioned here. There will be a reluctance on the part of even some good and zealous Christians to engage in the propagation of the Gospel in Africa on the ground " that its ultimate tendency must be to subserve the objectionable scheme of African colonization." But surely any one can see that such an objection is wicked. The Gospel *must* be preached in all the world. The Master commands it. The history of the Church shows that it does not necessarily, if generally, carry colonization with it. But even if in this particular case it does so, no Christian has a right to shrink from his duty. And that man must be demented who cannot see God's beneficent providence in colonization,—that man blind who does not recognize good and mercy in its work, civil and religious, on the coast of Africa! The duties of our present state are not to be determined by imaginary results or prospective issues. They always grow out of the positive commands of the Bible, or manifest human relations; and *both* fasten the duty upon us to care for the heathen in general, and for our heathen kin in particular.

I have no doubt, however, that every effort that is henceforth made to spread the Gospel in Africa, will bring many, from the impulse of emigration, to Africa. Up to a certain future, but I hope not distant, point in American sentiment, there will be, I feel quite certain, a large exodus of the better, more cultivated, and hence more sensitive minds, partly to Africa, Hayti, Brazil, and the British colonies. Those who " having done all," still STAND, must bear with those who leave. Hayti *needs a* PROTESTANT, Anglo-African element of the stamp Mr. Holly will give her. Jamaica is blessed by the advent in her midst of such a strong-minded, open-eyed, energetic spirit, as my old school-mate and friend SAMUEL R. WARD. And Liberia's wants in this respect are stronger than either of the above. You should learn willingly to give, even of your best, to save, and regenerate, and build up the RACE in distant quarters.* You should study to rise above the niggard spirit which grudgingly and pettishly yields its grasp upon a fellow laborer. You should claim in regard to this continent that " THIS IS OUR AFRICA," in all her gifts, and in her budding grace and glory. And you should remember, too, with regard to emigrants, the words of that great man, EDMUND BURKE,—" the poorest being that crawls on earth, contending to save itself from injustice and oppression, is an object respectable in the eyes of God and man."

But it is time that I should draw to a close, for I have fallen into a too common fault: I have made too long a " palaver." My letter has run out to a greater length than I intended. And now I shall weary you no longer.

For near three centuries the negro race, in exile and servitude, has been grovelling in lowly places, in deep degradation. Circumstance and position alike

---

* The 2d article of the Constitution of African Civilization Society sets forth my views in better language than my own : "The Evangelization and Civilization of Africa and the descendants of African ancestors, *wherever dispersed.*"

have divorced us from the pursuits which give nobleness and grandeur to life. In our time of trials we have shown, it is true, a matchless patience, and a quenchless hope: the one prophetic of victory, and the other the germ of a high Christian character, now developing. These better qualities, however, have been disproportioned, and the life of the race, in general, has been alien from ennobling and aspiring effort.

But the days of passivity should now come to an end. The active, creative, and saving powers of the race should begin to show themselves. The power of the negro, if he has such power, to tell upon human interests, and to help shape human destinies, should, at an early day, make full demonstration of itself. We owe it to ourselves, to our race, and to our generous defenders and benefactors, both in Europe and America, to show that we are capable " of receiving the seed of present history into a kindly yet a vigorous soil, and [that we can] reproduce it, the same, and yet new, for a future period " * in all the homes of this traduced yet vital and progressive race.

Surely the work herein suggested is fitted to just such ends, and is fully worthy the noblest faculties and the highest ambition. If I were aiming but to startle the fancy, to kindle the imagination, and thereby to incite to brave and gallant deeds, I know no theme equal to this in interest and commanding influence. And just this *is* the influence it is now exerting upon passionate and romantic minds, in England and the United States, in France and Germany, in

* Dr. Arnold. Inaugural Lecture.

Austria and Sardinia. These civilized States are sending out their adventurous travellers to question, on the spot, the mysterious spell which seems to shut out Africa from the world and its civilization. These enterprising spirits are entering every possible avenue to the heart of Africa, anxious to assure the inner tribes of the continent that the enlightened populations of Europe would fain salute them as brethren, and share with them the culture and enlightenment which, during the ages, have raised *them* from rudeness and degradation; if they can only induce them to throw aside the exclusiveness of paganism and the repulsiveness of barbarism.

But the enlightened sons of Africa, in distant lands, are called to a far higher work than even this; a work which as much transcends mere civilization as the abiding interests of eternity outvie the transient concerns of time. To wrest a continent from ruin; to bless and animate millions of torpid and benighted souls; to destroy the power of the devil in his strongholds, and to usher therein light, knowledge, blessedness, inspiring hope, holy faith, and abiding glory, is, without doubt, a work which not only commands the powers of the noblest men, but is worthy the presence and the zeal of angels. It is just this work which now claims and calls for the interest and the activity of the sons of Africa. Its plainest statement and its simplest aspect are sufficient, it seems to me, to move these men in every quarter of the world to profound sensibility, to deep resolve, to burning ardor. Such a grand and awful necessity, covering a vast continent, touching the best hopes and the endless destiny of millions of men, ought, I think, to stir the soul of many a self-sacrificing spirit, and quicken it to lofty purposes and noble deeds. And when one considers that never before in human history has such a grand and noble work been laid out in the Divine Providence, before the negro race, and that it rises up before them in its full magnitude now, at the very time when they are best fitted for its needs and requirements, it seems difficult to doubt that many a generous and godly soul will hasten to find its proper place in this great work of God and man, whether it be by the personal and painful endeavors of a laborer in the field of duty, or by the generous benefactions and the cheering incitements which serve to sustain and stimulate distant and tried workers in their toils and trials. "A benefaction of this kind seems to enlarge the very being of a man, extending it to distant places and to future times, inasmuch as unseen countries and after ages may feel the effects of his bounty, while he himself reaps the reward in the blessed society of all those who 'having turned many to righteousness, shine as the stars forever and ever.'"*

I am very truly,
   Your servant,
      ALEX. CRUMMELL.

* Bp. Berkley: "Proposal for supplying churches."

HOPE FOR AFRICA.

A SERMON ON BEHALF OF THE LADIES' NEGRO EDUCATION
SOCIETY.

*Preached at Hotwell's Church, Clifton, Bristol, England,
April 21st, 1852.*

"Shall drink at noon . . . . .
The palm's rich nectar; and lie down at eve
In the green pastures of remembered days;
And walk, to wander and to weep no more
On Congo's mountain-coast, or Guinea's golden shore."
—Anon.

"In the unreasoning progress of the world
A wiser spirit is at work for us,
A better eye than ours."
—Wordsworth.

SERMON.

PSALM lxviii. 31.—"Ethiopia shall soon stretch out her hands unto God."

I AM requested to plead this evening on behalf of the Society established in this country, for the education of the Negro race in the British West Indies. I most readily comply with this request, because I regard this as one of the *chief* among the charities of England; and because I feel, that to advocate the claims of this Society is, as it were, to plead for my own life and blood, and to vindicate my own personal interests and advantages.

I use the paragraph which I have announced as my text, since it is singularly appropriate to the objects of this excellent association, and, also, remarkably coincident with the train of thought I purpose presenting to your consideration. The Ladies' Negro Education Society aims at and desires the mental and spiritual regeneration of the Negro race in the

West Indies; but it also entertains another important purpose, in close connection with this high end. It is a cherished idea of many of its supporters, that by their endeavors, and through the objects of their benevolence, they may send abroad healthful influences and a saving power, far beyond the limits of their immediate field of labor;—even to the benighted father-land, whence the ancestors of the sable dwellers upon these islands were first brought; and thus help to raise up the great African family, in its several sections, to civilization and enlightenment;—to bring up a people, who for centuries " have lain among the pots," * to the fine adornment, and the beauteous proportions of grace,—and to aid in that which seems just now, the GREAT WORK OF CHRISTENDOM—the regeneration of a continent!

Falling in with these purposes and aims, I wish to avail myself of the prophetic announcement I have quoted, by calling attention to some facts, in order to show, *first* of all, that in the work of the Divine Providence, this withered arm of the human species—the Negro race—is gradually, nay rapidly, resuming life and vitality, and hastening with a pace quick beyond all precedent, to the open day of the Gospel: and then I wish to employ the evidences of this fact which I may present, as the grounds for increased zeal and energy, in the particular department this Society aims to fulfil.

The term Ethiopia is, in the original, Cush. This Cush was one of the four sons of Ham. His descendants, in part, settled in Asia between the Euphrates

* Psalm lxviii. 13.

and the Tigris, and there first distinguished themselves. There Nimrod, his son, laid the first foundations of empire of which we have any record, and founded Nineveh. Subsequently, the Cushites spread themselves abroad through Arabia, from the Persian Gulf to the Red Sea. By and by, in process of time, a portion of them crossed the Red Sea and settled in Africa; and afterwards, as the remainder of the Cushite amily, who were settled in Asia, were gradually merged into other races, the seat of their strength and empire was transferred to Africa: and consequently in history, the African section of the Cushite family stands forth as the representative of the race. For although two other of the sons of Ham, that is, Mizraim and Phut, settled in Africa; yet they have had but little to do with generating that mighty hive of human beings which peoples the continent of Africa, whose numbers seem ever to swell more and more beyond all ordinary calculation as the missionary or the traveller advances toward the interior. The name Mizraim and his race seem connected only with ancient Egypt; for, from a very early period down to the present, the invasion of the Persian, the Greek, the Roman, and the Turk, has obliterated the distinctive marks of the sons of Mizraim: and hence in these our modern days, we find in Egypt a mixed race of people, and only the faint memory and the doubtful tracings of the aboriginal population. And so, to a certain extent, was it with Phut; he settled in the northwestern part of Africa; and although his family, too, in a partial degree, have remained intact, yet the presence, the influence, and the power of the Moors and the Romans can be seen in their mixed blood and the foreign control to which they are subjected.

The history of the Cushites, in its African section, has been entirely different. Shut in by the great desert from the rest of the world, and, until the discovery of America, protected from foreign aggression by the then, to them, mysterious ocean, they have peopled the vast interior of the African continent with numerous tribes and nations; of most of whom we have but vague, indefinite, and almost fabulous reports, and concerning whom the world is now in nearly as much doubt and incertitude, as it was two thousand years ago, in the time of Herodotus and Ptolemy.

This ignorance, with respect to the Cushite or Negro family, long continued as it was, has in more modern days become greatly lessened. It was broken up by that remarkable activity of the human intellect which the discovery of the magnet, the invention of printing, and the geographical adventures of Columbus, produced in the fifteenth century. These events led to a complete acquaintance with the coast of Africa, and the tribes dwelling thereon. Another influence tended to the same result: the peculiar social condition of the newly-discovered islands in the West—a condition produced by the ruthless waste of aboriginal life by Spain—caused a strong demand for a new supply of labor. In this originated the Slave Trade: and this effectually broke the spell of African seclusion. The demand for West Indian labor was met by the forcible substitution of the Negro for the Indian.

And thus the children of Cush are scattered over the face of the whole earth. The Negro race is to be found in every quarter of the globe. Stolen from their homes, and reduced to abject vassalage, they are gathered together by thousands and tens of thousands, and even millions, in lands separated, by thousands of miles, from the primitive seat of their ancestors, and the rude hamlets of their sires.

Now it is with respect to the Negro race, as thus scattered abroad through the world, as well as dwelling in their homes in Africa, that I shall apply my text: my purpose is to show that, in the merciful providence of God, the Negro race is fast approaching the day of complete evangelization. And as proof of this position, I shall call your attention,—

I. To *secular* evidences of its correctness and truth, manifested during the last fifty years.

II. To the spiritual progress of the Negro race during the same period.

III. To the unusual spiritual solicitude exhibited in the race, during this period, and at the present time.

I. In the *first* place, I am to refer you to secular evidences—to some temporal providences, that are alike recent and remarkable; which show that the day of the regeneration of Africa and her children is fast drawing nigh.

We stand now, my hearers, in the central period of the present century: we are living in the year of grace eighteen hundred and fifty-three. Now just go back with me to the commencement of this century, and look at this race of which we are speaking. What then meets our eyes? Why we find one universal fact connected with the Negro race—the fact of universal slavery, and the slave trade. If we turned to the West Indies, whether under Danish, Spanish, Dutch or English rule, the black man, everywhere, was a chattel. If we turned to the American continent, we would have found the race in the same position there, whether under the Protestant rule of the North American colonies, or under the Romish rule of the South American States. If we turned to Africa herself, we would have seen the whole extent of that vast continent given to the spoiler, robbed of her children—the vast interior converted into a hunting-ground for capturing miserable and wretched human beings;—drenched on every side with fraternal blood; —and the long line of the coast, for thousands of miles, evidencing, at every point, how prolific was the slave trade, in woes and agonies and murders, by the bleached bones, or the bloody tracks of its countless victims!

And what was the *status* of the Negro race at this time, in either Europe or America? It is one of the sad results of crime that its deadly influences strike down deep into every part of the human constitution: it both dementates and demoralizes men. The slave trade not only lowered the nations that engaged in it, in the scale of humanity, and in the tone of their morals, but it robbed them of the clearness of their mental vision. They not only robbed the Negro of his freedom—they added another crime thereto: they denied his humanity. Yes, at the commencement of this century it was a debated question among cultivated, thoughtful, nay even scientific minds, whether the Negro was indeed an integral member of the human species.

This, then, was the condition of the Negro race fifty years ago—this the estimation in which that race was held.

And now I desire to call your attention to the great change which has taken place in both these respects, since that period.

Since the commencement of this century, the leading European and American Governments have renounced all participation in that nefarious traffic which has barbarized Africa; and some of them have declared the slave trade piracy. The black man, thus held in a state of servitude, has been emancipated. The cheerful voice of freedom has been heard all around the islands of the Caribbean Sea; and eight hundred thousand human beings, under British rule, have been awakened by its grateful tones, to liberty and manhood. Influenced by this gracious example, France has stricken the shackle and the fetter from the limbs of three hundred thousand men and women. And Denmark has given the promise that she too will follow, at an early day, in the same benevolent pathway.

In America, the civil condition of the Negro race presents, in many places, the same signs of a half century's progress. From Mexico,* Bolivia, Peru,

* Slavery was abolished in Mexico, September 15, 1829, by the following decree:—" Slavery is forever abolished in the Republic; and consequently all those individuals who, until this day, looked upon themselves as slaves, are free."

Columbia, and Guatemala, the signs and tokens of Negro slavery were obliterated long before the system was abolished in your own western possessions. And although it still exists in Brazil, in the United States, and in Cuba, we have nevertheless some few signs of advancement, some evident indications that it must ere long yield and come to an end: for the commerce of the world is against slavery; the free-trade principle of the age is against it; science in her various developments is against it; the literature of the day is just now being brought to bear, in a most marvellous manner, against it; and the free sentiments of the world are against it, and doom it to an early utter oblivion!

Turning again to the coast of Africa we meet with most cheerful evidences of progress. Along a coast extending some two thousand five hundred miles in length, the slave trade has been entirely uprooted and destroyed; and from "more than three-fourths of the strongholds"* once occupied by the traders, they have been driven out, never more to return. Along this region—including some of the richest and most productive portions of the African continent—legitimate trade has sprung up; and instead of a revolting commerce in the "bodies and souls of men," and women, and even babes, we see industrious communities springing up, civilization introduced, and a trade commenced which already has swelled up, in exports alone to Europe and America, to more than two millions of pounds per annum.†

* The "British Squadron on the Coast of Africa": by the Rev. J. Leighton Wilson, an American Missionary, p. 10.
† Ibid., p. 18.

In connection with these general facts of African improvement, there are a few particular details which deserve special notice. One of these is, that from the midst of this race, various individuals have arisen who, on many accounts, merit consideration. If I had time, I could mention the names of scores of negroes who have achieved fame and celebrity: philanthropists like Howard; scholars, classical and mental; scientific men—one, a Doctor of Philosophy in a German university; distinguished painters and artists; officers, well known in Europe;* and ONE—a statesman, a general, and a hero, now a historical character, who was the father of his country, and achieved her liberties; one of the ablest commanders of the age; a man for whom the highest notes of minstrelsy have been struck, around whose name and history all the attractions of romance have hung. I mean the great and mighty chief of Hayti, Toussaint L'Ouverture.†

* EUSTACE, a Negro of the Island of St. Domingo, was an eminent philanthropist: he devoted all his means to providing for the sick and needy, nursing and sheltering orphans, and apprenticing destitute youth. He lived and labored only to make others happy. In 1832, the National Institute of France awarded him the sum of 1,000 dollars. JOB BEN SOLOMON; ANTONY WILLIAM AMO, (of the Universities of Halle and Wittenburg,) Doctor of Philosophy; IGNATIUS SANCHO, and FRANCIS WILLIAMS; ranked high as scholars: ANNIBAL was a Lieutenant-General in the Russian Army; LISLET GROFFROY was an officer of artillery in the Isle of France.

† Lamartine and Miss Martineau have both made Toussaint the hero of one of their works; and most readers are acquainted with the fine sonnet of Wordsworth, which I cannot resist repeating:

"Toussaint, the most unhappy man of men!
Whether the whistling rustic tend his plough
Within thy hearing, or thy head be now
Pillowed in some deep dungeon's earless den;—

Besides these various evidences of the progress of my race during the last half century, I must not fail to notice one striking fact: that is, that within this period, the black government of HAYTI has come into existence; the African colony of SIERRA LEONE has been established—a colony which has already become the cradle of missions, the mother of churches, the parent of colonies. And, moreover, we see now rising with, we trust, hopeful indications, on the western coast of Africa, the lone star of the black REPUBLIC OF LIBERIA.

And still another movement of a similar character is now projected by Englishmen, from your own West India Islands: a movement of brightest promise, even while yet in the bud; which contains within its folds the germs of a new African nationality of a civilized and Christian type. In the island of Barbadoes a society has been formed, under the patronage of the Governor, the Bishop, and other chief personages, whose object is to transplant colonies of black men from the West Indies to the coast of Africa. The black population have become interested, and have formed societies, and declare their strong spiritual

> O miserable Chieftain! where and when
> Wilt thou find patience! Yet die not; do thou
> Wear rather in thy bonds a cheerful brow:
> Though fallen thyself, never to rise again,
> Live, and take comfort. Thou hast left behind
> Powers that will work for thee; air, earth, and skies—
> There's not a breathing of the common wind
> That will forget thee; thou hast great allies;
> Thy friends are exultations, agonies,
> And love, and man's unconquerable mind!"

yearnings for Africa. They are to go in communities with clergymen, physicians, mechanics, and laborers, and form themselves at once into organized settlements. An agent has been in this country seeking funds for the foundation of a college. An important society has been formed in England, under the patronage of the Archbishop of Canterbury, and the leading dignitaries of the Church, and great statesmen. Already two African youths are under a system of instruction for missionary usefulness.

The locality they have chosen is that rich and precious portion of the coast which lies south of Liberia, and which is contiguous to the powerful kingdoms of Ashantee and Dahomey; and thus, in a corporate state, they will be enabled, at an early day, to act with a civilizing power and a Christian influence upon all the wide spaces, yea, at the very heart of the great life which beats in that vast continent. And here you cannot but notice that which has struck my own mind as one of the most distinct, unequivocal, and peculiar providences of the Almighty, which has been seen during the last three centuries. It is now three hundred years since the commencement of the slave trade. During this period millions of negroes have been stolen from Africa, and subjected to all the bitter but unimaginable horrors of domestic slavery on the American continent and its isles. Why all this agony and anguish—continued from generation to generation, to the only portion of helpless humanity—dragging down the people of a single race on two continents;—why all this agony and anguish should have been permitted by the Divine will and providence, has been perhaps the most puzzling question which ever agitated the mind of Christian men, who could not doubt the justice and equity of Heaven. Well, three centuries have passed, and the mystery is being solved: the recaptured Africans taken to Sierra Leone, civilized and Christianized, feel all of a sudden, an irresistible desire to return to the land of their birth: they charter vessels, and a large number go down the coast a thousand miles and more, bearing the Gospel to Abbeokuta.*

Again, emancipation takes place in your British West Indian Islands, and eight hundred thousand men, women, and children are changed, by a single act in one day, from chattels into men. So soon as they are freed from the fetter and from thraldom, a strong spiritual yearning arises in their souls for their father-land, and they stretch forth the arms of a sacred affection for Africa. The feeling is so wide, so general, so earnest, that an organized system is fallen upon; and soon Christian communities of black men in large numbers from your British West Indies, will be seen planted on the west coast of Africa, proffering the boon of salvation to all the large tribes and nations of that continent.

And yet again: the children of Africa have been sojourning nigh three centuries in America, and in

* This Emigration commenced in 1839. I shall not enter into the particulars pertaining to it: but I would beg the reader to procure a copy of "Abbeokuta, or Sunrise within the Tropics," by the accomplished and philanthropic Miss. Tucker, author of "South India Sketches" and the "Rainbow in the North." Chap. III. gives a full account of the "foundation of Abbeokuta," and the "Sierra Leone Emigrants."

the course of time, large numbers of them have become free. The free blacks of America are a disturbing element in the midst of the white inhabitants of the paradoxical Republic; and hence, by the force of the oppressive principle, thousands of them have been led to emigrate to the coast of Africa. There they have formed a Republic—the Republic of Liberia, with free institutions, with schools and churches, and missions to their heathen kin.

Here, then, in the providence of God, we see *three* distinct movements, in the Negro race itself, of a civilized and Christian character, tending towards the coast of Africa; and it presents this singular, this cheering and auspicious aspect, that after three centuries of slavery and outrage, this people are emerging from the shades, and, all at once, from three different quarters of the globe, are carrying in a combined and organized manner, in three different streams, civilized institutions and the Gospel of our Lord Jesus Christ, not only to the coast of Africa, but to the banks of the Niger—to the very heart of that vast benighted continent!

II. I must not dwell any longer upon these topics of temporal regard. Interesting and gratifying though they be, they are not nigh so grateful to the Christian mind, as the facts which pertain to the spiritual progress of the Negro race during the last fifty years.

The contrast I have just presented between the commencement of this century and the present moment, holds in an equal degree with respect to the spiritual condition of this race, as to their civil and political status.

Prior to the commencement of this century, the Negro race had been left in a state of almost absolute spiritual neglect. Along the whole line of the west coast of Africa, not a mission had been commenced to evangelize nations; not a spire pointed its silent finger, with a heavenly significancy, to the skies. The masses of the black population of America and the West Indies were in a state of heathenism, though surrounded by the Christian institutions of the whites. Both custom and law forbade the instruction of Negroes, and superadded fear prevented the formation of schools. Nay, more than this: the conquerors of the black race were as yet undecided whether their bondmen were capable of spiritual illumination, or were heirs of immortality.

Now let us take a general view of the advance which has been made in the Negro race in Christian culture and enlightenment. I have not time to trace the stream of improvement, from the first flowings of the generous waters to the present full and grateful supply. I cannot linger on my way to mark the first signs of a noble revolution of feeling on this subject —to note the kindly endeavors and the zealous efforts which ensued, the encouraging fruits which they yielded, and the present state of cheering advancement and hopeful promise. Let it suffice that I present the more notable changes—the almost incredible contrast which meets our eyes this day almost everywhere where the children of Cush, the Negro race, are living.

Fifty years have sped their flight, and now, at the present day, there is not a spot on earth where members of the Negro race are gathered together in any considerable numbers, but what there enlarged facilities are now opened to them for mental and spiritual culture, or where their religious interests have not become questions of vast importance. Turn to the West India Islands. Immediately on emancipation, nay, in justice it must be said, *before* that glorious event, efforts had been commenced to give religious instruction to the black population. Even then this Society had commenced its benign and saving labors; and now, in all the lovely isles of the West, where "Britain's power is felt," there are hundreds and thousands of African youth who this day have been appropriating the rich advantages of mental and spiritual instruction. During the few years which have elapsed *since* emancipation, there has been a marvellous increase of schools, and churches, and chapels. A number of intelligent and thoughtful African young men, among the different bodies into which Christendom is unfortunately divided, have been trained up as teachers and ministers. In the Church a class of this kind act as catechists and lay-readers. Some of the children of these people have been sent to Europe, to avail themselves of the higher discipline of education in the universities of the old world, and have returned home again to serve their people in civil and spiritual functions. A few have remained in Europe. I know myself of three of these sons of Africa now in England, who, having taken orders, are acting as curates in the Church;

another, a personal acquaintance, has recently commenced his ministry in one of the West India Islands.

In the United States of America, although wicked laws and a bad public sentiment have seriously retarded the spiritual progress of the African race, yet in the slave States a greater attention is now paid to this duty than ever before; and in the North a class of free black men has arisen, who, as ministers and teachers, in their own persons vindicate their race, and at the same time elevate and bless it.

And now, when we turn to Africa, how great the change! How wonderful and pleasing the contrast! "Previous to the year 1832, there was not a mission anywhere between Sierra Leone and the Cape of Good Hope." Now, "during the last fifteen or sixteen years"—I use the words of another*—"there have been established as many as twelve independent missions, at the distance of 100 or 200 miles from each other, embracing three times that number of outstations along the coast, and a still greater number of outstations interiorward." To hundreds of thousands of the nations, on the coast and in the interior, the Gospel of glad tidings is regularly preached. Its life-giving power is manifested in the marked revolution which is going on in their tastes and habits, and in the change of their customs. Christian communities are being gathered together; civilized and Christian institutions are formed, and are extending themselves. Christianity has made itself felt in the family, in the domestic relations of life, in trade, in law, in the

* The "British Squadron on the Coast of Africa": by the Rev. J. Leighton Wilson, an American Missionary, p. 24.

"modus operandi" of their Governments. Thousands of children are now regularly receiving instruction in our holy religion, and the enlightenment which comes from mental training.* Already one highschool has furnished a score and more of catechists and teachers; has produced three native young men, fit candidates for holy orders in the Church, who are preaching the Gospel to their own kith and kin in heathen darkness. This same school—the Fourah Bay Institution—has now a dozen young men fit candidates for holy orders; and another set of youths trained in the languages and in science, also preparing for sacred duties and the ministerial call. At another place on the coast, two other high schools are already in operation; two colleges, one on a large scale, are projected, and will soon commence operations. Indeed, so great, so increasing, and so important are the spiritual interests of the nations, that the Episcopal Church of America is now strengthening all its posts on the coast of Africa; and, to use the words of its Foreign Secretary, in a letter to myself, she expects that the Church there, that is, in Liberia, will soon be permanently established; and last year she commissioned a Bishop to head her movements in the mission there, in the Republic of Liberia. And since the consecration of Bishop Payne, the mother Church of England has met the needs and the demands of your own missions and African colonies by the consecration of the Bishop of Sierra Leone.

* Mr. Wilson says, (p. 24,) "more than 10,000 youths are now receiving a Christian instruction in the schools connected with the missions."

III. In the third and last place, I beg to direct your attention to the unusual spiritual solicitude now everywhere manifest in the Negro race.

This characteristic has had its chief manifestation during the half-century which has just expired, and seems peculiar to it. There is a stirring up now in the spiritual desires and yearnings of this race, such as the world has never before witnessed. From every side we hear the earnest call, from yearning hearts, for Christian light. There is no quarter of the globe, where the children of Africa are gathered together, but where we see this trait of character more discovered than any other. Indeed, risking the imputation of partiality of race, I think I may say that religious susceptibility and moral dispositions are the more marked characteristics of the Negro family, and the main point in which they differ from other races. There is a peculiar fact which proves this point: where the white man goes he first builds a bank or a trading-house: the first effort of the black man is to erect a meeting-house. The enlightenment of the one seeks, first of all, to express itself in mere civilization: the native disposition of the other tends toward some religious manifestation.

During the last few years there has been a more than usual—a most marked expression of these features of character. We have the testimony of West Indian pastors, missionaries, and teachers, to the eager craving of the African peasantry for instruction. In America, the gravest hindrances cannot repress this desire; and among the free black population, I can testify from personal acquaintance and observation that this, the religious solicitude, is the master principle of that people. Turn to Africa, and there we see almost fulfilled the prediction of the Prophet—"The Gentiles shall come to thy light, and kings to the brightness of thy rising." * I doubt much whether, if ever, the history of missions has discovered such a wide-spread and earnest seeking for Christian knowledge, as is seen among the Pagan tribes on that suffering coast. A missionary on his way down the coast, lands at a certain spot. The news of a God-man, as they term him, having come, flies like lightning through the neighborhood. Three kings visit him; several chiefs bring him their sons, and desire him to take them under his care for instruction; numbers of the people assemble, all expressing their sorrow that he will not abide with them, and teach them. When Mr. Freeman went some two hundred miles in the interior to visit the king of Ashantee, the whole kingdom was thrown into excitement. "Never since the world began," said the king, "has there been an English missionary in Ashantee before." Thousands of troops attended him on his approach to the sable monarch; and in the midst of the grossest superstition and most cruel rites, the ambassador of Christ was received with the most marked respect; and full permission was given him to establish Christian institutions in the capital of the kingdom.† All along the coast where missions are established, kings and princes and great men are bringing their children

---

* Isaiah lx. 3.
† See "Journal of various Visits to the kingdoms of Ashantee, &c.," by the Rev. Thomas B. Freeman.

forward to be trained up in our holy faith. I do not know of a single mission but where there are two or three or more of these youthful princes, who are intrusted to the care of these missionaries. Sometimes their parents come from the far interior with their children—so great is their desire; and so numerous are the requests of this kind, that, not unfrequently, the missionaries are obliged to decline receiving them. In several cases they have sacrificed their parental feelings—parted with their little ones, and sent them across the ocean for instruction. In England, at the present time, there cannot be less than a hundred Negro children at school, in different parts of the country. Nor does this solicitude spend itself in anxieties for the young only—it is fully participated in by the adult population. The missionary, wherever he goes from his station, is sure to get a large, patient, inquiring auditory, whether in a hut, or in a rude heathen temple, or in the temporary Christian Church, or beneath the shade of the palm, upon the passing highway. Sometimes the chief of a tribe refuses an escort through to a neighboring town, lest the missionary should stay with the other people and not come back and proclaim the good news to him and his people. At times it is both ludicrous and tearful to hear of a missionary being kept captive by a heathen king, for fear that, should he suffer him to depart, he might never come back again to preach the Gospel. It is only last year that the people of a village formed a stratagem to keep a travelling missionary to themselves. They attempted to bribe his boatmen to go away, so that he would be obliged to remain with them. And what is singular is, that this desire for the Gospel, vague, undefined, and ignorant as it surely is, comes from every quarter—from the north and the south, the east and the west. The missionaries on the Gambia find themselves utterly unable to meet the earnest solicitations of the Foulahs, the Jalofs, and other tribes in Senegambia. The American missionaries in Liberia are pleading with tears for more help—for more teachers —for more clergymen. The call is so earnest at Lagos, at Abbeokuta, and in the interior from the banks of the Niger, that Mr. Townsend sends the cry across the ocean for a band of many missionaries; and the Church Missionary Society is using every possible effort to meet the call.*

At Calabar, and at the Gaboon, the missionaries have been obliged to refuse the earnest request of the natives for more teachers and ministers. You are, doubtless, aware of the fact that the chiefs in South Africa, in many places—chiefs representing tens of thousands of needy men, have gone hundreds of miles to the Bishop of Cape Town for teachers and clergymen,—yea, have written across the ocean to the Queen, pleading for help. And Dr. Krapf, that modern Paul, has the kings of mighty nations in Zanguebar—nations extending four and five hundred miles in the interior, numbering millions of people—

* The *root* of all this disposition seems to be the yearning of the native African for a *higher* religion; and it is illustrated by the singular fact that Mohammedanism is rapidly and *peaceably* spreading all through the tribes of Western Africa, even to the Christian settlements of Liberia.

begging him to come and settle in their midst; and he is almost the only man in East Africa, to meet the demand!

I have brought these facts before you, Christian friends and brethren, because to my mind they assume a most marked importance, and seem to me to have a most clear and striking significance. It is but probable that to your minds their import may seem less weighty, and that through peculiarity of position, my own view of them may appear exaggerated. I think, however, that a few considerations will show that I ought not to be regarded as sanguine; and will cause the remarks I have made to stand out before your own minds as possessing an almost wondrous significance, and as being among the first marked fulfilments of the prophecy, that "Ethiopia shall soon stretch out her hands unto God." Just look at these facts—note the great progress of the African race. See the civil and religious improvement they have made alike in Africa and in the lands of their captivity. Mark the religious solicitude they are manifesting on every hand. Observe the peculiar providences which are just now occurring in connection with them; and then remember that nearly all these events, all this progress, has taken place during the short period of fifty years; while in all the centuries past of the race, from the very dawn of history, the intellect, the moral nature, society, and civil government, had remained dormant and inert! In his "History of the Decline and Fall of Rome," Gibbon remarks that "the rude ignorance of the Negro has never invented any effectual weapons of defence or of destruction: they appear incapable of forming any extensive plan of government, or of conquest; and the obvious inferiority of their mental faculties has been discovered and abused by the nations of the temperate zone." * Gibbon made this assertion as a fact of history, not many years before the commencement of this century. Never before had the nations beheld any thing the reverse of his description. Nigh thirty centuries of the world's existence had rolled along, and yet an almost palpable gloom had brooded over the multitudinous masses of that thickly crowded continent. During the flight of those dark ages, not a healthful motion was given to the almost deadened life of its crowded population. The discoveries of Columbus took place, the Reformation ensued, and the art of printing was invented. These events revived the languid pulse of Europe, and stirred into activity the energies and skill of India, and broke up the perpetual solitudes of America, and poured therein life, civilization, and enlightenment.

But to my poor father-land they brought chains and slavery, and the cruel desolations and the harrowing atrocities of the slave trade, and the untold horrors of the mid-passage, and a deeper depth of misery and anguish than Africa had ever known in all her dark histories before. And thus from 1562, down to the commencement of this century, the dark and bloody history of Africa was lengthened out and

---

* Book 5. In quoting this remark, I would be understood as referring it to the tribes and nations south of the desert only.

prolonged, with, alas! aggravations and intensities unknown in all her long previous eras.

And now but fifty years have elapsed, and all this history is being reversed. The dark curtain is removed, and a brighter scene meets the view. God seems to have compressed in this single half-century the work and the blessings of thousands of years.

And now I say that, looking at these facts as they stand before us—comparing them with the history of Africa, nigh three thousand years of a previous era—they appear marked, distinct, and marvellous. I say, that if the providences of God may be regarded as indications of His purposes and will; then, inasmuch as *these* providences are, in a marked degree, peculiar, so we may regard them as highly significant.

I am aware that it is the part of a wise man not to be too sanguine. I know, too, that, looking at the untold, the unknown millions in Central Africa, upon whom the eyes of civilized man have never fallen, the work is yet but begun. But when I note the rapidity of God's work during the brief period I have mentioned, and know that God allows no obstacles to stand against Him and His cause, whether it be a pestilential shore, or a violent population, or a sanguinary king, or vindictive slave-dealers, or a slave-trading town like that of Lagos; when I see these things, I cannot but believe that we are now approaching the fulfilment of this prophecy. When I see, moreover, how this great continent is invested on every side by the zealous ardent missionary or the adventurous traveller; how, almost weekly, something is brought to our ears across the ocean, of new discovery, or of startling incident; how that now there is every probability that soon the very heart of that continent, and all its centuries of mystery, will be revealed to the gaze and scrutiny of the civilized world; and then, that by the common road, by trade, by commerce, by the flying wings of steamers, by caravans, by converted Africans, by civilized and pious Negroes, from the West Indies or America, the Bible, the Prayer-Book, and Tracts, and the Church in all her functions and holy offices, will almost at once be introduced among the mighty masses of its population;—when I see these things, my heart is filled with confident assurance—I cannot but believe that the day of Africa's redemption fast draweth nigh! And vast and extensive as the work may be, it seems that it will be a most rapid one; every thing gives this indication: for first, you will notice, that since the abolition of the slave trade, this race, in all its homes, has been going forward: it has had nowhere any retrograde movements. And next, you will notice, that the improvement of this race, social, civil, and religious, has been remarkably quick, and has been, almost all, included in a very brief period; and therefore I think that the work of evangelization in this race will be a rapid one. So God, at times, takes "the staff of accomplishment" into His own hand, and fulfils His ends with speed. The children of Israel were thirty-nine years performing a journey, which could have been accomplished in a few days: but in the fortieth year they marched a longer distance than all the years preceding, and entered, in a few weeks, at once, into the Promised

Land. So God, now, unseen to human eyes, may be leading on His hosts to a mighty victory over Satan; and in the briefest of all the periods of the Church's warfare, may intend to accomplish the most brilliant and consummate of all His triumphs. And this is my conviction with regard to Africa. In my soul I believe that the time has come. I have the strongest impression of the nigh approach of her bright day of deliverance. The night, I am convinced—the night of forlornness, of agony and desolation—is far spent, the day is at hand! The black charter of crime and infamy and blood, which for nigh three centuries, has given up my father-land to the spoiler, is about to be erased! The malignant lie, which would deliver up an entire race, the many millions of a vast continent, to rapine and barbarism and benightedness, is now to be blotted out! And if I read the signs of the times aright—if I am not deceived in supposing that now I see God's hand graciously opened for Africa—if to my sight now appear, with undoubted clearness,

———" the baby forms
Of giant figures yet to be," .

what a grand reversal of a dark destiny will it not be for poor bleeding Africa! What a delightful episode from the hopeless agony of her unmitigated, unalleviated suffering! For ages hath she lain beneath the incubus of the "demon of her idolatry." For ages hath she suffered the ravages of vice, corruption, iniquity, and guilt. For ages hath she been "stricken and smitten" by the deadly thrusts of murder and hate, revenge and slaughter. Fire, famine, and the sword have been her distressful ravaging visitations. War, with devastating stride, has ravaged her fair fields, and peopled her open and voracious tombs. The slave trade—that fell destroyer! has fired the hamlets of her children—has sacked her cities—has turned the hands of her sons upon each other—and set her different communities at murderous strife, and colored their hands with fraternal blood! Yea, every thing natural has been changed into the monstrous; and all things harmonious turned into discord and confusion. Earth has had her beauty marred by the bloody track of the cruel men who have robbed my father-land of her children: and the choral voice of ocean, which should lift up naught but everlasting symphonies in the ears of angels and of God, has been made harsh and dissonant, by the shrieks and moans and agonizing cries of the poor victims, who have either chosen a watery grave in preference to slavery, or else have been cast into its depths, the sick and the emaciated, by the ruthless slave-dealer! And then, when landed on the distant strand—the home of servitude, the seat of oppression—then has commenced a system of overwork and physical endurance, incessant and unrequited—a series of painful tasks, of forced labor, of want and deprivation, and lashings, and premature deaths, continued from generation to generation, transmitted as the only inheritance of poor, helpless humanity, to children's children!

But now there is a new spirit abroad—not only in the Christian world, but likewise through the different quarters of her own broad continent. There is an uprising of her sons from intellectual sloth and spritual inertness; a seeking and a stretching forth of her hands, for light, instruction, and spirituality, such as the world has never before seen; and which gives hopes that the days of Cyprian and Augustine shall again return to Africa; when the giant sins and the deadly evils, which have ruined her, shall be effectually stayed; and when Ethiopia, from the Atlantic to the Indian Ocean—from the Mediterranean to the Cape, "shall stretch out her hands unto God!"

But it may be asked, What relation have the remarks I have made this evening, to the subject of the Ladies' Negro Emancipation Society? Much every way: and I proceed now to point out this relation, and the obligation which it appears to me to ensue thereon.

I have endeavored to show this evening that God is laying bare His arm just now for Africa and the Negro race;—is bringing to a rapid end their long and grievous servitude;—and is showing, in His mysterious providence, that, however grievous, in the past, to flesh and blood, has been their lot, that He meant it for good. Now the Almighty has placed a very considerable section of this race under your care, control, and government. They inhabit all those islands in the Caribbean Sea, which have come into your possession by discovery, or which have been purchased by the heroic sacrifice of blood, or won by bravery or prowess. They are the dwellers of some of the most productive portions of the globe, lying in the bright and genial bounds of the tropics.

They are the laboring population of lands which yield those articles, once termed luxuries, but which are now the most important and lucrative articles of commerce. And they are the peasantry of provinces which soon will be the high road of the globe—the central depots of the world's trade; and through which, ere long, will be poured the vast and magnificent treasures of the East.

These islands must, without doubt, be held in high estimation by you as their owners and proprietors. It may be, however, that you have adopted the new and current dogma, that is, that colonies are a useless, costly burden, which should be disposed of as soon as possible; and, if you have, then there is no need that I should further press this subject upon your attention. But if you have not adopted this opinion, and if you *do* value your colonial possessions, then you must see the need that these people —the Negro peasantry—should be trained to be honest, moral, industrious, intelligent, and thrifty. But in order that they may become fixed in moral and industrious habits, they must receive a moral and religious training. Heretofore, as you know, the school in which they have been educated was the school of slavery—a school which yields naught but the productive spawn of vice, and sloth, and ignorance, and superstition—a school in which indolence was respectability, and labor was degradation and vileness. Since emancipation, however, vigorous efforts have been made to extend to them the advantages of education. To a very large extent this has been done by the Ladies' Negro Emancipation

Society, with zeal and with success; for hundreds of schools have been founded by them, thousands of children have been instructed, churches and chapels have been called into existence, and teachers and ministers have been supplied. These have been the direct and the indirect results of this Society's efforts. But what is remarkable is, that while the wide and merciful blessings of this Society have been falling "like gentle dew from heaven" upon the objects of its benevolence, its work has been silently done; its operations have been carried on quietly and unostentatiously; so much so, indeed, that thousands of intelligent persons do not know of even the *existence* of the Ladies' Negro Emancipation Society. But however much like gentle woman it may be that these generous Christian ladies should thus, at once, "silent and unseen," exert themselves, it can be so no longer. Events have occurred which drive them before the public, and which require them to make most earnest appeals for aid. Formerly they were aided by grants from Government and from the Colonial Legislatures, and they received considerable contributions from the emancipated blacks themselves. But now the sad wreck of pecuniary resources, the blight of bankruptcy which has fallen upon the West India proprietors, has completely cut off these sources of aid and assistance. The planters and the Local Government can no longer help them; the Home Government has withdrawn its grants. And though I must say, as my firm belief and conviction—a conviction founded on a careful study of reports and documents—that amid the general wreck the black population, *on the whole*, is rising, yea, in some places, rising on the ruins of the planters,* yet it is also the sad fact, that, in some places, they are going down to ruin with the proprietors: a ruin, alas! which

* This I believe to be a true statement of the case: the black population generally, are advancing, to the disadvantage of the planters. The West Indian party in this country, and the pro-slavery party in the United States, maintain, that emancipation is a failure, and that the black population are fast degenerating into barbarism. As proof of this, they refer to JAMAICA:—in the other islands the proprietors have suffered but little; but in Jamaica there has been an almost utter prostration of this class. The inference drawn from this is, that emancipation is a failure.

A few items will enable us to see whether this representation is altogether correct:

1. For whose benefit was emancipation effected? For the planting population only, or the black also? The census of the island of Jamaica will help decide this matter, if even the past history and injuries of the Negro race do not. According to the received estimate of 1850, of the 400,000 people in the island, 16,000 were white, and 384,000 black and colored. It is but fair, then, that this large black and colored population should have a very considerable interest in the results of emancipation.

2. Have the black and colored population received any advantage through emancipation? In 1833, they were, nearly all, "chattels," "marketable commodities," poor, penniless,—not even possessing themselves. Is their condition any better now? I answer this question, by quoting from a valuable and impartial work entitled "JAMAICA IN 1850," by J. Bigelow, Esq., an American gentleman. He says: "I was surprised to find how general was the desire among the Negroes to become possessed of a little land, and upon what sound principles that was based," (see p. 115.) "I was greatly surprised to find the number of these colored proprietors—OVER ONE HUNDRED THOUSAND, and constantly increasing," (p. 116.) "When one reflects that only sixteen years ago there was scarcely a colored landholder upon the island, and that now there are a hundred thousand, it is unnecessary to say that this class of the population appreciate the privileges of free labor, and a homestead, &c.," (p. 116.) "They raise not only what they require for their own consumption, but a surplus which they take to market, &c., &c.," (p. 117.) "Of course it requires no little self-denial and energy for a Negro, upon the wages now paid in

involves the wreck of immortal souls, with the lesser evil of confused and disastrous material interests. And surely this melancholy state of affairs cannot

Jamaica, to lay up enough with which to purchase one of these properties," (p. 118.)

3. POLITICAL POWER. "The political power of the island is rapidly passing into the same hands, (the black people's.) The possession of four or five acres of land confers a right to vote on the selection of members of Assembly. The blacks are ambitious to possess and exercise this privilege; it causes them to be courted and respected. It is only a short time since there were no colored people returned to that body. *In the last Assembly there were a* DOZEN. No Negro ever had a seat there till the session before the last, when one was returned. In the last session there were three. It is safe to say, that in a very few years the blacks and browns will be in a clear majority. They already hold the balance of power," (p. 157.)

4. DISTINGUISHED NEGROES AND COLORED MEN. "One of the most distinguished barristers on the island is a colored man, who was educated at an English University, and ate his terms at Lincoln's Inn," (p. 23.) Speaking of the Surrey Assize, he says, (p. 25:) "Two colored lawyers were sitting at the barristers' table, and the jury-box was occupied by twelve men, all but three of whom were colored."

In a statement made by G. W. ALEXANDER, of London, who recently visited the West Indies, I find that there are between 30 and 40,000 black voters in Jamaica.

The Rev. Mr. Dowding, who has lived many years in the West Indies, thus speaks of the black population in general: "They are now in the fullest career of improvement, and after knowledge of them, as parishioners, both young and old, in the school, in the family, and at the sick bedside, it is impossible not to call them a most promising people; intelligent, orderly, and (for the most part) religious.

"It is not necessary for our purpose that we should make out a case, and I have no wish to hide either their foibles or their faults. It would be strange indeed if they had not both; but let it be remembered that *within the last twenty years* these people were salable like the brutes that perish; suffered (almost encouraged) to live as the brutes; and it needs must be considered a most significant fact, that they have risen to the requirements of their condition so rapidly, and taken possession of

but have its due and powerful influence upon your minds and upon your charity.

But besides this claim upon your interest, your generosity, and your zeal, as Englishmen, there is another earnest consideration, and one which appeals to you on a higher principle, that is, as Christians.

When I commenced my remarks I said that it was a cherished idea of many of the supporters of this Society, that their labors might eventually tell upon Africa. Christian friends, this is no longer a mere idea. It is, in very deed, one of the results

their freedom with so little effort. Whilst in these regions many are still thinking of the Negro as an animal who wears a monkey-face, and says 'massa,' with just wit enough to be cunning, and just English enough to lie, there is a race growing up in those Western Islands, seemly in their bearing, and very often handsome, (civilization and improvement fast *creolizing* their features, and effacing the uncomeliness of the African type;) their peasants as intelligent and intelligible as our own; their advanced classes already a powerful *bourgeoisie*, of whose future position we have an instalment in *this*, that even now (and I pray it be carefully marked) it has its merchants, its barristers, its clergymen, its magistrates, its members of Assembly, and (even) its members of Council."—" Africa in the West," by Rev. W. C. Dowding, M. A.

Both Mr. Dowding and Mr. Bigelow speak impartially of the character of the West Indian blacks, and mention their failings as well as their virtues; yet their common testimony evidences the improvement of my race in the British West Indies. But why is it, it may be asked, that so many writers declare emancipation a failure, and that the Negro race is degenerating? The reasons are briefly these: 1. Because most persons think that the *only* important parties in the British West Indies, are the planters; and consequently that the ruin of this small item of the population, is the ruin of the population itself; forgetful of the fact that their numbers are inconsiderable; that they have always been in pecuniary embarrassment; and above all that, *from the nature of the case*, there is no hope for slave-holders: they must go to ruin!

which God's providence has already wrought, in a partial degree, for Africa, through your West Indian islands. The ways of God are most mysterious—past finding out! He sees what man's short sight cannot perceive; and takes the direst human workings into his own hands, for enlarged and most beneficent ends. And herein we may see the plastic power and the transforming energy of that perfect wisdom and that omnipotent hand, which knoweth all things, and which worketh as it wills, His own great ends. It seems now quite clear that the children of that very people, who for nearly three centuries have been passing through the dread ordeal of slavery in your West Indian colonies, are yet to be the special messengers of glad tidings to their father-land. Already several missionary companies of black men from your islands have gone to the land of their fathers. One case I may mention: some African converts from Jamaica, feeling that they ought to do something for their father-land, went, four years ago, as teachers, to the Calabar, at the mouth of the Niger; and already as the first fruits of their labors, the king of one of the small tribes has been converted, and is attempting to introduce civilized habits, and has already established the observance of the Sabbath. Indeed, so important has this movement become, that a Society has been formed, as I have before remarked, to give it form, order, system, and distinctness; and there is every probability that soon it will become one of the great colonizing movements of this colonizing age, with this difference, that is, *that it will be conducted on a* PRINCIPLE, *and that it will have as its main object the* GLORY OF GOD!

The train of thought I have presented this evening furnishes ground, I think, for the following suggestions:

1. It shows, *first* of all, that the Negro race possesses strong vital power. I think the facts to which I have already called your attention evince this: they show that, amid the most distressful allotments, this race clings to life; and that God has most benignantly cared for them, in times past, notwithstanding all their fiery trials. The contrast between this people, in this respect, and some others, is most striking. Wherever European civilization has been planted, there generally the natives have vanished, as the morning mist before the rising of the sun. The Indians of North America are fast fading away. The natives of Van Dieman's Land are gone. The many millions that once peopled the clustering islands of the West Indian Archipelago have vanished before the presence and the power of the white man, and will never again return from the deep repose of the tomb, until they arise at the final day for accusation as well as for judgment. The aborigines of the South Sea islands, of New Zealand, of Australia, are departing, like the shadow, before the rising sun of the Anglo-Saxon emigrant. It is said that no statesmanship, no foresight, no Christian benevolence can preserve the Sandwich Islanders. There is something exceedingly sorrowful in this funereal procession of the weak portions of mankind, before the advancing progress of civilization and en-

lightenment! But amid all these sad general facts there seems to be one exception—the NEGRO! The ravages of the slave trade would seem sufficient to produce extermination: the mid-passage alone is enough to destroy any people! It has not destroyed the vitality of the Negro! The vast interior of Africa teems with the countless millions of an unnumbered population; and in the land of the Negro's enthralment, the race increases with a rapidity which surprises the keenest calculator, and which carries fear to the heart of the oppressor. These facts I take and mention as indications that Divine Providence designs a FUTURE for this people. They appear to me tokens and evidences that this particular section of the human species is not doomed to destruction, but that the elevation, the civilization, the evangelization of the Negro are determined purposes of the Divine mind for the future. "Ethiopia SHALL stretch forth her hands unto God."

2. The remarks I have made show us, in the second place, that God has given this race a *strong moral character*.

Although the Christian zeal and endeavor of the Church are by no means to be determined by the richness or the hardness of the soil in which the truth is to be planted, still it is cause of great encouragement, and an incentive to higher effort, when we find a people in whose nature there is congruity, so far as that *can* be in wretched humanity, with the spirit of our Holy Faith, and who desire the possession of it. The Negro race manifests this peculiar trait of character: it is a race, I think I may say, remarkably

among the charities of England; and therefore, as a son of Africa, deeply interested in the welfare of a race which, of all others, may be called the "suffering race," anxious that the precious things of Jesus may be known of them for comfort and for consolation, I venture to ask you this evening most generous contributions to this important Society, and a zealous, affectionate interest in Africa and the Negro race. If an English Christian grieves at the remembrance of wrongs inflicted upon Africa;—if his deepest sensibilities are affected at the darkness and the sin which still prevails through all her borders;—if he anxiously desires the spread of the Gospel through all her quarters;—if he wishes to see her sons, in every part of the earth, stand up erect, blessed with the liberty wherewith the Gospel makes men free; then, I say, that by participating in the labors, and sharing the burdens of this Society, he is privileged, in the Divine providence, to realize, to a measurable degree, all his desires. For thereby he can be giving to the children of Africa the best compensation, even the Gospel; and be turning back the stream of misery into a tide of blessing; and joining in with God in directing most marvellous purposes, and proclaiming abroad, through those who—by birth and color, by the sympathy of suffering, by common hopes and aspirations—seem pointed out as the fittest agents, the marvels of that grace, and the wondrous efficacy of that blood, and the power of that name which is above every name —even of Him "who is above all, and through all, and in you all." "To whom," &c.

docile, affectionate, easily attached, and when attached, ardently devoted—a race with the strongest religious feelings, sentiments, and emotions—a race plastic in nature, with a native mobility and adaptedness which at once saves them from those deadly shocks and antagonisms which destroy races when placed in juxtaposition with elements diverse from and stronger than their own—a race patient and enduring; ambitious as any other for freedom; but when, in the stern collisions of this forceful, heartless life of ours, stricken down by the iron hand of mere brute power, not given to despair, but content to use the genial teachings of Hope, and to wait for the future, in calm abidance and with confident assurance. These elements of character—these qualities and dispositions, show that God has kindly bestowed a nature upon this race, which is a gracious preparation for the entrance of His Gospel—a nature which seems the highest *natural* type of Christian requirement.

3. I remark, in the last place, that in His gifts of nature and in His preserving favor upon my race, we may see the training hand of God upon them, in all their scattered homes, for high ends and purposes, in the future, and also the Church's opportunity and her duty.

I need not dwell upon this point, for I have already, in a general way, disclosed the wondrous providences of God upon the race, in every quarter of the globe where they are living. Dark and dreary has been their way through their many avenues of pain, and distress, and agony, during the long centuries of their distressful pilgrimage, and yet they have not been deserted of God. Surely their history warrants the affirmation that "the angel of His presence saved them;" and now, when all His purposes of trial and of training, of suffering and of sorrow, are well nigh fulfilled, the Almighty casts down all the barriers of restraint: a light seems of a sudden to shine into their dark prison-house, and a divine voice to say unto them, "Arise up quickly; and their chains fall off from their hands;"* and a mission appears to be given them, whether in Sierra Leone, or the West Indies, or America, to start up from the ashes, and go forth to their needy kin in heathenism:—"Go stand and speak . . . to the people all the words of this life." †

This aspect of the matter, that is, God's training of the people for His own great work in Africa, I have brought before you already in preceding remarks; and in it you can easily see the importance of your black West Indian population with reference to Africa, and likewise the Church's opportunity and duty for the glory of God and the honor of our Lord Jesus Christ. You see herein also the great value and importance of this Society for which I am pleading. In aiding the Society, you are not only building up your own possession, but you are also becoming co-workers with God in some of His greatest purposes. In contributing to the funds of this association, you touch, with a gracious saving influence, the needy people of two hemispheres. In joining in the labors of these benevolent ladies, you are evangelizing both the West Indies and Africa.

I repeat, therefore, that this is one of the chief

* Acts xii. 7. † Acts v. 20.

EXAMINATION, ETC.*

The chief object of this paper is to show the falsity of the opinion that the sufferings and the slavery of the Negro race are the consequence of the curse of Noah, as recorded in Genesis ix. 25. That this is a general, almost universal, opinion in the Christian world, is easily proven. During the long controversy upon the slavery question which has agitated Christendom, no argument has been so much relied upon, and none more frequently adduced. It was first employed in vindication of the lawfulness of the slave

---

* This paper was originally written as a letter, in reply to another from an eminent philanthropic lady in Cheltenham, England. She communicated it to the then Editor of the London "Christian Observer," in which monthly it was published in September, 1852. Subsequent to this, in compliance with the request of many persons, it was rewritten and prepared, in its present form, for publication as a tract. Perhaps the Author may be permitted to say here, that it has had the advantage of being read by the late Rev. G. Stanley Faber, D. D., of Sherburne, the distinguished author of many learned works, who expressed his approbation of it, and presented the writer with his learned and able work, "Prophetical Dissertations," in which the writer found that Mr. Faber had, several years ago, taken the same view of Gen. ix. 25, as is contained in this article.

trade. When the slave trade was abolished, and philanthropists commenced their warfare against the system of slavery, the chief pro-slavery argument brought forward in support of that system was this text. The friends of the Negro race have had to meet it when asserted by statesmen in the Legislature, and they have had to contend against the earnest affirmation of it by learned divines. And now, although both slavery and the slave trade are condemned by the general sentiment of the Christian world, yet the same interpretation is still given to this text, and the old opinion which was founded on it still gains credit and receives support. Its insidious influence relaxes the missionary zeal of even many pious persons, who can see no hope for Africa, nor discover any end to the slavery of its sons. It is found in books written by learned men; and it is repeated in lectures, speeches, sermons, and common conversation. So strong and tenacious is the hold which it has taken upon the mind of Christendom, that it seems almost impossible to uproot it. Indeed, it is an almost foregone conclusion, that the Negro race is an accursed race, weighed down, even to the present, beneath the burden of an ancestral malediction. The prejudice against this race seems as wide, as absolute, and as decided, as that entertained by the Jews against the Samaritans.

2. THE OPINIONS OF COMMENTATORS AND THEOLOGICAL WRITERS.

A very few references to writers in the past and at the present will show the prejudiced views of even

THE
NEGRO RACE NOT UNDER A CURSE.

An Examination of Genesis ix. 25.

REPRINTED, WITH CORRECTIONS AND ADDITIONS, FROM
THE LONDON "CHRISTIAN OBSERVER" OF
SEPTEMBER, 1850.

"And God blessed Noah and his sons."—Gen. ix. 1.

"And God spake unto Noah, and to his sons *with him*, saying, And I, behold, I establish my covenant with you and with your seed after you. * * * * And God said, This is the token of the covenant which I make between me and you, and every living creature that is with you, for perpetual generations."—Gen. ix. 8, 12.

"And in thy seed shall all the kindreds of the earth be blessed."
—Acts iii. 25.

"And there shall be no more curse."—Rev. xxii. 3.

eminently good men upon this topic. POOLE admits the primary and pointed application of the curse to Canaan; he also acknowledges the subsequent power and greatness of the other three sons of Ham, and the spiritual blessedness which ultimately attended them; yet, with singular inconsistency, in another place, he involves Ham, the father, in the curse, which he declares to have been pointed at his son Canaan. He says: "When Canaan is mentioned, *Ham* is not exempted from the curse, but rather more deeply plunged into it; whilst he is pronounced accursed, not only in his person, (which is manifestly supposed by his commission of that sin for which the curse was inflicted,) but also in his posterity, which doubtless was a great aggravation of his grief." *

The learned and pious MATTHEW HENRY says: "He (that is, Noah) pronounces a curse on Canaan, the son of Ham, in whom Ham himself is cursed; either because this son of his was now more guilty than the rest, or because the posterity of this son were afterward to be rooted out of their land, to make room for Israel." † Again, in another place, speaking of the division of the families of the earth, he says: "The birthright was now to be divided between Shem and Japheth, *Ham being utterly discarded.*"

BISHOP NEWTON, in the first place, applies this prophecy to Canaan and his descendants; but he afterward gives a fanciful correction of the text, on the authority of the Septuagint and the Arabic version; and then asks: "May we not suppose that the copy-

* Poole on Gen. ix. 25.
† See Henry's Commentary on Gen. ix. 25.

ist, by mistake, wrote only *Canaan,* instead of *Ham, the father of Canaan,* and that the whole passage was originally thus: And Ham, the father of Canaan, saw the nakedness of his father, &c. &c. And he said, Cursed be Ham, the father of Canaan, &c.?" He then goes on to remark: "By this reading all the three sons of Noah are included in the prophecy, whereas otherwise Ham, who was the offender, is excluded, or is only punished in one of his children. . . . . The whole continent of Africa was peopled principally by the children of Ham; and for how many ages have the better parts of that country lain under the dominion of the Romans, and then of the Saracens, and now of the Turks! In what wickedness, ignorance, barbarity, slavery, misery, live most of the inhabitants! And of the poor Negroes, how many hundreds every year are sold and bought like beasts in the market, and are conveyed from one quarter of the world to do the work of beasts in another! Nothing can be more complete than the execution of the sentence upon *Ham,* as well as upon Canaan."*

The excellent Rev. THOMAS SCOTT says: "The frequent mention of Ham as the father of Canaan, suggests the thought that the latter was also criminal. . . . . . . Ham must have felt it a very mortifying rebuke, when his own father was inspired, on this occasion, to predict the durable oppression and slavery of his posterity; Canaan was also rebuked by learning that the curse would especially rest on that branch of the family which would descend from him; for his posterity were no doubt *principally,* though not *ex-*

---

* See Newton on Prophecies, Dissertation I.

clusively, intended. . . . . . . True religion has hitherto flourished very little among Ham's descendants; they remain to this day almost entire strangers to Christianity, and their condition, in every age, has remarkably coincided with this prediction." *

Similar views are expressed by KEITH, who remarks: "The unnatural conduct of Ham, and the dutiful and respectful behavior of Shem and Japheth toward their aged father, gave rise to the prediction of the future fate of their posterity, without being at all assigned as the cause of that fate. . . . . Though long banished from almost all Europe, slavery still lingers in Africa. That country is distinguished, above every other, as the land of slavery. Slaves at home, and transported for slavery, the poor Africans, the descendants of Ham, are the servants of servants, or slaves to others." †

In a popular work much used in the schools and the universities of England, this comment upon the curse of Noah is found: "These prophecies (Gen. ix. 25–27) have since been wonderfully fulfilled; the Egyptians were afflicted with various plagues; the land of *Canaan*, eight hundred years afterward, was delivered by God into the hands of the Israelites under Joshua, who destroyed great numbers, and obliged the rest to fly, some into Africa, and others into various countries; what their condition is in Africa, we know at this day." ‡

---

* Scott on Gen. ix. 24, 25.
† See Keith on the Prophecies.
‡ Analysis of Scripture History, by Rev. W. H. Pinnock, B. C. L.
"*What their condition is in Africa, we know at this day.*" *Whose* con-

The Rev. Dr. Cumming, of London, thus discourses upon this subject:

"Read the predictions respecting *Ham*, that his descendants, the children of Africa, should be bondsmen of bondsmen. England nobly sacrificed twenty millions, in order to wash her hands of the heinous crime and horrible abominations of slavery, and sent her cruisers to sweep the seas of every craft that ventured to encourage the inhuman traffic. But while God is not the author of sin, nor man irresponsible for his crimes, slavery has grown under all the attempts to extinguish it, and shot up in spite of the power of Britain and the piercing protest of outraged humanity, the hour of its extinction not having yet come; thereby showing that heaven and earth may pass away, but that one jot or tittle of God's word cannot pass away." *

3. THE REAL STATE OF THE CASE.

The writer of this paper differs from the distinguished persons here referred to. He regards the prevalent opinions upon this subject a sad perversion of Biblical history on the part of the intelligent minds that have stereotyped them, during the last century and a half, in the literature and theology of the English language.

In considering this subject, there is one material point which should be carefully noticed—a point upon which nearly all writers upon the subject have greatly

---

dition? Some would suppose that Africa was peopled in the mass by Canaanites. Surely this is loose writing, and inaccurate history.

* Exeter Hall Lecture.

erred : THE CURSE WAS PRONOUNCED UPON CANAAN, NOT UPON HAM. "And he said, Cursed be Canaan, a servant of servants shall he be unto his brethren." Gen. ix. 25. This is the utterance of the Divine word, clear, plain, distinct. There may be differences of opinion as to the cause, the nature, the extent, the justice, and the influence of this judgment; but as it respects *the person* who is cursed, the word of God is specific and pointed : " CURSED BE CANAAN ; " and in this we have the curse, *direct*.

No one, indeed, can deny that learned and distinguished divines have thought that *Ham* fell under the dire influence of this strong malediction. The suppositions of such most eminent divines as Poole, and Henry, and Newton, have already been presented. But what are they when contrasted with the distinct and emphatic word of God? They *suppose* that Ham was cursed ; the word of God says, " CURSED BE CANAAN."

But, as though the Holy Spirit intended that there should be no error or mistake in the matter, we find the curse upon Canaan repeated, that is, by implication, again and again, in this same chapter, (chap. ix.,) both in the context and sub-text. In the 18th verse of this (ix.) chapter it is written : " And the sons of Noah, that went forth of the ark, were Shem, and Ham, and Japheth ; and *Ham is the father of Canaan*." Why are Shem and Japheth spoken of *individually*, while Ham is mentioned *in relation to his son Canaan?** Why, there can be no doubt that this

* Mr. Faber asks, "Why Ham should be specially distinguished as the father of Canaan, while, *in the very same prophecy*, his two brothers

form of expression was *designed* to point out *Canaan* as a marked individual.

In verses 26 and 27 we find the same form of expression *twice*, "and Canaan shall be his servant." We now have the curse *indirect*. In both cases, however, it is manifest that Canaan was the person subjected to this curse. Neither directly nor indirectly is Ham, the father, denounced by Noah; and therefore we have the authority of the word of God, for the affirmation that the curse was *not* pronounced upon Ham.*

Now, in order to involve the Negro race in this malediction, one of two things must be proved: either,

1st. That Noah, in mentioning Canaan, intended to include *all* the children of Ham; or,

2d. That the Negro race, in Africa, are the descendants of Canaan.

4. THE WHOLE FAMILY OF HAM NOT ACCURSED.

It cannot be proved that *all* the sons of Ham were included in the curse pronounced upon Canaan. Ham had four sons: "And the sons of Ham, Cush, and Mizraim, and Phut, and Canaan." Gen. x. 6. Ca-

---

are simply mentioned as Shem and Japheth, without any parallel genealogical adjunct to their names." See "Prophetical Dissertations:" Dis. ii. p. 102, note.

* In an old work entitled "The General History of the World," I find the following sentence: "Some have believed that Noah cursed Canaan because he could not well have cursed Ham himself, whom God had not long before blessed." And he refers to Sermon 29, Chrysostom. in Genesis.

naan, it is evident, was the *youngest* of these sons, and Cush the *eldest*.

Now, the common rule among men is that "THE GREATER INCLUDES THE LESS." If, therefore, Cush, the *eldest* of the sons of Ham, had been the person cursed, then there would have been some strength and plausibility in the plea, that, according to this principle, a curse upon him, that is, Cush, as the head and representative of the family, involved a curse upon his three younger brothers. But the curse was upon the youngest, *Canaan*. And there is no received rule among men, the reverse of that here quoted, that is, that "the less includes the greater."

So, also, if Ham himself had been the person designated by Noah, then all disputation upon this matter would be, at once, at an end; for then the inference would be natural, legitimate, and indisputable, that *all* his posterity were implicated in the curse which fell upon himself. But this fact is nowhere stated in Scripture. IT DOES, INDEED, RECORD GOD'S BLESSING UPON HAM AND HIS POSTERITY;* although

---

* It is objected to the view taken, in this paper, of Gen. ix. 25, that Ham is left neither blessed nor cursed; and hence divines include him in the curse on Canaan. But it is a singular fact, that all the commentators neglect to notice the fact that Ham had just received a blessing from God.

In Genesis ix. 1, we read: "And God blessed Noah and his sons, and said unto them, Be fruitful," &c., &c. And in verses 8 and 12 it reads: "And God spake unto Noah, and to his sons *with him*, saying, And I, behold, I establish my covenant with you, and with your seed after you. . . . . . And God said, This is the token of the covenant which I make between me and you, and every living creature that is with you, *for perpetual generations.*"

The question here arises, "Does Noah's curse (*incidental to Ham's*

this is universally passed over and ignored; but that he was cursed by Noah is only one of the conjectures of men. In the sacred record we find Canaan's name, and his only, mentioned as the person cursed.

It is mentioned, moreover, in such a way as though the Divine mind intended there should be a marked significance connected with it. For why, when the Scripture narrative is so careful to give the names of Ham's four sons, according to seniority, why is *Canaan's name*—the name of the youngest —selected, singled out, and repeated, no less than *five* different times, in the brief narrative which records this remarkable event?* Surely for no other reason than to mark HIM distinctly as *the* individual referred to, and to separate his three elder brothers from the curse.

The argument of an American writer upon this point is of great force, and deserves notice. He adduces "two rules of law and logic, viz.: enumeration weakens, in cases not enumerated; exceptions strengthen, in cases not excepted. In the curse Canaan is enumerated, and therefore the probability of its application to his brothers is *weakened* by this enumeration, and in the blessings bestowed upon Shem and Japheth, in the next two verses, Canaan, and not Ham and his posterity, is excepted; and therefore the prob-

---

youngest son) override the blessing of God, for perpetual generations, to Ham and his seed, in the general and particular blessings of Gen. ix. 9 and 12? Does the curse of *man* supersede and set aside the *covenanted* blessings of God?

* See Genesis ix. 18, 22, 25, 26, 27.

ability of the exclusive application of the curse to Canaan is strengthened by this exception." *

The testimony of Jósephus accords with this theory. He says: "Noah spared Ham by reason of his nearness of blood, but cursed his posterity; and when the rest of them (*i. e.*, of the children of Ham) escaped that curse, God inflicted it on the children of Canaan.†

This argument is strengthened and confirmed by a reference to the counterpart of this curse, which is seen in God's dealings with the Canaanites. It is seen in those severe commands to the Hebrews on their entrance into the promised land, to expel and destroy the devoted Canaanites. The indictment against this wicked and profane people is written, in fearfully descriptive terms, in the 18th chapter of Leviticus, which enumerates the aggravated crimes on account of which the Almighty was about calling them to judgment.‡ The events which followed, in consequence of the commands of Jehovah to the Hebrews, have always been taken as the fulfilment of this prediction of Noah. By Jew and Christian Gentile, in the early periods of the Church, and in more recent times by writers upon prophecy, and by commentators upon the Bible, the havoc and destruction visited upon the Canaanites have been regarded, not only as a punishment for their wickedness, but also as the counterpart to the prediction of Noah, and as a

---

* I cannot give the name of the writer of the above. I found this extract in the fragment of a newspaper.

† Josephus, "Antiquities of the Jews," B. i. Ch. vi.

‡ See Lev. xviii. 24–28.

complete fulfilment of his prophetic curse upon Canaan.

To sum up, then, we have, for the application and *limitation* of this curse to Canaan and his posterity only, the following facts and arguments:

1. The text of Genesis.
2. Two fundamental rules of law and logic.
3. The testimony of Josephus.
4. The Scriptural account of the fate of the Canaanites.

5. THE NEGRO RACE NOT THE DESCENDANTS OF CANAAN.

But, in reply to the above arguments, it may be said that, granting that the three elder sons of Ham were not under the curse, nevertheless the Negro race may be the descendants of Canaan, and hence under the infliction of this prophetic judgment.

The facts of the case warrant the most positive denial of the assertion that the Negro race are the descendants of Canaan. In fact, of all the sons of Ham, *Canaan was the only one who never entered Africa.* Of this there is abundant evidence, sacred and profane.

The evidence, so far as *Scripture* is concerned, is given us in Gen. x. 19: "And the border of the Canaanites was from Sidon, as thou comest to Gerar, unto Gaza; as thou goest unto Sodom and Gomorrah, and Admah, and Zeboim, even unto Lasha." The locality here designated is evidently the land of Palestine, and in Asia; and in the Pentateuch, this region is frequently called the land of Canaan.

A reference to the names of the descendants of

Canaan will tend to place this still more distinctly before us. In Gen. x. 15–18, we find the following statement : " And Canaan begat Sidon, his first-born, and Heth, and the Jebusite, and the Amorite, and the Girgasite, and the Hivite, and the Arkite," &c., &c. These names, most surely, are not African, nor do they indicate African localities. We recognize in SIDON the name of that city, celebrated in history for its commerce and luxury, which stood on the Mediterranean, at the north of Palestine. The Hittites were the descendants of Heth, and lived in nearly the same quarter. The Jebusites were the descendants of JEBUS, and their locality was the spot on which Jerusalem was built. And the Amorites, Girgasites, &c., are frequently mentioned in the Old Testament as inhabitants of the land of Canaan.

The *profane* historical evidence is brief, but clear, weighty, and decisive: it is the evidence of Josephus, who says : " Canaan, the fourth son of Ham, inhabited the country now called Judea, and called it, from his own name, Canaan." *

It appears, then, from the evidence adduced, that this curse, in its *significance* and LOCALITY, is altogether Asiatic, and not African. Asia was the field on which the Canaanites moved, and whence their history is derived. The Canaanites of old were Asiatics, that is, so far as residence is concerned ; and the mass of their descendants, if existing anywhere, are the modern Syrians.

Again, the above facts and arguments may be opposed by some, by the fact that *some* of the Canaan-

* Josephus, " Antiquities of the Jews," B. i. Ch. vi.

ites established themselves on the north coast of Africa, in a colony. But it is quite evident that the Negro race, which mostly peoples that vast continent, could not have proceeded from them:—

1. Because the establishment of Carthage, the great Phœnician (Canaanitish) colony, was at a late period in the history of the world;* but the permanent division of races had been formed centuries anterior to this event; and the Negro race, as a race, had long before sprung into existence.

2. If this were not the case, the probability is that the great desert would have prevented their being mingled with the mass of the aborigines who live south of the desert; and it is almost certain that the interior of Africa was first reached by the way of Egypt.

3. History informs us that Carthage, a colony, grew up, *by itself*, in one locality; flourished for a space, and then sank to decay; while it does *not* inform us that Carthage was the mother of nations, the founder of a race.

Moreover, the fact should not be forgotten that the blood of the Canaanites was more mingled with that of Europeans than with Africans; for they formed *more* colonies in Europe than in Africa, and their influence was stronger in Europe than in Africa; and they have left behind more numerous marks and monuments of their power in Europe than in Africa. Indeed, almost every vestige of their former might, in Africa, has been obliterated.

* The foundation of Carthage, Utica, Septis, &c., took place, according to Heeren, between 1000—500 B. C. See "Heeren's Historical Researches," Vol. i. Ch. ii.

When the Israelites entered the promised land, they broke up the political establishment of the Canaanites, destroyed large numbers of them, and drove many of them out of the land. These latter went northward, and at first settled in the country called Phœnicia; and from this they received the name Phœnicians. And here it was that the Canaanites gave evidence of being a wonderfully active, enterprising, ingenious, and intellectual people—as much, if not more so, than any people of ancient times. They were a maritime nation, and their adventurous spirit led to the far regions of the North, and southward around the Cape of Good Hope, which they doubled, traversing thence the countries bordering on the Indian Ocean.* They had commercial intercourse all through the Mediterranean Sea. Their ships and trade reached all along the coast of Europe, even beyond the pillars of Hercules, to Britain and Ireland. In many of these places they planted colonies, on both sides of the Mediterranean; carrying with them arts, letters, commerce, and civilization, to people yet rude and uncultivated. It appears to be an established fact that one of their colonies was planted on the coasts of both Spain and Ireland; and thus some of the Celts of the present day may now have some of the blood of the Canaanites flowing through their veins.†

"The establishment of a Canaanitish colony on the coast of Africa is no more evidence that the Afri-

* See Heeren's Historical Researches, Vol. i. Ch. iii.
† See Heeren's Historical Researches, Vol. i. Ch. ii. Also, Ezekiel xxvii.

can race proceeded from Canaan, than the similar fact in Ireland and Spain is evidence that Europeans had such an origin.

6. WHENCE IS THE ORIGIN OF THE NEGRO RACE?

Here it may be well to give a passing notice to the question, Who were the progenitors of the Negro race?

The writer of this paper does not pretend to speak with certainty upon this question. The following, he thinks, is a true statement of the matter.

Africa was originally settled by the descendants of Ham, *excepting his son Canaan.* Ham himself is supposed to have emigrated to Egypt; and Egypt, in Scripture, is called the "land of Ham." * There he attained to state and eminence; and after his death, it is said, was deified by his descendants. The supreme deity AM of the Egyptians, it is stated, signifies his name: e. g., (H)AM; and the Jupiter AMMON, in honor of whom a temple was erected, is supposed to indicate HAM.

Africa was peopled by Ham in the line of his *three* sons, CUSH, MIZRAIM, and PHUT.

1. Cush, the eldest, and undoubtedly the most distinguished of all the sons of Ham, appears to have been the great progenitor of the Negro race. His name is also associated, with distinction, with Asia. The records of these early periods of the world's history are by no means clear and distinct; but Cush appears to have gone, at first, into Arabia, between the Euphrates and the Tigris, the country sometimes

* Ps. cvi. 22.

called Chaldea, and in Scripture, Shiraz. Thence his descendants spread themselves abroad through the beautiful and luxuriant region of "Araby the blest," and eastward, by the Persian Gulf, to the Orient. Here, in the first place, Cush and his children distinguished themselves. Here Nimrod, his son, became the first of kings, and reared up the mighty city of Babylon, and founded Nineveh. In the course of time some of the descendants of Cush crossed the Straits of Babelmandel, turned their steps southward toward the sources of the Nile, and settled in the land south of the Mountains of the Moon ; and from them the Negro race has sprung, although the Cushites were, undoubtedly, greatly mingled in blood with the children of Mizraim and Phut.

2. Mizraim was the father of the Egyptians. Wherever, in our version, we find the name Egypt, in the original it is Mizraim.

3. Of Phut, the *third* son of Ham, we have but little more than conjecture. It is the generally received opinion that his descendants settled on the northern Atlantic coast of Africa—Libya, and the adjacent parts, the country of the Moors.

7. SLAVERY NOT PECULIAR TO THE NEGRO RACE.

But there may be persons who will still object that the severities of the African slave trade, and the horrors of Negro slavery, are peculiar and significant, indicate something special in their inflictions, outweigh all theory and argument, and give strength and authority to the opinion that the curse was pronounced upon Ham, and that the children of Africa have participated in its consequences. The reply to this is:

1st. That the severities of the African slave trade, and the horrors of Negro slavery, as exhibited in European colonies and possessions, are entirely *modern*—confined to a short period in the history of the world, and therefore not a true exemplification of the *general* condition of the Negro race.

2dly. That while it is true that servitude and slavery have existed in some form throughout Africa, in every stage of its history, it is also true that *servitude and slavery have been the general condition of society, in all nations, in all countries, at all periods of time*, and are not in any manner peculiar to the black man, or the Negro race.

In connection with this fact I remark:

3dly. That if the general existence of slavery in a race, or among a people, is to be taken as an indication that a curse has descended upon them, then the mass of the Turks, Poles, Russians, Circassians, are lineal descendants of Canaan, and therefore "doomed races." And in the same category the larger portion of even Anglo-Saxons must be placed; for, but a short time since, a multitude of Britons were absolutely "goods and chattels," under the name of "villeins."

8. THE UNIVERSAL PREVALENCE OF SLAVERY.

Those persons, surely, display great ignorance, who associate the system of slavery, specially and alone, with the Negro race, and who are not aware of its existence in other races, and in all periods of history. There are no people, whether ancient or modern, with whom slavery has not been, at one period or other, a national institution. Indeed, how very little freedom has ever been enjoyed in this sin-ridden world of ours! Among the various evils to which society has been subjected, none have been more general or more deadly than slavery. No portion of the globe has been exempt from this curse. Slavery existed among all the nations of antiquity of whom we have any knowledge. It was maintained among the Assyrians and Babylonians. That slavery existed among the Egyptians is evidenced by the testimony of the Bible. Joseph was sold by his brethren; and sold again to an officer of Pharaoh's household. The Canaanites, after they were driven from the land of Canaan, and set up empire in Tyre and Sidon, trafficked in the bodies of men. The Greeks and Romans held vast numbers of slaves; they were great traders in human flesh, and distinguished themselves beyond all other people as cruel slave-holders; they kept their slaves in the deepest subjection, and visited upon them the most horrible cruelties, as is instanced in the condition of the Helots.

In more recent times, we see the same prevalence of slavery among the nations. The whole western part of Europe, not long since, was in a state of abject vassalage. In Russia, twenty millions of serfs, even *now*, in wretchedness and poverty, suffer the infliction of the knout, and are subject to irresponsible power and unrestrained tyranny. And if all the truth were known, it would, no doubt, be seen, that some of the convulsions which have recently occurred on the continent, were, in fact, insurrections of slaves battling for personal freedom.

The same state of things has existed even in England. A few centuries since, Saxons were bought and sold in Ireland and Rome. At one time slaves and cattle were a kind of currency in the land; and down to the period of the Reformation, human beings were " marketable commodities."

In the light of these facts, how ignorant and idle is it to regard the children of Africa as the subjects of a peculiar curse, because, in the mysterious providence of God, they have participated in the miseries and the sufferings of a cruel system, which has existed from the dawn of history, *in every quarter of the globe*, among every people under the sun.*

9. THE CAUSE OF THE SLAVE TRADE, AND OF NEGRO SLAVERY IN CHRISTIAN COUNTRIES.

It was the discovery of America, and the development of the treasures of the New World, which led to all the accumulated horrors of the slave trade, and the dreadful barbarities of Negro slavery, in Christian lands. The system took its rise in the sixteenth century. Since then the shameful fact has been witnessed, by earth and by heaven, of men, civilized men, men born and reared in Christian lands and under Christian influences, tearing their fellow-creatures from home, and friends, and country; carrying them across the

---

* With reference to the general prevalence of the system of slavery, see a very able article in the " Life and Remains of Rev. B. B. Edwards, D. D.," late of Andover Theological Seminary.

wide ocean; trading in the flesh and blood of human beings! The system of slavery, *as thus marked and distinguished*, is a MODERN affair—was unknown anterior to the discovery of America; and therefore, as such, not a fact of history—not the general, universal state of the Negro race.

10. THE SLAVE TRADE DOUBLY DISASTROUS.

But it should be remembered that this event did not bring distress and slavery upon the Negro race only; it struck at once, with deadly, blasting influence, upon two races of men,—the Indian as well as the Negro; and if, because of its destructive and enslaving influence, we are to infer a people's descent from Canaan, then the American Indian is of his seed, as well as the Negro. So soon as the European planted his foot upon the western continent, he seized upon the aborigine as his instrument and property. Before there was any thought of stealing the African and making him a slave, the Indian was enslaved and overworked; until, at last, he sank down, spent and overwearied, into the grave. And then, when the Indian was exterminated, the Negro was torn from his native land, brought across the water, and made to supply the red man's place. It is difficult to tell which has suffered the more from the discovery, and the slavery which has grown out of it—the Indian or the African. "In the West Indies," to use the words of another, "the whole native population became speedily extinct; the ten millions of that almost unearthly race, the gentle Caribs, vanished like a morning mist before their oppressors. They bled in war; they wasted away in the mines; they toiled to death in the sugar mills."* And then, when their spirits had fled from earthly thraldom, the "conquerors of the New World" turned toward the vast African continent for new victims to fill up the places they had made vacant by their murderous treatment of the natives.

11. Whence this perversion of Scripture?

A consideration of this subject would be altogether incomplete, without an attempt to account for the origin of this perversion of the word of God, that is, that the Negro race is under a curse, and devoted to slavery. The writer of this article is fully aware of the responsibility he assumes in making the assertions which follow; but it is his deliberate conviction that this perversion of Scripture originated,

1st. In the unscriptural dogma, still maintained by Christian men, and even ministers, that slavery is consistent with, nay, authorized by, the word and will of God, and that it existed among the Jews under the divine sanction.†

---

* Rev. J. S. Stone, D. D.

"Las Casas and Vieyra might be quoted to show the cruelties which stimulated them in their unwearied efforts to save the original inhabitants from servitude. The Indians vanished from the scene, giving way to a more enduring race, who were thenceforward to monopolize the miseries of slavery."—"Friends in Council," p. 121.

† The mind of God upon this subject, so far as the *Old Testament* is concerned, is thus expressed in Exodus xxi. 16: "He that stealeth a man, and selleth him, or if he be found in his hand, he shall surely be put to death." Can any thing be more explicit?

So far as the *New Testament* is concerned, one distinct, unambiguous,

2d. In the natural disposition of our corrupt nature to justify a committed wrong, and, if possible, to claim the authority of God's word for it; and this is the peculiarity which characterizes this great and deep-seated error. It had its origin in the rise and influence of the system of slavery; and this system has appropriated for itself no stronger support than this, and those other staple arguments, wrenched from the Scripture to vindicate and sustain the whole fabric of Negro slavery.

Christianity, in the abstract, is a pure and perfect gift from God to man. But Christianity is a deposit from heaven, in the hands of sinful men; and consequently, in all its ages, Christianity has suffered the loss which is the natural result of being entrusted to this agency, and of being transmitted through this medium. History proves this; for no one need be told that Christianity, in every age, has partaken of the prevailing spirit of that age, whatever it might be. In a philosophical age, it has been influenced by the philosophical spirit and dogmas of that age. In the middle ages, Christianity was influenced by scholasticism. In the age of wars and crusades, she produced Peter the Hermit, and her prelates led forth mighty armies to battle. In an age of luxury, its rigid tone has been relaxed by the enervating influence of wealth, and ease, and refinement. That Christianity has suffered in a like manner, in a slave-trading and a slave-

and positive utterance would seem to be sufficient. St. Paul furnishes us with such an one in 1 Timothy i. 9, 10: " Knowing this, that the law is not made for a righteous man, but for . . . . . . MENSTEALERS"— ἀνδραποδισαις. See "Conybeare and Howson" upon this verse.

holding age, no one need wonder who looks at the wide and withering influence which the slave trade and slavery have exerted, in all the countries of Christendom, during the last three hundred years. During this period, nearly all the literature of the chief European nations was a Negro-hating and a pro-slavery literature. The institution of slavery, wielding a most potent and commanding authority, brought every thing, in politics, science, philosophy, and letters, to bear in support of the slave trade, in maintenance of the institution of slavery, and to uphold the dogma that the Negro was but an inferior animal. The aid of science was invoked; philosophy trimmed her lamps; literature poured forth whatever treasures she could possibly command. The period has but recently passed since distinguished men in England and France exercised the keenest wit and the subtlest genius to prove that the Negro differed physically from the rest of the human species, and had a *distinct* organization. The puzzling questions concerning the cuticle, the coloring membrane, the "woolly" hair, the facial angle, the pelvis, and all the other supposed characteristic differences of the Negro race, have only recently been settled in a sensible, reasonable manner. In such a state of public sentiment in the Christian world, what wonder that the Church herself should have become tainted and infected by the deadly touch of slavery? And she did not escape; she, too, fell into the common sentiment of the age; she has not yet entirely unschooled herself from it; * and hence it was that,

* See, as a most lamentable instance, a recent scriptural defence of Negro slavery, by the venerable Rt. Rev. Bishop Hopkins, of Vermont.

to a very considerable extent, for nigh three centuries, the black man has had a pro-slavery theology pressing him to the earth, as well as the all-grasping cupidity of man:

"Trade, wealth, and fashion asked him still to bleed,
And holy men gave Scripture for the deed."

To this prevailing sentiment we owe the fact that nearly all interpretations of Scripture, commentaries, works on prophecy, dissertations on Jewish servitude, sermons and theological treatises elicited by the anti-slavery struggle in England and America, nearly all are pervaded by a pro-slavery tone.

In legal matters it is an assumed principle "that in doubtful cases the advantage of the law shall be in favor of the prisoner;" but Christian men have reversed this principle, and in their treatises have assumed, as a foregone conclusion, that the spirit of the Bible was in favor of slavery, and *not* for freedom, and hence ingenuity has been exhausted in order to show the exact similitude between Jewish servitude and Negro slavery; and to prove that when Noah cursed Canaan he was looking right down the track of time upon some fine specimens of " Ebony," in the barracoons of the Gallinas, or some "fat and sleek " Negroes in the slave-shambles of Virginia!

CONCLUSION.

In conclusion, the author submits that the preceding examination authorizes the following conclusions:

1. That the curse of Noah was *pronounced* upon Canaan, *not* upon Ham.

2. That it *fell* upon Canaan, and was designed to fall upon him only.

3. That neither Ham, nor any of his three sons, was involved in this curse.

4. That the Negro race have not descended from Canaan; were never involved in the curse pronounced upon him; and their peculiar sufferings, during the last three centuries, are not the results or evidences of *any* specific curse upon them.

5. That the fact of slavery in the Negro race is not peculiar to them as a people; but a *general* evil existing in the whole human family; in which, in God's providence, the Negro family have latterly been called to suffer greatly, and doubtless for some high and important ends.

6. That the geographical designations of Scripture are to be taken in good faith; and that when the "*land of Canaan*" is mentioned in the Bible, it was not intended to include the Gold Coast, the Gaboon, Goree, or Congo.

This examination furnishes us with suggestions upon a few *collateral* subjects which have been more or less associated with, or deduced from, the false interpretation thus noticed:

1. We see that *whatever* may be the significance of Gen. ix. 25, *it does not imply mental degradation and intellectual inaptitude.* The curse of Noah did not rob Canaan and his descendants of their brains. The history of the Phœnicians gives evidence of as great creative faculty, and of as much mental force and energy, as that of any other people in the world.

It would seem that they, of all the ancient world, were only *second* to the Romans in that commanding national influence which begets life in distant quarters, starts enterprise in new regions, and reproduces its own force and energy among other peoples. Of course, it follows legitimately from the above, that the *whole* Hamitic family are under no Divine doom to perpetual ignorance or endless moral benightedness.

2. The history of the Canaanites serves to show that the "*principle of chattelism*" *is not the correlative of the curse of Canaan;* this was neither their doom nor their destiny. Neither in sacred nor profane history do we find them bought and sold like cattle. Driven out of Canaan, they themselves traded in "the bodies and souls" of men, but *not* so others with them.* The nearest approach to any thing of this character is the condition of the Gibeonites, who deceived Joshua; but their condition was that of *servants.*† Although subjugated and humbled, yet their personal and family rights were preserved intact, and none of the aggravations of slavery were permitted to reach themselves or their children. When set upon, at times, by lawless and ruthless men, both Divine and human power interposed for their protection and preservation.

3. This examination *nullifies the foolish notion that the curse of Canaan carried with it the sable dye which marks the Negro races of the world.* The de-

---
* See Ezekiel xxvii.
† See Joshua ix. 21. 2 Samuel xxi. 3, 4, 5, 6.

scendants of Canaan in Palestine, Phœnicia, Carthage, and in their various colonies, were not *black*. They were not Negroes, either in lineage or color.

NOTE.—The article "Hope for Africa," has been inserted in the place of the "Eulogium on Clarkson," as being more pertinent to the object of this work.

THE END.

www.ingramcontent.com/pod-product-compliance
Lightning Source LLC
Chambersburg PA
CBHW030300240426
43673CB00040B/1017